PSYCHOLOGICAL
GAMES

Nicola Alberto De Carlo

PSYCHOLOGICAL GAMES

Facts On File Publications
New York, New York • Bicester, England

Color photographs
Stelvio Andreis and Elvio Lonardi,
Deltaprint s.r.l. Verona
with the exception of the photographs on the
following pages:
  17: Alvaro Frigeri, Verona;
  18: Raghubir Singh, Magnum Photos, Paris;
171: W. Kennedy, Image Bank, Milan;
172: Sybille and Klaus Kalas, Grünau, Austria

Translated from the Italian by Maria Piotrowska

First published in the United States by
Facts On File, Inc.
460 Park Avenue South
New York, N.Y. 10016

Library of Congress Cataloging in Publication Data

De Carlo, Nicola.
  Psychological games.

  Translation of: Giochi psicologici.
  1. Psychological tests. 2. Psychology—Popular works.
I. Title.
BF176.D43   1984   150'.28'7   84-4194
ISBN 0-87196-188-1
ISBN 0-87196-983-1(pb)
Printed and bound in Italy by Arnoldo Mondadori Editore, Verona

Contents

A contribution to the art of being

But still I'm troubled by one thing:
time is short and art is long.
I'd think you'd let yourself be taught.
Associate yourself with a poet and let
him gallop through the fields of thought
and heap all noble qualities on your honoured head:
the lion's courage, the stag's speed,
the fiery Italian blood, the Northman's fortitude.
(Johann W. von Goethe, Faust)

An eminent example

Sir Francis Galton was rather alarmed. Wherever he went—be it in the streets or at home—he had the distinct impression he was being carefully watched by animals. Worse still, they seemed to study him furtively, deliberately looking the other way whenever he glanced at them. As you can well imagine, going to the country was sheer torture, and perhaps that is why (although history does not actually tell us this) Galton tried to confine his walks to the main streets of London, concentrating all his attention on objects while making mental notes of the associations they provoked in him. However that may be, his walks generated some valuable scientific work and cured him of the unpleasant sensations he associated with the animal world.

As a scientist, Sir Francis was not unacquainted with paradox. For example, when he was trying to empathize with the feelings a savage had for an idol, he trained himself to believe that Punch was a god capable of chastisement and punishment. Unfortunately, the experiment was so successful that, from then on, Sir Francis could never see the puppet without experiencing an undercurrent of respect and faith. As for his notion about animals, that too, was the result of his

trying to see the world through the eyes of someone else, in that instance a mentally ill person who believed everything was conspiring to spy on him.

An eccentric with a taste for the extraordinary and an overwhelming love of science, Galton was awarded a baronetcy for his eminence as a scholar. Indeed, today, seventy years after his death, his insights and discoveries are still topical in the fields of anthropology, statistics and psychology.

Galton also had a passion for gambling, from which he learned the versatility and inventiveness he considered fundamental characteristics.

Who knows which was the strongest in Galton, the instinct of the scientist or the gambler; he was probably one because he was also the other.

As for us, what is the fascination with the mind? Are we trying to tax ourselves mentally, or merely while away the time, or are we trying to emulate Sir Francis?

Enough of such speculation. Most of us can devote just a few hours every now and then to card games, billiards, tennis or whatever, and perhaps when we do we feel guilty about stealing the time. But games can only do us good. They are a breath of fresh air to those of us who spend our hours with the noise, rush and stress that pollute everyday life. This is why we suggest we play more games, and that we play them together.

Our aims

This book is far more than a compendium of diversions for entertaining guests, or wiling away the time on rainy days. It is intended as a source of pleasure that will also help us to know ourselves and our fellows better. We suggest that you "play games" which make use of your knowledge of human behaviour, your intelligence, feelings and motivations, in other words, play games with psychology.

The joy of knowing yourself

If we observe children while they are playing games, we quickly see the pleasure they get from identifying with interesting characters, their fun in trying out new personalities by dressing up as cowboys, Indian chiefs, robots or spacemen. There is a mixture of wonder and satisfaction in a child who watches a friend perfectly at ease in the guise of an astronaut or a Sioux warrior; children will do all they can to take part in make-believe. In short, they play at getting to know themselves and each other.

However, in time, this changes. Teenagers and adults rarely let themselves go and "dress up," and when they do, it is seldom spontaneous. A special point is made: A host issuing invitations to a costume party, for instance, or perhaps carnival, a time for disguise that is celebrated the world over. And what about adult games and parties? The purpose of sport tends to be the satisfaction of a need for self-assertion, whereas children play games mainly for the pleasure in the game itself, and as a means of discovery. Then too, adults often see parties more as social obligations than as fun.

What opportunities do adults have to really observe one another and unearth new feelings and behaviour patterns? Not many, if truth be told.

Adults have lost the joy of getting to know one another.

Of course lovers, and those who are falling in love are an exception. A sign of interest leads a man or woman to emphasize those qualities that are most likely to please; a smile may be used to give hope or to disconcert. However, with familiarity, the behaviour we associate with infatuation, with all its signals and nuances of expression, tends to give way to somewhat passive acceptance.

Yet, although a degree of placidity is necessary for two people to live together in harmony, it is still quite possible to remain interested in the other person; problems and responses, after all, are constantly changing.

This is true in other relationships as well, not simply those between men and women. We are used to thinking of other people in terms of ourselves and often we do not know *how* to approach someone with genuine attention and curiosity. Hence, we may overlook a rich source of interest and human warmth without even realizing it. Games can help us.

Play and reality

Does an elegant, self-confident woman choose her clothes after a specific appraisal of their shape and colour, or does she tend to create an overall image designed to draw the attention of others? Examining it on another level, what factors determine success in a particular person? Is it analytical intelligence and great strength of will, or the capacity to grasp the essentials of a problem and entrust them to the right people?

Further, will childlike qualities add to, or detract from, the fascination of such a person? Again from another vantage point, what choices are open to the teenager about to finish school and torn between a love of literature and the desire to help her fellow man? Will she devote herself to classical studies and become an educator or writer, or will she become a doctor and lead a markedly different life?

These are only a few examples of the problems on which we might be able to throw some light.

First we might ask, and answer, two questions:
1. To what extent can our games contribute to greater self-understanding?
2. Is it right to tackle important matters, like some of those we have just discussed, through games?

As to the first question, the tests in this book often involve making choices, just as we must do in everyday life: You will have to reflect about your own or other people's reactions and, through that, reach a better understanding of yourself and others.

Many of the games are, in fact, psychological tests and we illustrate their uses and limitations. On the whole, however, these tests are not used in medical practice. Indeed, we have avoided reproducing those that are commonly used for diagnostic or therapeutic purposes.

We would like to emphasize the need to perform the games after a careful reading of the explanations and comments. Responses to the games are merely pointers which should then be assessed with reference to current methodological and interpretative theories.

This book contributes to a keener self-knowledge in that *every* aspect of our behaviour is scrutinized; very little of human behaviour is predictable or easily comprehended, and no more importance should be attached to the results of any single test than it is due.

The second question, of whether it is right to deal with matters of personal and social importance through games, requires further consideration.

These pages do not claim to offer definitive evaluations of people. Nothing is immutable or conclusive. What we are today and what we will be tomorrow, how our behaviour and feelings will change, are determined by conditioning and the continuous pressures to which we and those around us are subjected. A background of hardship and poverty for example, can either be a springboard for social mobility, or impel us to escape from reality. It is not easy to predict the reaction of someone brought up in this kind of environment, or to determine whether that reaction will be temporary, cyclical, or permanent.

The interpretation of reality demands a dynamic perspective, which we have tried to generate. Hence, we have avoided giving rules that pin the reader down to set scores. No black and white judgements should be made. To do so would impose an excessive strain on whoever participates in the games, and would only create anxiety and frustration instead of good humour. Along with scientific accuracy, this, then, is the spirit of the book. The lightheartedness of the evaluations—and more generally, an awareness of our behaviour and the way we are—depend on our individual personalities, our environment, and our luck.

The science of behaviour

All research techniques are founded on theories. For example, there is little sense in discussing scores on a scale of aggression without first specifying what is meant by aggression, and what criteria produce the grading system. Such precaution is, in fact, indispensable in all areas of science, but often it is forgotten in work on human behaviour, and hence leads to suggestive or dogmatic judgments rather than ones solidly based. It is as if scientific methods were not congenial to the study of man.

For the scientist in human behaviour, the situation is indeed a difficult one. We are strongly influenced by our feelings, emotions and ideals. We are attracted by art and ideology. We are subject to a morality that is both individual and collective. Yet we try to disregard the contradictory nature of reality and to establish certainties based on the analytic methods of reasoning. By so doing, the study of man could then follow the structured path taken in physics, chemistry and biology, or so it would seem.

But this is the sticking point. The "human" sciences (and we use the term conventionally) have not yet accumulated sufficient data to either explain or predict our behaviour. And, if by behaviour we mean both our actions and our interior lives, which add up to the way we behave, then we must admit we have a long way to go before realizing truly satisfactory objectives. Thus far, there have been only partial successes, and those have been limited to a few theoretical fields (e.g. perceptual psychology, and the study of attitudes) and to some practical areas such as the prediction of certain consumer trends, and insurance company assessments.

Understandably, though not justifiably, short cuts have been taken. In many instances, we have settled for a mixture of science, art, ideology and various other human spheres, and this mixture continues to be adopted precisely because of the changing nature of its methodology, in short, its refusal to submit to scientific norms.

Each one of us has a desire to comprehend the gamut of human behaviour, perhaps in the hope that a full understanding of behaviour mechanisms will eventually allow us to control our destinies. Much of the temptation to produce "global" explanations which are wholly or largely unprovable, is based, in part, upon such an aspiration. Indeed it smacks a bit of the diabolical.

Of course there is no egregious wrong in considering extrascientific reasoning. Faith, passion and the metaphysical permeate human life and we cannot deny their importance, nor would we wish to, or the fact that they are essential for the task of getting on with life. After all, the works of the great poets are the very spice of life.

However, we must not allow ourselves to put the seal

of scientific approval on theories of human behaviour that are still largely unconfirmed, or are nothing more than opinions that yield only partial explanations.

To dispel any potential misunderstanding and to immediately establish the proper approach, we would like to stress the fact that certain assumptions are purely hypothetical.

Both science and philosophy are necessary, but they should coexist harmoniously, and not in a state of reciprocal confusion. In this book, we will try to point out certain advances in psychology and at the same time indicate those areas where hypotheses of varying degrees of reliability have a practical application. The reader will easily see which areas are scientifically proven, and which are particularly resistant to scientific research.

We also need a little air in our lives. According to Erich Fromm, the conflict between "to be" and "to have" characterizes our daily lives, and "to have" is often of first priority: *One has* certain capacities, *we have* good characters, *you have* an infectious smile, *they have* good friends. These expressions underline the essentially acquisitive nature of normal human experience, and it is the acquisitiveness that frequently retards true growth. Too often our relationships are based more on antagonism than on solidarity; they are competitive and cloaked in fear rather than open and sharing. We dare not risk appearing less intelligent, less productive or less creative than others. To do so might adversely affect our images and, as a result, our careers, salaries and social status. This leads to a perception of ourselves as trapped in constant, and perhaps tragic, competition with others.

Modern man must work *to be* rather than *to have*. Fromm wrote that one must find "security, sense of identity and confidence based on faith in what one *is*, on one's need for relatedness, interest, love, solidarity with the world around one, instead of on one's desire to have, to possess, to control the world . . . Love and respect for life in all its manifestations, in the knowledge that not things, power, all that is dead, but life and everything that pertains to its growth are sacred . . . Developing one's imagination. . .knowing oneself, not only the self one knows, but also the self one does not know, even though one has a slumbering knowledge of what one does not know. . .making the full growth of oneself and of one's fellow beings the supreme goal of living."

But can our book be seen in such a broad perspective? In our opinion it can, because games can be seen as microcosms of everyday situations.

All games require of their players an awareness of undertaking an important (we might even say serious) activity governed by its own rules of interaction with others (and with oneself), and a particular mode of behaviour: During a game, you must pay attention to what you are doing, you should respect the game's conventions and rules, and if you win you should not appear openly superior to, or look down, on the loser. Indeed, a game is an analogy of real life. Sociologist and anthropologist Erving Goffman described games as activities that build worlds, and should there be boundaries between them and everyday existence, those boundaries act as a kind of sieve, selecting, transforming and modifying everything that passes through.

Games give us the chance to distance ourselves from much of the conditioning to which we are subjected in the course of daily life, and they provide a context in which the acquisition of self-knowledge is not inspired simply by our desire to gain prestige. We hope these pages are a stimulus and serve as a means to improving one's self-knowledge—a source of pleasure in itself. You come to life when you begin to discover yourself and those around you in a variety of situations. In short, discovery is a form of growth.

This, then, is how a book of games can contribute to the art of being.

Creativity and intellectual level

"It requires productive activity to give life to the emotional and intellectual poten-
tialities of man, to give birth to his self. It is part of the tragedy of the human
situation that the development of the self is never completed...Man always dies
before he is fully born." (Erich Fromm, Man for Himself)

To a large extent, our time is spoken for minute by minute. Very early on we learn to get up when the alarm rings and go to school, fair weather or foul, whether we want to or not. The time we spend having breakfast, in school, returning home, the afternoon hours spent studying for the next day, and our free time in the evening stretching into the night (until the alarm goes off again in the morning), set our daily rhythm for many years to come. Later, we work in factories or offices, line up in banks and post offices, go to church or relax in a bar with friends. In short, our behaviour is standardized in a myriad ways; we know the rules inside and out that we are expected to follow, and that, in turn, we expect others to follow. Our thoughts, too, follow a standardized pattern, imposed both by nature and necessity.

We try to concentrate on the immediate problem, frequently stopping our minds from wandering so we do not forfeit a moment's attention.

Teachers' reprimands, setbacks at school and a variety of professional difficulties frequently stem from a limited capacity to discipline our attention and apply ourselves to the problem at hand, which, as formulated by Hans J. Eysenck in his *principle of reality,* usually requires one specific mental activity. An example of this principle as it operates in everyday life might be a mathematics teacher who has little interest in whether one of his pupils develops a love for modern literature. At any given moment, the teacher is interested only in whether the student knows how to solve a specific geometry problem, and woe unto him should he get it wrong, even if he is considered so gifted that he could become one of the future's noted engineers. Similarly, it is not very important for a bookkeeper to have brilliant ideas on a company's expansion strategy when all that is required is simply accuracy in classifying or calculating.

Mental application, in the sense we have been discussing it, tends to be judged in terms of what is specifically needed in a certain social context at a certain time. Quite often, those who meet these requirements and are most diligent, are looked down on by their peers. The majority of people, even while recognizing (more or less willingly) the importance and necessity of such work, normally take every opportunity to ridicule excessive activity and devotion to duty: The student who always completes his homework and the employee who is always available and hard working are commonly accused of lacking independence and a free spirit.

Although the implications of this last notion certainly bear more discussion, we hasten to point out that, to some extent it is necessary to conform to the demands of our technologically oriented and organized society, and therefore such behaviour should not be scorned.

Creativity is among the most highly valued of human qualities. Indeed, artists are forgiven practically everything provided they give us "something new." All of us

Interpret the Drawings in the Circles.

Fig. 1

1 example

A worm doing
gymnastics. A twisted
paper clip.

put great store in originality. The schoolchild who neglects some subjects (and, of course, earns bad marks) to develop the areas that interest him most, frequently wins the respect of fellow students. Similarly, a manager's shortcomings become insignificant if he is capable of bringing valid and substantial change to a production line, or of increasing a company's sales.

Creativity is associated with freedom and intelligence. We might define it as the *capacity to see new relationships, to entertain out-of-the-ordinary ideas and to free our intuition from traditional ways of thinking.*

There is a contradiction between the commonly held view that only the elite are endowed with creativity—hence people who have achieved fame and public recognition are considered creative—and the experience of the ordinary individual. The calmer your emotional life is, with no peaks or troughs, and the more repetitive your work, the more you tend to appreciate your free time and to use it creatively, perhaps adopting a hobby such as gardening, needlework, sailing or mineral study. The fact is that creativity is deep within all of us, albeit to different degrees.

Through our appearance and our conversation, we can strike other people as creative; this is precisely because it is the unique and the unpredictable that are most apt to capture attention.

Creativity is expressed when solving a problem, straightening out an emotional entanglement, bringing together elements thought to be dissimilar and unconnected, or just simply in being able to see and recognize an object, a person, or a pattern of behaviour. It combines intelligence, sensitivity, originality, and a capacity for analysis and abstraction. In short, it encompasses the many variables that together form the personality.

Later on, we shall discuss the difficulties that arise in trying to pursue an empirical approach in psychology. Much useful research has been done based on the methodological point of view, which assumes that to different degrees everyone is endowed with the same abilities, including creativity. While those who are recognized as creative may have more of this attribute than others, the difference does not hinge on a dichotomy of all or nothing. Hence, creative acts can be expected from everyone, no matter how faint or infrequent their expression; some may gain recognition and appreciation in the social context, whereas others may remain part of an individual's private experience, but they are nonetheless important.

To a large extent, then, creativity lies in our ability to shed the almost automatic responses inculcated in us by everyday demands; the more we understand what is new in ourselves, in others, and in the many situations in which we find ourselves, the better we will understand who we are and who our fellow men are.

An example of how this book can be used to stimulate our own creativity and that of our friends, is the amusing game in Figure 1. Try it. The thirty circles illustrated all contain images for us to interpret. According to the book from which this game is taken (which is cited on page 179, as are all the articles and books we have used as sources for the tests and games), there are no "right" answers, only witty, daring or unusual interpretations, depending on who is playing, e.g., no. 10 could be "pedantry," no. 22 "two boomerangs in love," no. 20 "a three-way tug-of-war," and no. 17 "a honeymoon on snow."

These are entertaining examples to be sure, but the credit, or responsibility, for the interpretations is the author's. Now let us put ourselves to the test and see if we can come up with funnier and even more unexpected interpretations. Play the game alone, or with others, and then compare your respective answers. If you like, you can use dice to allot circles to each person. It is wonderful to discover that friends have flashes of brilliance and a sense of humour we can share. Besides, confiding what is in your imagination to someone else could be, in itself, a new form of dialogue as it can touch on subjects not often talked about openly; if they are, we tend to be guarded, usually making certain we or the other person can retreat. But through this game, it is possible to communicate in a different and more satisfying fashion, in effect, to turn a deaf ear to the hubbub of the outside world.

Fantasies are built on such games, wild guesses are made about the present and the future, and love, business and reputations are gossiped about or planned.

Figures 2 and 3 offer a framework that can be used to predict possible situations regarding ourselves or other people. A seemingly innocent activity is to classify people on the basis of a combination of qualities. Figure 4 is an example of how to set about determining a person's ideal qualities (and their opposites), and it leaves one circle to be filled in. Good luck to those who are about to be classified.

As we have said, these games can be a source of amusement, an unusual entertainment for guests, and a pleasant way of deepening your friendships. Indeed, they can perform many functions that you might conjure up. Whatever their aim, they enable us to appreciate the *flexibility* of the mind and its capacity to *work things out,* and they serve as examples of *converging* and *diverging* thought. The tests also give us the chance to develop our own faculty to move past the

Fig. 2

We are now in the future. This apparently absurd game is based on our abilities, desires and plans, so try to imagine what else might happen and what external influences, chance situations and possibilities might affect us. With just a little imagination, you can write your memoirs.

1. Describe your professional situation in 1985.

2. Describe your personal situation in 1987.

3. Describe your holiday travel in 1990.

4. Describe your interests, desires and aspirations in 1992.

5. Describe your home in 1995.

6. Describe what you think your place of work will be like in 1999.

7. Describe a party with friends in 2001.

8. Describe a weekend in 2003.

9. Describe your house in 2007.

10. Describe your personal experiences in 2010.

11. Describe what you do in your spare time in 2012.

12. Describe your memories in 2015.

Fig. 3

This game is an invitation to play around with what might happen in the future, something like a juggler throwing balls in the air. First of all, choose an area that interests you in terms of your future: Do you want to learn about your job prospects or your domestic arrangements? Describe the situation you are starting with. What could change in the immediate future? What depends on you; on external circumstances? Make brief notes about the consequences, then repeat the process for the period immediately following. The table below gives an example of Mr/Mrs X's chances of success in their friendships.

Initial Situation	What happens in the 1st year	Consequences	What happens in the 2nd year	Consequences
Mr. X has a female friend or Mrs. X has a male friend.	The friend wants to get married.	Look for another friend.	Don't find one.	Continue looking.
	The friend gets married to someone you know.	Look for another friend.		
	The friendship doesn't change.	Intensify the friendship.		

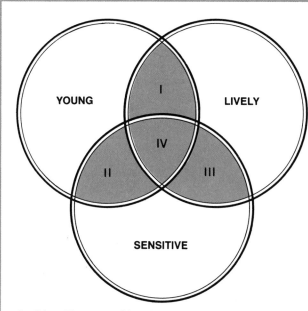

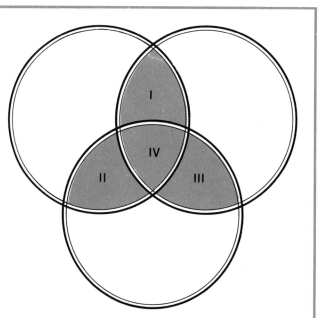

1. Classify your friends according to their age (young, not-so-young), temperament (lively, quiet) and how emotional they are (cold, sensitive). Write one of the qualities inside each circle, as in the example. The overlapping sections give four possible combinations.

I —Young, lively, but cold
II —Young, quiet and sensitive
III—Lively and sensitive, but not-so-young
IV—Young, lively and sensitive

2. Now you can substitute different qualities or use your friends' ambitions, experiences and interests as a basis for classification. Write one characteristic feature inside each of the empty circles above and then form new groupings, again like the example. Decide what points of view you will adopt as the basis for the classification and use them to describe the widest variety of people or objects. In this way, you can group things, ideas, aims (or anything that comes to mind) on the basis of their salient features, and produce a variety of permutations.

commonly accepted interpretations and to probe for answers, from which, in turn a variety of conclusions and implications can be drawn. For example, look at no. 3 in Figure 1. Some people might see it simply as a target, but others might see a car wheel, or even the hat Princess Margaret wears at the Ascot races; such interpretations could then lead to discussions about the superiority of solid wheel hubs over perforated types, or comical comparisons with manners of dress. To some extent, this is an example of diverging thought, which expresses itself not only in a search for the exact answer but also in the multiplicity and originality of solutions, in a wealth of ideas and the possibility of restructuring a subject. It is determined by such factors as fluency with words and expression,

and mental flexibility; to a great extent, such a definition coincides with the concept of creativity. Converging thought, on the other hand, is concentrated and limited, we might even say "sacrificed," to one specific aim.

Later in the book, we will deal with the problems implicit in these determining factors and their analysis, and with the subject of fluency with words and expressions. To fully understand the numerous limitations of assessments made on the basis of the games discussed so far, let's consider the concept of a test. Most often tests, including psychological tests, are used to measure intelligence, which is one of the variables that is quite important in creativity.

Evaluating our intellectual level (I)

Instructions
All the tests should be finished in thirty minutes. Write the answers to each question without looking up the answers. If you finish ahead of time, go back to the questions you might have been unable to answer.

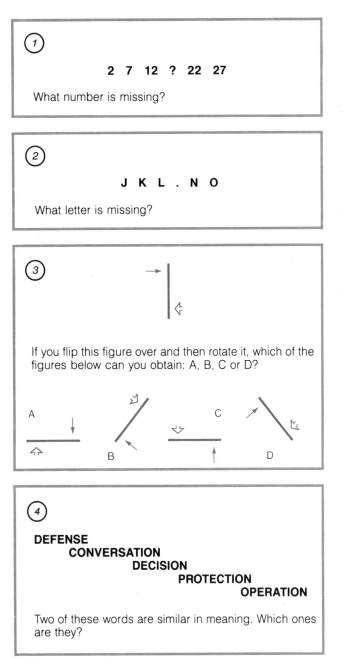

(1)

2 7 12 ? 22 27

What number is missing?

(2)

J K L . N O

What letter is missing?

(3)

If you flip this figure over and then rotate it, which of the figures below can you obtain: A, B, C or D?

A   C   B   D

(4)

DEFENSE
    CONVERSATION
        DECISION
            PROTECTION
                OPERATION

Two of these words are similar in meaning. Which ones are they?

When you put on a mask with a sad or happy face, or garb yourself as an aristocrat or a tramp, you choose a role. Anyone who has ever dressed up for a costume party, a carnival or a parade knows that you tend to adopt the behaviour of the character you represent. A clown is expected to be happy, a vampire horrific, Mata Hari to be seductive, and a king to be regal.

Playing a part expresses a search for a new identity, a desire to try out a different way of life, if only for a short time and in a special context. It has been thus throughout history. We see it in the very existence of the dramatic arts and also, perhaps, in our readiness to disguise ourselves. Dressing up is a serious thing; both those who take part and those who watch must play the game. It can be cathartic and release us from the ever-present tensions of reality: The company president emerges as a court jester, the teacher as a bandit. In a similar fashion, a physics student might masquerade as Einstein, revealing an ambition he could not confess even to himself, or a bank clerk might act out his grandiose dreams as Genghis Khan. This is perfectly acceptable for a few hours, or even a day. It is the chance to divulge a secret part of yourself without triggering a sense of anxiety—after all, it is not really you in the spotlight.

Other people do not recognize you; you can laugh and talk loudly, tell a few risqué jokes. And even if they do recognize you, it's of little matter as everyone is in on the game.

It may be that this complex intermingling of one's own and other people's feelings is what makes carnivals, which each year involve millions in a riot of song, colour and noise, so immensely popular. Yet the release of inhibitions can also lead to dangerous antisocial extremes; it is no accident that at certain times, governments have forbidden the wearing of masks in public.

To adopt a tragic or comic image, if only by wearing a mask, or to fully disguise oneself as another person, is a way for ordinary people to let go. Otherwise, how could those of us who are not professional actors play out different states of mind, characters and situations and still maintain our dignity? The mask gives you security: Put it on and you slip into your chosen role; take if off and you return to your normal self.

To be an actor, on the other hand, requires not only training but an interpretative sensitivity. Actors must know how to convey those actions that people perform naturally (movements, words, speeches); and they must be able to differentiate between gestures in order to convey the motivations behind an action. By accentuating certain gestures instead of others, actors can interpret various human types.

In his observation of other people's behaviour, an actor functions much like an ethologist, carefully noting characteristic actions, attitudes and gestures.   The last of these is central to the actor performing mime, for he communicates with his audience through appropriate visual signals. These signals, according to the classifications of the famous ethologist Desmond Morris, fall into the categories of expressive, schematic, symbolic, and mimic gestures. The first group incorporates smiles, grimaces, winks, shrugs of the shoulders, whispers, hand gesticulations, and the many other forms of expression all of us use. They may vary slightly, but they are universal.

The face communicates most nonverbal signals precisely and

clearly. Indeed man's facial muscles are the most complex in the animal kingdom. It is as if some people "speak" by means of their facial expressions.

A good mimic acquires such facial suppleness that he can literally transfigure himself, depending on what message he means to convey. His face comes to resemble Plasticine which may be moulded according to his needs.

The environment, too, influences expressive gestures. In some parts of the world there is a veritable "smile culture"; in others people are so reserved that any outward display of pleasure is rare.

Schematic gestures depend on the specific and immediate experience of the person using them and on the experience of those to whom they are directed. Hence, the ease with which they can be interpreted is linked to the extent that what they represent, or the realities they describe, are general. Some schematic gestures are almost universally understandable: The actions of eating, drinking and smoking can be expressed by certain rhythmic movements of the hands toward the mouth with the fingers in particular positions; a gun can be simulated by using the index and middle fingers and the thumb. While these are direct, incisive signals, their immediacy robs them of subtlety and the possibility of extension.

Symbolic gestures are those that indicate abstract qualities such as being a little "crazy" (expressed by tapping the index finger on the forehead), and to a great extent they are determined by cultural traditions. In fact, an "abstract" concept can be interpreted in a variety of ways, hence the same gesture can convey different meanings depending on the environment in which it is used.

Finally we come to mimic gestures as they are employed by professional mimes. Their skill in imitating human actions is the result of careful study and close observation of the ways in which people use their bodies and faces to talk. Feelings, states of mind, and diverse forms of behaviour, are portrayed through a combination of facial techniques and body postures, expressive, schematic and symbolic gestures, more or less codified signals, and other variants generated by the situation and the interpreter's sensitivity.

An important area of expression is the representation of nature, ideas and animals by using the hands and, to a lesser extent, the body. It is quite possible to communicate complex, and abstract notions such as dawn, the tide coming in, a flight of seagulls, a snow-capped mountain, a flowering bush, ectasy, dejection or euphoria. Unfortunately, no description of a gifted mime can adequately relate the harmony of his movements and expression, or the feelings he can arouse. To understand this, you must see for yourself—in short, you most play your part.

(5)

2   5   15   18   54   57   171 . . .

How does this series of numbers continue?

(6)

C is to **E**
as **L** is to . . .

(7)

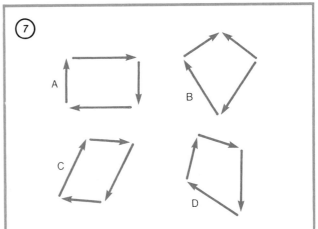

Which of these figures does not belong?

(8)

Change the position of two of the circles so each of the five radii forms a complete word.

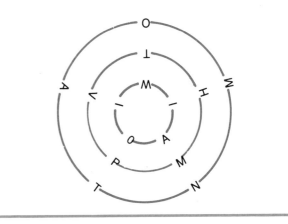

(9)

12

8

17

5

23

3

What number do these arrows lead you to?

(10)

BORDER

AVENUE

TAPE

RIM

SCEPTER

Two of these words are similar in meaning. Which ones are they?

(11)

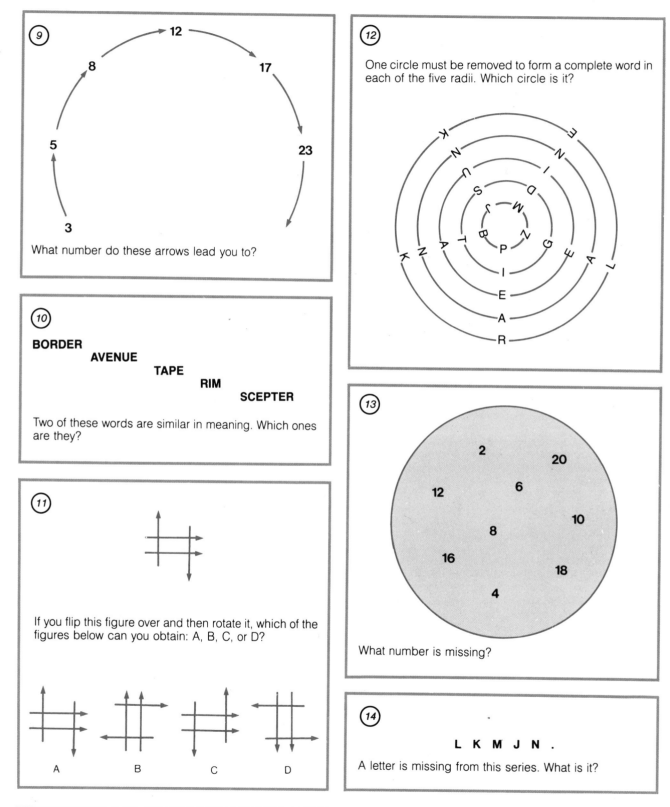

If you flip this figure over and then rotate it, which of the figures below can you obtain: A, B, C, or D?

A   B   C   D

(12)

One circle must be removed to form a complete word in each of the five radii. Which circle is it?

(13)

2   20

12   6

10

8

16   18

4

What number is missing?

(14)

L K M J N .

A letter is missing from this series. What is it?

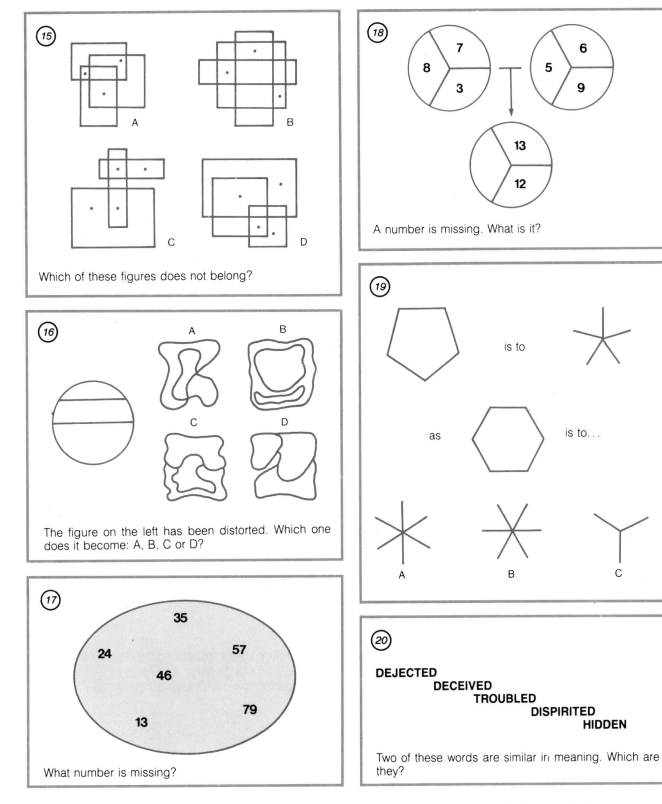

15 Which of these figures does not belong?

16 The figure on the left has been distorted. Which one does it become: A, B, C or D?

17 What number is missing?

18 A number is missing. What is it?

19 is to ... as ... is to...

A   B   C

20

DEJECTED
     DECEIVED
          TROUBLED
               DISPIRITED
                    HIDDEN

Two of these words are similar in meaning. Which are they?

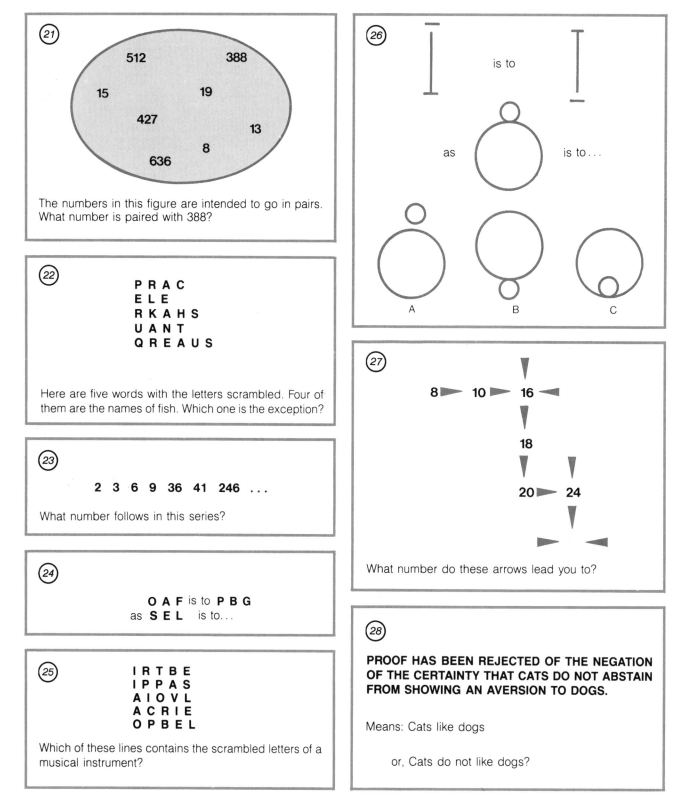

21

512   388

15   19

427

13

8

636

The numbers in this figure are intended to go in pairs. What number is paired with 388?

22

P R A C
E L E
R K A H S
U A N T
Q R E A U S

Here are five words with the letters scrambled. Four of them are the names of fish. Which one is the exception?

23

2 3 6 9 36 41 246 . . .

What number follows in this series?

24

O A F is to **P B G**
as **S E L** is to. . .

25

I R T B E
I P P A S
A I O V L
A C R I E
O P B E L

Which of these lines contains the scrambled letters of a musical instrument?

26

is to

as   is to . . .

A   B   C

27

8 ▶ 10 ▶ 16 ◀

18

20 ▶ 24

What number do these arrows lead you to?

28

PROOF HAS BEEN REJECTED OF THE NEGATION OF THE CERTAINTY THAT CATS DO NOT ABSTAIN FROM SHOWING AN AVERSION TO DOGS.

Means: Cats like dogs

or, Cats do not like dogs?

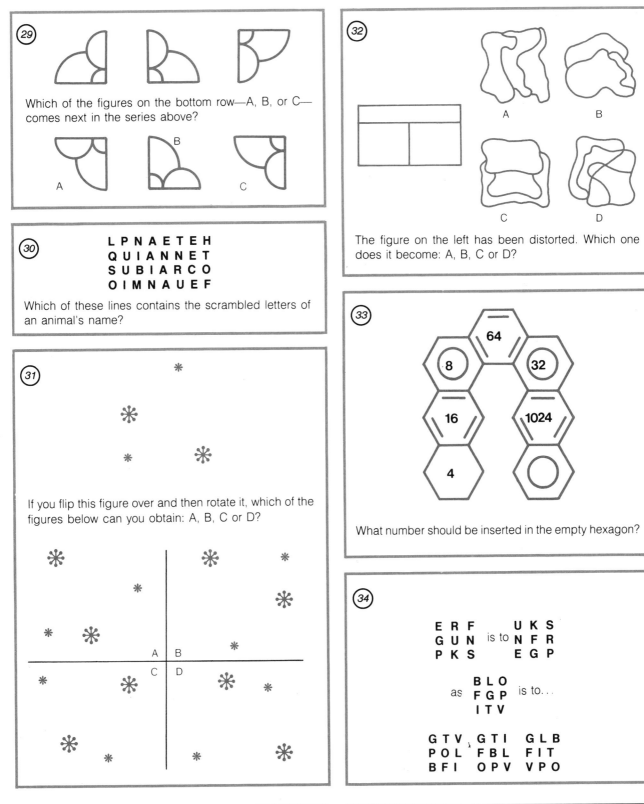

(29) Which of the figures on the bottom row—A, B, or C—comes next in the series above?

(30)
LPNAETEH
QUIANNET
SUBIARCO
OIMNAUEF

Which of these lines contains the scrambled letters of an animal's name?

(31) If you flip this figure over and then rotate it, which of the figures below can you obtain: A, B, C or D?

(32) The figure on the left has been distorted. Which one does it become: A, B, C or D?

(33) What number should be inserted in the empty hexagon?

64 8 32 16 1024 4

(34)

ERF   UKS
GUN is to NFR
PKS   EGP

as BLO
    FGP is to...
    ITV

GTV   GTI   GLB
POL   FBL   FIT
BFI   OPV   VPO

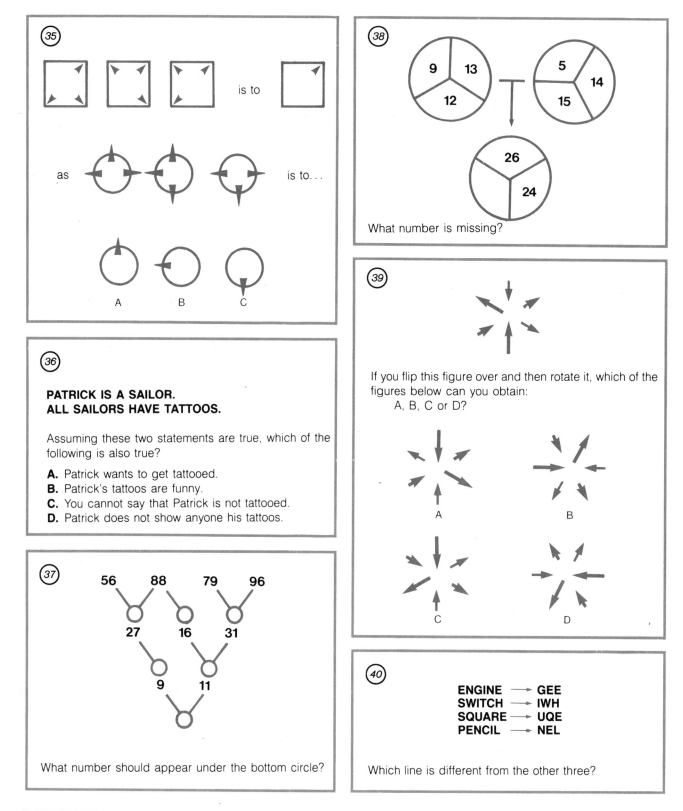

(35)

is to

as

is to...

A B C

(36)

**PATRICK IS A SAILOR.
ALL SAILORS HAVE TATTOOS.**

Assuming these two statements are true, which of the following is also true?

A. Patrick wants to get tattooed.
B. Patrick's tattoos are funny.
C. You cannot say that Patrick is not tattooed.
D. Patrick does not show anyone his tattoos.

(37)

56 88 79 96

27 16 31

9 11

What number should appear under the bottom circle?

(38)

9 13 12

5 14 15

26 24

What number is missing?

(39)

If you flip this figure over and then rotate it, which of the figures below can you obtain:
A, B, C or D?

A

B

C

D

(40)

ENGINE ⟶ GEE
SWITCH ⟶ IWH
SQUARE ⟶ UQE
PENCIL ⟶ NEL

Which line is different from the other three?

Answers

1. 17: The numbers increase by fives.

2. M: The series is in alphabetical order.

3. C

4. DEFENSE and PROTECTION

5. 174: The number three is alternately added to and multiplied by the previous number. Hence:

   $2 + 3 = 5$; $5 \times 3 = 15$; $15 + 3 = 18$; $18 \times 3 = 54$...

6. N: In alphabetical order, it is the second letter after L.

7. B: Not all the arrows point in the same direction.

8. Invert the order of the first and second circles from the center to form:

   HIM
   TWO
   VIA
   POT
   MAN

9. 30: The arrows add 2, 3, 4, 5, 6 and 7 respectively to the previous numbers.

10. BORDER and RIM

11. D

12. The second circle from the center.

    MINE
    ZEAL
    PEAR
    BANK
    JUNK

13. 14: It is the only even number between two and twenty that is not in the figure.

14. I: Alternate letters are arranged alphabetically, but go in opposite directions:

        L M N...
    ...   K J I

15. B: In figures A, C and D, each rectangle contains two dots.

16. D: It is the only one in which the central area touches two noncontiguous areas.

17. 68: The figure contains all the numbers in which the second digit is equal to the first digit plus two.

18. 13: The numbers in the corresponding areas of the first two circles—8 + 5—are added together.

19. A: The radii are perpendicular to the sides.

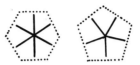

20. DEJECTED and DISPIRITED

21. 19: In each pair, the sum of the three digits in the first number is equal to the second number.

22. The last one: SQUARE.

23. 253: The numbers 1, 2, 3, 4, 5, 6...are alternately added to the previous number and multiplied by it. Hence:
    $2 + 1 = 3$; $3 \times 2 = 6$; $6 + 3 = 9$; $9 \times 4 = 36$...

24. TFM: Each of the three letters in the second group is the next in alphabetical order to the corresponding letter in the first group.

25. The third line: VIOLA.

26. B: The figure is simply inverted.

27. 30: Each arrow adds two, therefore:

                    +2
        8 + 2 10 + 2 16   + 2
                    +2
                    18
                    +2   +2
                    20   +2   24
                         +2
                 +2   30   +2

28. Cats do not like dogs.
    "Proof has been rejected of the negation of the certainty..."
    = "It has been confirmed that..."

29. C: The pairs of figures must be symmetrical.

30. The first line: ELEPHANT.

31. A

32. B: Three areas meet at one central point.

33. 512: The numbers in the hexagons with lines are the square of the previous number; those in the hexagons with a circle are half the previous number.

34.
ERF		UKS
GUN	is to	NFR
PKS		EGP

	BLO	GTV
	FGP	POL
as	is to	
	ITV	BFI

35. B: The figure on the right of the top line contains the only element common to the other three figures.

36. C

37. 11: Each number is the sum of the digits in the numbers above it to which it is connected.

38. 18: The two circles at the top were rotated (the first by half a turn clockwise and the second by a quarter turn counter-clockwise), and then placed one on top of the other. The digits in the sectors were then added together.

39. C

40. The first: In the other three lines, the letters on the right are the third, second and sixth letters of the word on the left.

Evaluation of results
Less than nine correct answers: modest.
Between ten and twenty-four: good.
Twenty-five and over: excellent.

It is most unlikely that in 1831 when the *Beagle* set sail from England on a surveying expedition with the young Charles Darwin as its official naturalist, anyone imagined the ship carried the father of the theory of evolution and future author of *Origin of Species* (1859). It is even less likely that anyone foresaw that the intelligence test would grow out of the expedition. But, in fact, it did. The relationship between animal and human evolution posed by Darwin, implied a fundamental continuity in mental characteristics, and it was just a short step from there to an active consideration of the mental similarities and differences in individuals.

Such a step was taken by Sir Francis Galton, a cousin of Darwin's who studied heredity, among other subjects, and to whom we referred in the early pages of this book. To support his theory, tendered in *Hereditary Genius* (1869), that individual excellence was closely linked to genetic heritage (a point we shall come back to later), Galton developed statistical methods using the properties of the normal distribution curve, to measure physical and mental performance. This made it possible to predict, in any given test, the number of people who would fall within the average range and the smaller number of those who would produce excellent or poor results. Frequently, observations of the natural world follow this kind of distribution; by demonstrating that data relative to man also lends itself to such methods, Galton came to define the correlation between human and natural phenomena.

This methodology based on the normal distribution curve is still used to assess the validity and reliability of *intelligence tests.*

Sir Francis examined thousands of subjects, employing instruments designed to measure their ability to discriminate between sounds, colours, smells, the characteristics of their visual perception and many other anthropometric and psychometric variables.

The aim of Galton's program, as explained by D.P. Schultz, a noted American professor of psychology, was to determine, through mental aptitude tests, the range of human capacities in relation to a range of attributes and types of performance. Indeed, it could be said that Galton actually invented the idea of the intelligence test (although the term itself was not introduced until later).

The first time the phrase "mental aptitude test" was used publicly was in an article written in 1890 by J. M. Cattell, in which he described a series of tests designed to measure the intellectual level (i.e., intelligence) of university students. The word "test" was used, as it is in a variety of fields, to signify a trial or an experiment.

However, it was some fifteen years later that French psychologist A. Binet made particular intelligence tests—still widely in use—familiar to experts and the public alike. "Even prior to the 1908 revision," according to A.A. Nastasi in his book, *Psychological Testing,* "the Binet-Simon tests attracted wide attention among psychologists throughout the world. Translations and adaptations appeared in many languages. In America, a number of different revisions were prepared, the most famous of which is the one developed under the direction of L.M. Terman at Stanford University and known as the 'Stanford-Binet.' It was in this test that the intelligence quotient (IQ), or the ratio between mental age and chronological age was first used.

We need to examine this in more detail. By mental age (MA), Binet meant the level of intellectual ability revealed in the tests. To determine this, Binet first grouped tests that proved to be adequately performed by children of certain ages into various classes. Then taking into account the chronological age (CA—the number of years and months which had passed from birth until that moment) of a given subject, he could deduce the mental age from the correspondence between the subject's test results and those normally produced by children of a certain chronological age.

The two ages do not necessarily coincide. The mental age and intellectual performance of some people can be ahead of or behind that of the majority in the same age group. The *intelligence quotient* (i.e., the ratio between MA and CA) is a *measurement of a subject's intellectual activity in relation to the average intellectual activity of others in the same age group.*

Evaluating our intellectual level (II)

Instructions
You have thirty minutes for the test; if you have time at the end, return only to those questions you were unable to answer.

(1)

17 19 22 16 . 13 32

What number is missing?

(2)

What letter is missing?

C F H . M

(3)

If you flip this figure over and then rotate it, which of the figures below can you obtain: A, B, C or D?

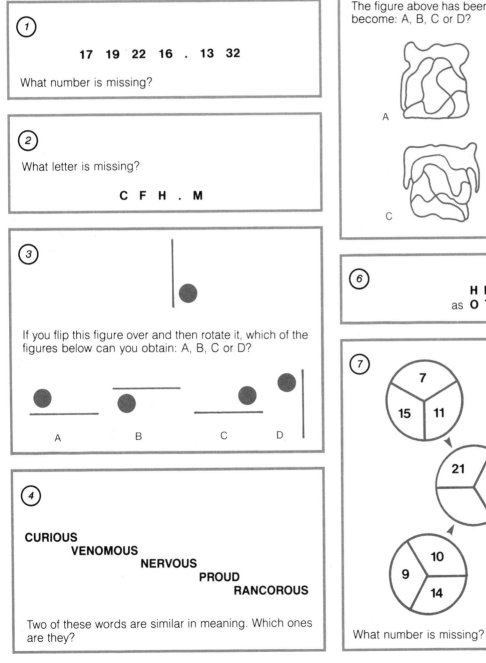

A   B   C   D

(4)

CURIOUS
   VENOMOUS
      NERVOUS
         PROUD
            RANCOROUS

Two of these words are similar in meaning. Which ones are they?

(5)

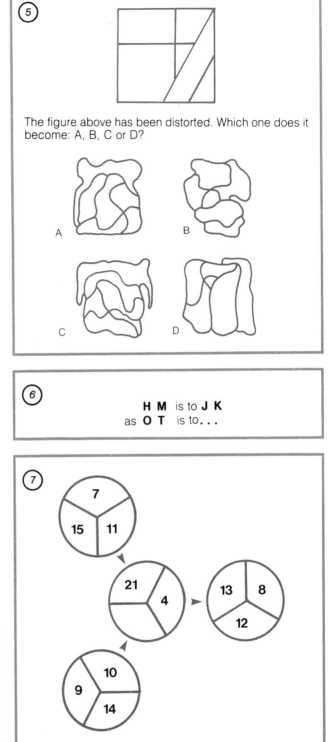

The figure above has been distorted. Which one does it become: A, B, C or D?

A   B

C   D

(6)

H M is to **J K**
as **O T** is to**. . .**

(7)

What number is missing?

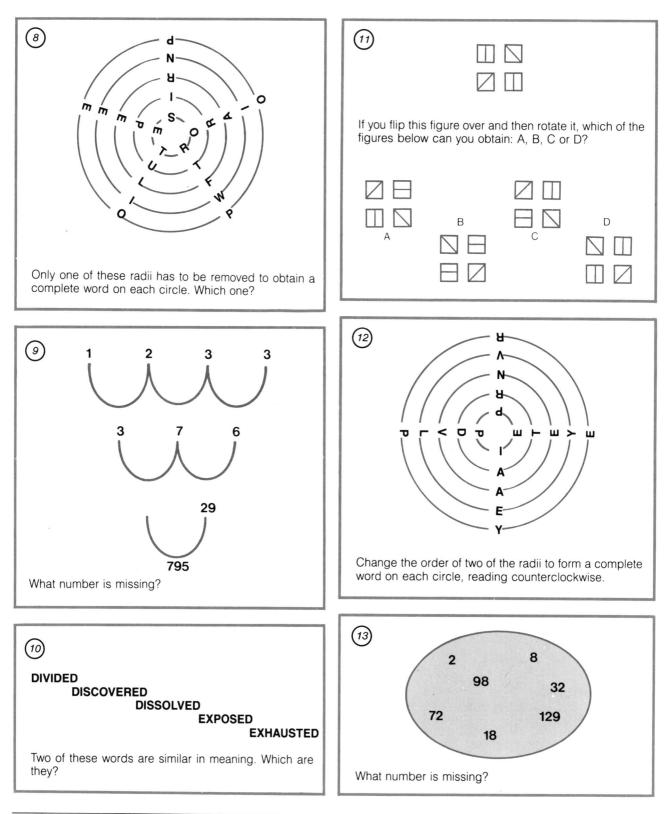

8

Only one of these radii has to be removed to obtain a complete word on each circle. Which one?

9

1   2   3   3

3   7   6

29

795

What number is missing?

10

DIVIDED
   DISCOVERED
      DISSOLVED
         EXPOSED
           EXHAUSTED

Two of these words are similar in meaning. Which are they?

11

If you flip this figure over and then rotate it, which of the figures below can you obtain: A, B, C or D?

A   B   C   D

12

Change the order of two of the radii to form a complete word on each circle, reading counterclockwise.

13

2   8
98
32
72   129
18

What number is missing?

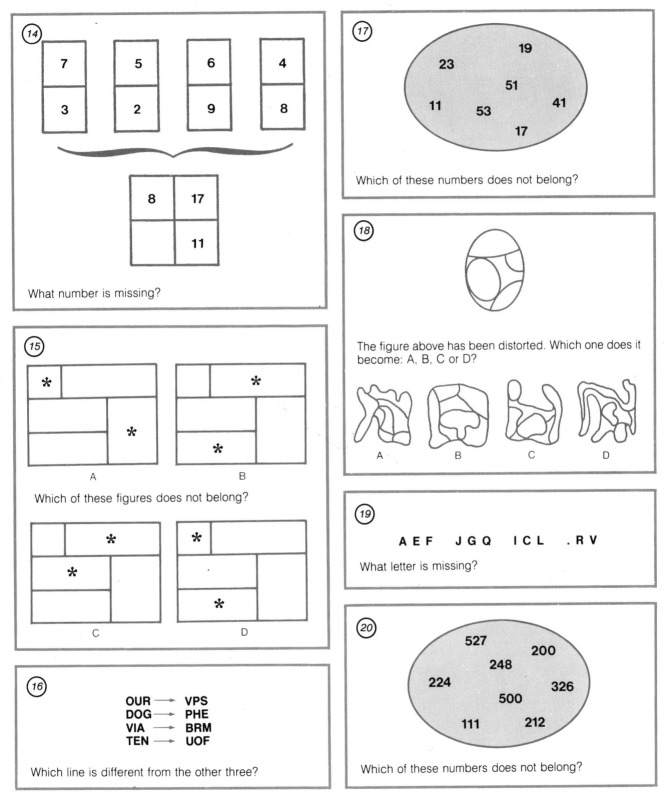

14

7		5		6		4
3		2		9		8

8	17
	11

What number is missing?

15

A

B

Which of these figures does not belong?

C

D

16

OUR ⟶ VPS
DOG ⟶ PHE
VIA ⟶ BRM
TEN ⟶ UOF

Which line is different from the other three?

17

19
23
51
11   53   41
17

Which of these numbers does not belong?

18

The figure above has been distorted. Which one does it become: A, B, C or D?

A   B   C   D

19

A E F   J G Q   I C L   . R V

What letter is missing?

20

527
248   200
224   326
500
111   212

Which of these numbers does not belong?

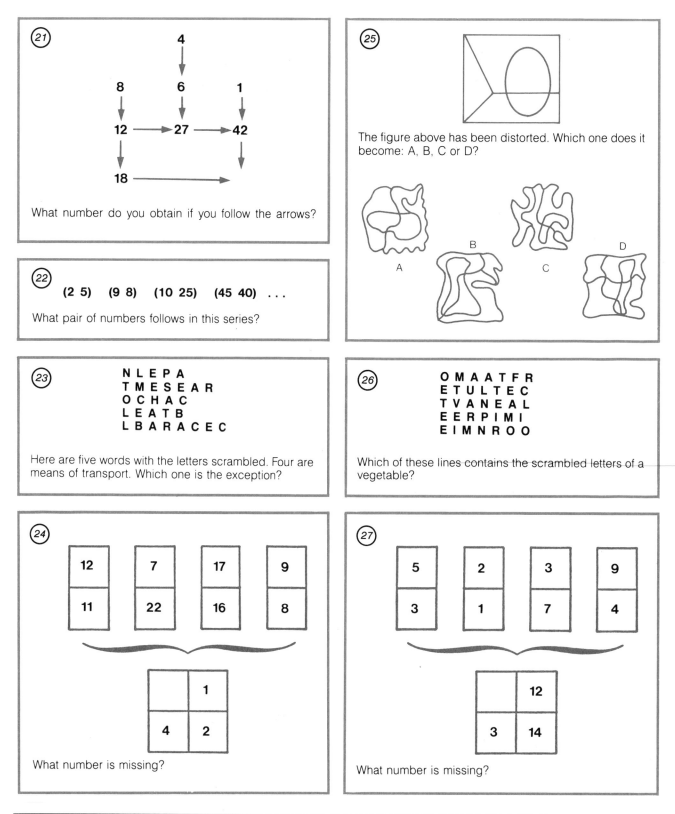

21

4

8   6   1

12 ——▶ 27 ——▶ 42

18 ————————▶

What number do you obtain if you follow the arrows?

22

(2 5)   (9 8)   (10 25)   (45 40) ...

What pair of numbers follows in this series?

23

N L E P A
T M E S E A R
O C H A C
L E A T B
L B A R A C E C

Here are five words with the letters scrambled. Four are means of transport. Which one is the exception?

24

| 12 | 7 | 17 | 9 |
| 11 | 22 | 16 | 8 |

| | 1 |
| 4 | 2 |

What number is missing?

25

The figure above has been distorted. Which one does it become: A, B, C or D?

A   B   C   D

26

O M A A T F R
E T U L T E C
T V A N E A L
E E R P I M I
E I M N R O O

Which of these lines contains the scrambled letters of a vegetable?

27

| 5 | 2 | 3 | 9 |
| 3 | 1 | 7 | 4 |

| | 12 |
| 3 | 14 |

What number is missing?

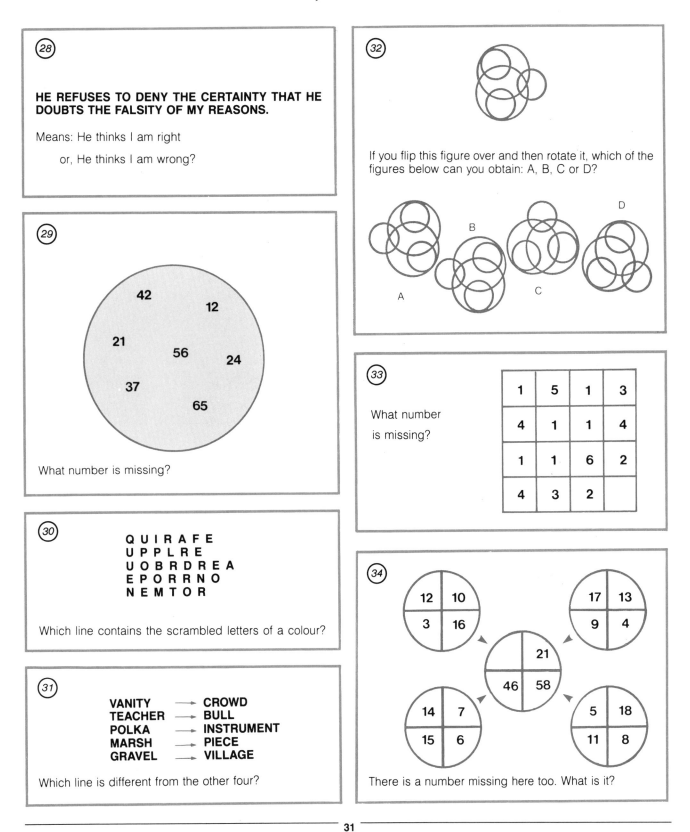

(28)

HE REFUSES TO DENY THE CERTAINTY THAT HE DOUBTS THE FALSITY OF MY REASONS.

Means: He thinks I am right

    or, He thinks I am wrong?

(29)

42

12

21

56

24

37

65

What number is missing?

(30)

Q U I R A F E
U P P L R E
U O B R D R E A
E P O R R N O
N E M T O R

Which line contains the scrambled letters of a colour?

(31)

VANITY   ⟶ CROWD
TEACHER ⟶ BULL
POLKA   ⟶ INSTRUMENT
MARSH   ⟶ PIECE
GRAVEL ⟶ VILLAGE

Which line is different from the other four?

(32)

If you flip this figure over and then rotate it, which of the figures below can you obtain: A, B, C or D?

D

B

A

C

(33)

What number is missing?

1	5	1	3
4	1	1	4
1	1	6	2
4	3	2	

(34)

| 12 | 10 |
| 3 | 16 |

| 17 | 13 |
| 9 | 4 |

| | 21 |
| 46 | 58 |

| 14 | 7 |
| 15 | 6 |

| 5 | 18 |
| 11 | 8 |

There is a number missing here too. What is it?

31

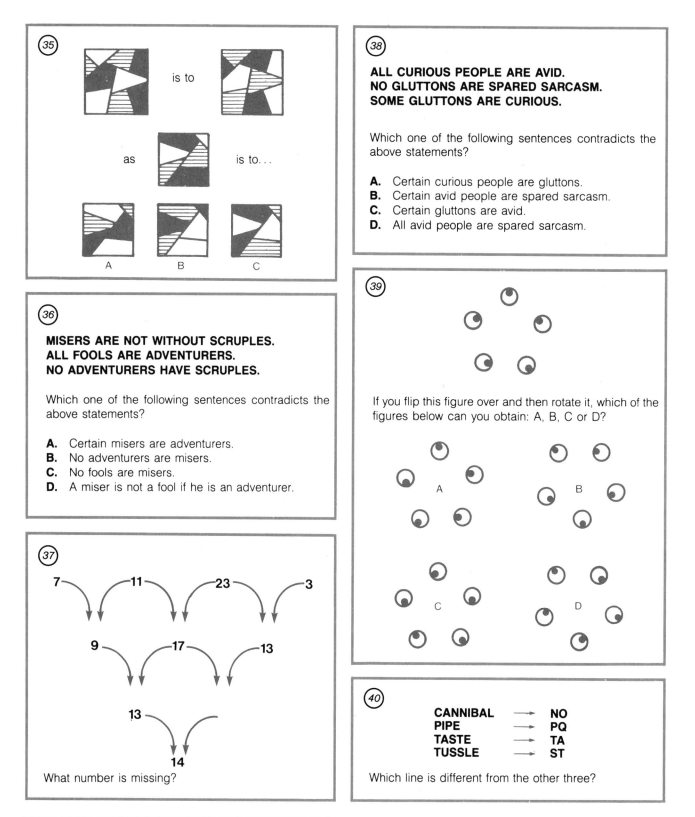

35

is to

as   is to. . .

A   B   C

36

MISERS ARE NOT WITHOUT SCRUPLES.
ALL FOOLS ARE ADVENTURERS.
NO ADVENTURERS HAVE SCRUPLES.

Which one of the following sentences contradicts the above statements?

A. Certain misers are adventurers.
B. No adventurers are misers.
C. No fools are misers.
D. A miser is not a fool if he is an adventurer.

37

7   11   23   3

9   17   13

13

14

What number is missing?

38

ALL CURIOUS PEOPLE ARE AVID.
NO GLUTTONS ARE SPARED SARCASM.
SOME GLUTTONS ARE CURIOUS.

Which one of the following sentences contradicts the above statements?

A. Certain curious people are gluttons.
B. Certain avid people are spared sarcasm.
C. Certain gluttons are avid.
D. All avid people are spared sarcasm.

39

If you flip this figure over and then rotate it, which of the figures below can you obtain: A, B, C or D?

A   B

C   D

40

CANNIBAL	→	NO
PIPE	→	PQ
TASTE	→	TA
TUSSLE	→	ST

Which line is different from the other three?

Answers

1. 27: There are two alternating series, one increases by five each time and the other is reduced by three.

2. K: The series is in alphabetical order, but alternately skips one and two letters.

3. A

4. VENOMOUS and RANCOROUS

5. B

6. QR: The first group of letters contains, in alphabetical order, the second group but with one letter missing on each side.

7. 8: The outer circles rotate and are placed on top of each other. The numbers in the outer circles on the left are added together while the numbers in the outer circle on the right are subtracted, hence:

8. TULIO, which produces ROSE, TRIP, FARE, WINE, POPE.

9. 46: Each number is the square of the number above and directly to the right of it minus the number above and directly to the left of it.

10. DISCOVERED and EXPOSED

11. D

12. By inverting ETEYE and PRNVR you get: PIPE, DART, VANE, LEVY and PYRE.

13. 50: The figure contains all the squares of numbers 1 through 9 doubled.

14. 8: The process can be visualized as follows:
The rectangle 9–6 moves to the top, with 6 on the left;
the rectangle 8–4 moves to the right, the 8 next to the 9; $8 + 9 = 17$;
the rectangle 2–5 moves to the left, the 2 next to the 6; $2 + 6 = 8$;

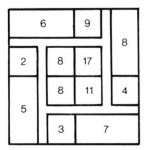

the rectangle 3–7 moves to the bottom, the 3 next to the 5; $3 + 5 = 8$;
the 7 is next to the 4; $7 + 4 = 11$.

15. C: It is the only one with dots in two contiguous areas.

16. The third: In the others, the element on the right is made up of the letters that follow alphabetically the letters on the left: OUR PVS VPS.

17. 51: The others are prime numbers.

18. A: It has three internal points of intersection (which rules out B and D) and six outer points of intersection (which rules out C).

19. D: In each group of letters, the numerical position in the alphabet of the first two letters is added together to produce the third letter, hence: A (first letter) + E (fifth letter) = F (sixth letter).

20. 527: In the other numbers the last digit is equal to the product of the first two digits.

21. 90: Each arrow adds $1\frac{1}{2}$ times the number from which it came.

22. (50 125): In each step, the difference between the two numbers is added to the higher number, and the sum of the two numbers is added to the smaller number, therefore:
$2 + (5 + 2) = 9$ and $5 + (5 - 2) = 8$
$9 + (9 - 8) = 10$ and $8 + (9 + 8) = 25$
$10 + (25 + 10) = 45$ and $25 + (25 - 10) = 40$
$45 + (45 - 40) = 50$ and $40 + (45 + 40) = 125$

23. The fourth: TABLE. The other words are PLANE, STEAMER, COACH, and CABLECAR respectively.

24. 5: The process can be visualized as follows:
The rectangle 22–7 moves to the top, with 22 on the left;
the rectangle 8–9 moves to the right, the 8 next to the 7;
the rectangle 11–12 moves to the bottom, the 11 next to the 9;
the rectangle 17–16 moves to the left, the 16 next to the 12 and the 17 next to the 22.
The smaller numbers are then deducted from the adjacent larger one.

25. B: It has three internal lines intersecting (which eliminates C and D) and, like the two halves of the ellipse in the original figure, it has two areas separated by one line that comes from only two other lines (which eliminates A).

26. The second: LETTUCE.

27. 45: The rectangle 4–9 goes to the top, the 9 on the left; the rectangle 7– 3 goes to the right, the 7 adjacent to the 14; the rectangle 3– 5 goes to the left, the 3 adjacent to the 3; the rectangle 1–2 goes to the bottom, the 1 adjacent to the 3.

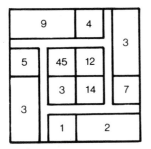

The contiguous pairs of numbers in the outer rectangles are then multiplied.

28. He thinks I am right.   "He refuses to deny" = to confirm; "…he doubts the falsity," is to believe true.

29. 73: The circle contains pairs of numbers; each pair has the same numbers in inverse order.

30. The second: PURPLE.

31. The fifth: In the others, none of the letters forming the word on the right appear in the word on the left.

32. B

33. 1: The sum of the numbers in each column is ten.

34. 43: The circles on the left were rotated and those on the right turned upside down. The corresponding segments were then added together to obtain the results in the central circle. Twenty-one is the clue to finding the answer, as it is the sum of only one permutation.

$$\frac{16\,|\,3}{10\,|12} + \frac{7\,|\,6}{14\,|15} + \frac{9\,|\,4}{17\,|13} + \frac{11\,|\,8}{5\,|18} = \frac{43\,|21}{46\,|58}$$

35. The black areas replace the shaded areas; the shaded areas replace the white areas, and the white areas replace the black areas.

36. A: Misers have scruples, adventurers do not.

37. 15: Each number is one-half the sum of the two numbers above.

38. D: Certain avid people are curious and gluttonous, so they cannot be spared sarcasm.

39. D

40. The third, TASTE. In the others, the first letter on the right is the one that appears twice in the word on the left; the letter next to it follows alphabetically.

Evaluation of results
Less than five correct answers: modest.
Between five and fourteen: good.
Fifteen and over: excellent.

Numbers are central to our lives. We use them to calculate expenses, balance our budgets, figure out our tax debt, or determine how many hours it will take to put up kitchen shelves. These situations lie well within our capabilities; we can work out the figures without too much difficulty and hence we are not afraid of them. But very often numerical calculations strike us as awesome, mysterious and, to say the least, terrifying. Depending on the circumstances, their import can be triumphant, abstruse or disturbing, as in the case of defense spending, when the reality of the numbers themselves is secondary to the effect of their implications.

An "inappropriate" sense envelops the vast numbers used to describe the macrocosm. The separation of the stars by millions of light years is a concept so far beyond most of us that it occasions feelings of wonder, and a measure of pride in the scientific and technological achievements of man which have enabled him to explore the mysteries of space. Indeed, we might say that here, the numbers bear a triumphant air.

It is much the same in the world of finance, where investments can be valued at billions of dollars, or man hours lost through strikes calculated in the hundreds of thousands. Such figures have been known to spark some fanciful impressions: One of Parkinson's laws (those humourous and quite discerning views on organizations and custom) which seems particularly applicable here, tells us that the higher the numbers, the less likely it is a board of directors will offer objections. Large numbers are daunting, especially when they involve money. Men save their quarrels for what they can comprehend; how much to expend on the repair of a generator can set off the most heated of debates between the parsimonious on a board and their more daring fellow members.

Actually, the only "proper" use of numbers is to convey the exact dimensions describing a given phenomenon. This requires the skills normally used in numerical aptitude tests: the ability to calculate, to grasp essential elements quickly, and to identify general aspects on the basis of the values given. For further discussion of this subject, see the chapter Intellectual Ability on p. 39.

Dealing with larger figures, calls for a certain aptitude and interest. How many trees are required to print a newspaper with a circulation of a million? All you have to know is the weight of the newspaper and the average amount of wood needed to secure enough pulp for one copy. Then you need only do a simple arithmetical calculation. How many floors are there in a given skyscraper? You can answer this by dividing the exact or estimated height of the building by ten feet which is the average height of a room. As an introduction to large figures, try to estimate the size of the box and of the small metal tubes seen in the photograph opposite. There are exactly 3,000 pieces.

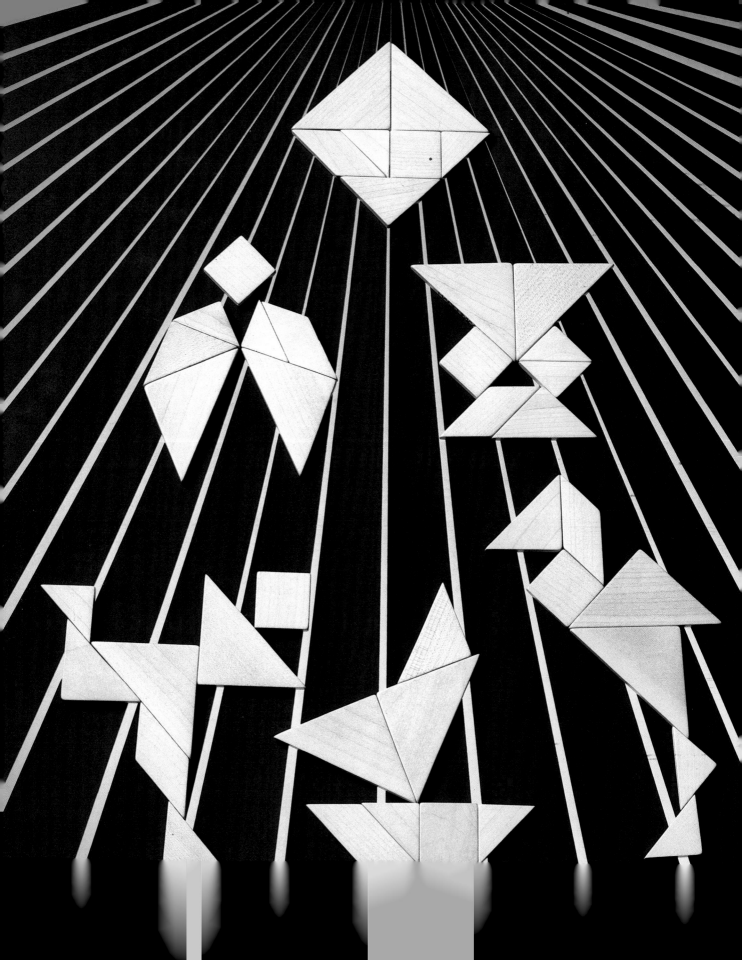

The author of a successful little book titled The Eighth Book of Tan, Part I, and published in 1903—one Sam Loyd, to be exact—was responsible for a stupendous hoax regarding games. According to Loyd, Tan was a legendary Chinese writer, venerated as a god, and the author of seven books about the seven stages of the world's evolution, from chaos and the primordial beginnings to the appearance of life, animals and man. The sage's eighth volume serendipitously fell into Loyd's hands, so he tells us, and he introduced it to the modern Western world. Primarily the book relates the legend of how the game Tangram came to be and why it is in seven pieces.

Loyd quoted liberally from Confucius, cited epigrams of ancient Oriental wisdom and the profundities of long-past philosophers—all of it pure fabrication. The Chinese writer never existed, and it is impossible to date the origin of Tangram beyond the last century.

The hoax was such a marvel of fakery that it beguiled everyone interested in the subject except Sir James Murray, editor of the Oxford English Dictionary. After much painstaking research, he delivered his authoritative opinion that the origins of the game were quite recent, and that its real name was a commonly used term in China, and meant an "intelligent seven-piece brain-teaser." It seems that "Tan" was derived from "tang," the Cantonese word for "Chinese," and coupled with "gram" from "anagram." Another theory holds that originally Tangram was played in houses of pleasure, for, in the vernacular, "tan" is a girl of "easy" virtue.

Before Sir James set the record straight, however, the hoax had already been widely accepted. Even today there are numerous books and even encyclopedias that still describe Tangram as a 4000-year-old game, often played in ancient China and preserved in its original form to the present day. Despite the hoax, or perhaps because of it, the seven-piece puzzle has enjoyed much success in its short lifetime of barely a hundred years. Indeed, Edgar Allan Poe, (1809–1849) that famed writer of the powers of darkness, ordered a set carved out of ivory.

The Tangram, which can be formed into a variety of shapes as shown in the illustration opposite, can serve a number of purposes. Among other things you can fashion human or animal shapes with it or simply aesthetically pleasing ones, experiment with different ways of creating a given image or solve problems of combinatorial geometry, such as how many geometric figures of a certain type can be obtained by subdividing certain pieces. And if you use more than one puzzle, you can increase the possible combinations as many times as you like and attempt more and more complex problems.

Tangram, like many another puzzle (see the caption on p.108), tests a number of interconnected abilities of perception, intelligence, analysis and synthesis, to say nothing of patience, but perhaps it is most interesting when used to design new and even more suggestive images than those shown opposite: Starting with the complete seven-piece puzzle at the top and moving counterclockwise, there is a jacket, a boy running, a boat, a stork and a goblet.

The concept of the intelligence quotient is still widely employed. The various levels of the intelligence scale are based on a series of questions which make up the IQ test.

The IQ is a number that gives an immediate and concise piece of information, which is certainly a major reason why the tests have been used so broadly. However, a measure of caution is necessary when drawing conclusions from the IQ. To sum up intelligence in a numerical value can be reductive in many cases. We will come back to this later, but here, we would like to point out that, in accordance with what we have been saying and in keeping with the spirit of the book, we have refrained from presenting the results to the sections "Evaluating our Intellectual Level" (I & II) in the form of IQ tables. Instead, we have given general indications. Naturally, you may or may not agree with our decision; the validity of intelligence tests and of psychometrics in general—that area of psychology dealing with mental measurement—and the best use of them (in a manner designed to stimulate improvement rather than cause frustration and add to existing problems), are topical subjects and open to much discussion.

Although Binet popularized a series of tests to measure intellectual levels (and used in the French school system to identify mentally handicapped children), which led to the development of other intelligence tests and their widespread application in schools and industry, intelligence tests can actually be used in a variety of ways and for a number of purposes: They can be individual or collective; they can test intelligence, attitudes or progress; they can even go so far as to measure personality.

Every intelligence test must contain certain basic characteristics, namely it must be standardized, reliable and valid.

The term standardization refers to the conditions under which the test is administered, which must be the same for everyone (it is not accidental that the tests are accompanied by instructions to be followed by both examiners and examinees); it also refers to the process of determining the statistical norms that govern the interpretation of the scores. In order to rank scores excellent, average or poor, you have to refer to the typical performances of "normal" people (normal meaning a set of characteristics shared by the majority of people); exceptionally good results are rare, as are exceptionally poor results, hence any given population tends to center around average values. Once the aims of a test are defined, its various components have to be evaluated in terms of their difficulty. Then too, the "control" group must be representative of every type of person who could be examined (called, in this case, a representative sample).

It should be emphasized again that, in themselves, the results of a test have no absolute value. They take on meaning only when they are compared to the scores—both potential and actual—of a majority of people in the same environment.

Reliability means that a test is stable and coherent to the extent that the same subject, if tested under different circumstances and at different times (in accordance with the standardized administration procedures), would produce identical results. Should this not be the case, the test would be considered flexible and elastic and its data somewhat unreliable.

Having said all this, we should make it clear that the tests given in Figures 1, 2, 3 and 4 did not contain the basic characteristics of standardization, reliability and validity to the extent that their results could lead to the construction of scales to measure verbal and emotional behaviour. Quite the contrary as a matter of fact, as these exercises give free rein to the imagination and provide an opportunity for moments of wit, laughter, curiosity and seeing how others react. And this, we maintain, has its own validity.

In Evaluating our Intellectual Level (I & II), the situation is different: The instructions are followed by a number of questions, each of which requires a right or wrong answer. The reliability and validity of the test—or, more precisely, the stability of the results that can be obtained and the extent of their effectiveness as a measurement of intelligence–have been carefully examined (although the relative processes, based for the most part on correlation, have not been explained), and the possible scores form interesting indices. These indices permit us to compare our results to those of a majority of subjects, be they adolescents or adults, who live in the same era and culture as we do, and hence, to legitimately rank scores, modest, good, or excellent.

Intelligence tests may create a sense of frustration: Perhaps we are disappointed in our results, or it may be that concentrating on specific problems which are of such limited use, makes us irritable.

Should this happen to you, we suggest an escape into the world of nonsense—the very stuff of Figure 5. Play with notions of factories that run on oil-lubricated flights of fancy, and mechanical ideas made out of rubber. It could prove quite beneficial!

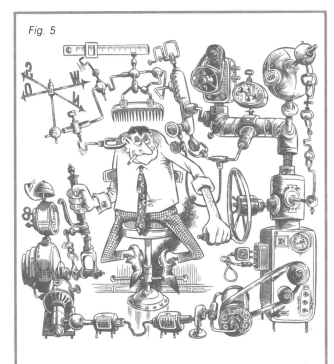

Fig. 5

Look at this picture from top to bottom. Try to follow all the mechanical connections, but, for the moment, disregard any thoughts that may come to mind.

Invent unusual combinations. Indeed, this is the realm of the absurd, but it is precisely from absurdity that you develop what is known as brainstorming—literally a storm of ideas.

Forget the old formulas. Assign each object a different purpose. Improvise. Get a pencil and piece of paper, and design even giddier machines. Connect basic parts of the machine to phantasmagoric accessory equipment to produce different results, just as the model machine designed to part the hair does.

For example, what might these look like?

A bottle opener and beer pourer,

A thought-and-smile extractor,

A nail cutter and cleaner,

A bed-mounted page turner,

A machine to polish shoes and put them on,

A bread slicer and butterer,

An alarm clock triggering device.

This is a good way to set the creative juices flowing; it combines technical knowledge with the satisfaction of doing it yourself. In fact, truly creative ideas can only spring from the fertile ground of observation and direct knowledge, but certainly a contributing factor is inspiration, and in this excerise, the player is free to indulge any and all flashes of inspiration.

Intellectual ability

G. Stanley Hall: His vocation and successes

Divergent thinking is expressed in a number of ways and under a number of conditions. Once, for example, G. Stanley Hall (1844–1924)—who at one time aspired to the priesthood but later, after much wavering and reflection, became both a doctor of theology and a noted psychologist—managed to turn an exam he was taking at New York's Union Theological Seminary into an impassioned sermon. When the moment arrived for his professors to set forth their evaluation, instead of announcing his marks, they fell on their knees and prayed for his soul.

An unusual sight, to say the least! If we asked why they reacted this way, we would have to admit there is no easy answer. The possibilities are numerous: irrational feelings combined with a rational appraisal of the arguments; pleasure in partaking of such high drama; a keen sense of ecclesiastical mission—all elements rooted in each personality of those involved. Indeed everything we do is to some degree, a reaction to the demands of the circumstances in which we find ourselves. It is a reaction drawn from our previous experience, our capacity to understand and act accordingly, and our emotions, our impulsiveness, self-control, and the faith we place in ourselves and in others. The list

could go on, but we will return to this later when we discuss personality. Although emotions and motivation must certainly be considered, in this chapter we want to concentrate on those particular elements that combine to form the intelligence.

Both Stanley Hall and his examiners shared intellectual qualities that were unquestionably above average, but what prevented the latter from achieving the same reknown their erstwhile pupil enjoyed? Does the answer lie mainly in their ambitions, or do the basic elements of their intelligences also play a part?

The answer is a foregone conclusion; intelligence as an independent entity that can be isolated from the individual's personality, is purely an abstraction. In reality, intelligence is the product of a synthesis of the many aspects of a person's nature and the diverse ways in which the intellect can function. Solving the logical problems encountered in a chess game, for instance, or tracking down the murderer in an Agatha Christie novel, call for a fluid and unrestrained approach. Taking an examination for employment, on the other hand, is quite different. Here emotion, anxiety, and indeed panic, can adversely affect our performance which under other circumstances, might have been completely satisfactory. Of course, individual reactions to these situations vary enormously.

Charles Darwin was not an exemplary student, yet the theory of evolution and much of his empirical research on vegetable genetics are true monuments to his intellectual ability. Stanley Hall dedicated himself to philosophy, theology, physiology and physics; he taught English and French—the languages as well as the literature; he studied experimental psychology in Germany, taught at Harvard University and other universities and organized a psychological laboratory at Johns Hopkins, the first of its kind in the United States. Because of his diverse interests and his independence of mind—on the one hand, he supported evolutionism in arguments with theologians, on the other hand, his study of religion made him suspect to many in the scientific community—his views were not rapidly accepted. Despite this, however, he became President of Clark University where he stayed for thirty-six years. In 1887 he founded the *American Journal of Psychology,* and in 1891 helped to organize and served as first president of the American Psychological Association. Quite a catalog of accomplishments for a man who chose to operate in a most unsystematic fashion.

If we recall our own school years, we will probably see that not all those who were "top of the class" went on to eminent careers. Indeed, it is quite possible for students who are less than brilliant, or employees whose work leaves much to be desired to achieve unexpected success with a change of environment or activity. This is not to say we think it is unnecessary to work hard at school and in your job—quite the contrary, in fact, for we believe this kind of commitment is the basis for both individual and collective progress and well-being.

Elements of the intellect

The Intelligence Quotient, derived by comparing a person's intellectual ability with his chronological age, is a general rather than a specific measurement. As early as the 1920s, after the enormous success of the "Army Alpha Test" and the "Army Beta Tests" used in World War I to select American soldiers, there was a growing awareness of the need for an analytical examination of that complex function which then, as now, is called "intelligence." It had been noted that someone could produce strikingly divergent results on two different parts of the same test. Hence, in order to assess how well they would do in a particular area, it was often necessary to evaluate answers to specific questions rather than rely on the overall score.

Furthermore, there was good reason to doubt whether IQ tests measured *all* the elements of the intel-

lect; it was correctly noted that only certain attributes—those that were of importance for particular purposes or activities—were highlighted. For example, the vocabulary needed to qualify for military training did not demand that one be a linguist, so while a candidate might have achieved excellent scores in the army's selection tests (giving him a high IQ), his performance could have been poor in more demanding vocabulary tests.

Much the same holds true for the tests in the earlier sections, Evaluating our Intellectual Level (I & II): You may have found a marked difference between your scores on tests requiring considerable language ability, and those requiring an ability to discriminate between shapes. Consequently any measurement of intelligence drawn from these games should be thought of as reflecting the limitations of the tests. However, even with these limitations the games are interesting because of their relative difficulty, and the dissimilar aptitudes they reveal. If, by intelligence, we mean a general *capacity to overcome difficulties and to resolve the problems encountered in new situations,* then we must identify the varied characteristics that join to create this capacity, through an analytical and investigative approach.

From the G factor to primary abilities

Of the numerous approaches to the study of that complex of abilities that constitutes intelligence, the one taken by Charles Spearman (1863–1945) is historically and conceptually of major importance. Spearman developed the system of factorial analysis and used it to isolate what is known as the G factor. He believed that all intellectual activities shared a common characteristic, on the basis of which a subject could be classified as more or less gifted, and that, in addition to this common attribute, each activity required a specific skill. The G factor therefore corresponded to "general intelligence" or, better still, "general intellectual energy."

Factorial analysis is a technique based on the mathematical-statistical examination of the correlations between scores from different intelligence tests, which makes it possible to identify a hypothetical common denominator for some of the correlations. By applying this technique Spearman's followers managed to isolate other factors in addition to the general factor, gradually narrowing the range until specific factors could be determined. In this fashion, the "verbal-educational" and the "practical" intelligence factors were isolated.

L. L. Thurstone (1887–1955), however, was responsible for a theory developed toward the end of the 1930s and extended in later years, which allowed the general measurement derived from intelligence tests (including the Binet-Simon tests mentioned earlier) to be broken down into a number of specific abilities. What was new about his theory was that it considered groups of factors instead of one general factor, hence a better evaluation of the scores obtained on the various items of one or more tests (some of which measure one factor and some another), was possible. Thurstone identified "seven factors as the *primary abilities* revealed by the items on intelligence tests. These seven are:

1. Verbal comprehension (V). Vocabulary tests represent this factor.
2. Word fluency (W). The ability to think of words rapidly, as in solving anagrams or in thinking of words that rhyme.
3. Number (N). Simple arithmetic tests, especially those calling for computations, represent this factor.
4. Space (S). Tests of this factor deal with visual form relationships, as in drawing a design from memory.
5. Memory (M). This factor is found in tests requiring memory for pairs of items.
6. Perceptual (P). Calls for the grasping of visual details and of the similarities and differences between pictured objects. (Tests for P are omitted from some forms of the Primary Mental Abilities batteries.)
7. Reasoning (R). Best represented by tests that call for finding a general rule on the basis of presented instances, as in finding how a number series is constructed from a portion of that series."

Verbal abilities

A handbook much favoured by the ladies of Piedmont, Italy in the 19th century, warned of the dangers of forming sentimental attachments to poets or writers. The author thoughtfully pointed out that to do so involved the risk of discovering one's intimate life serialized in magazines or recounted in enormous tomes. Even cavalry officers were potentially perilous—despite the fact that they rarely indulged in literary pursuits—given their penchant for making boastful toasts in the officers' club. As a result, the ladies were advised to frequent the nobility who were more reserved in their talk and unmotivated as scribes, or, failing that, to select their beaux from those among the bourgeoisie who were trained to keep secrets—.notaries, magistrates and doctors, for example.

Figs. 6 & 7   **The New Word**

The space between each set of two words should be filled in with a word that combines with the word before it, and with the word after it to form a new word or concept, as in the following example. The word "fish" forms a new word when added to "dog," i.e.,"dogfish," and to "wife," i.e.,"fishwife."

1. dog	fish	wife
2. master		work
3. letter		ache
4. silver		house
5. watch		hole
6. light		boat
7. bank		worthy
8. half		ward
9. blood		balance
10. letter		squad
11. blank		book
12. hair		work
13. broad		step
14. buck		gun
15. bottle		lace
16. fire		chair

(Answers in Figure 28)

Be that as it may, a good command of language remains a valued gift. Being able to express oneself convincingly and in appropriate terms is often essential for professional success, whether in politics, business or an academic career.

The saying, "speech is silver, but silence is golden" may be true for those unable to hold their tongues, but anyone able to use language to advantage is in a better position to give prompt and apt replies in any given situation. The game in Figures 6 and 7 exercises one's ability to construct compound words as a result of recognizing the possible connections between the words given and the missing link. The exercise can be made even more difficult by trying to find compound words in addition to those given in the answers. Figure 8 tests one's vocabulary; Figure 9 is an exercise in constructing sentences.

Fig. 8 **The Dictionary and You**

One of the four words in each line does not belong. Which one is it?

	A.	B.	C.	D.
1.	impeccable	senseless	perfect	irreprehensible
2.	fast	quick	swift	keen
3.	ill-bred	awkward	impolite	rude
4.	totally	widely	entirely	completely
5.	gigantic	colossal	violent	enormous
6.	to flash	to illuminate	to sparkle	to glitter
7.	cheerful	happy	jolly	satisfied
8.	to aid	to help	to supervise	to assist
9.	to restrain	to spy on	to prevent	to obstruct
10.	tediously	continuously	always	constantly
11.	tepid	boiling	temperate	warm
12.	hungry	poor	indigent	without means
13.	to buy	to pay	to purchase	to acquire
14.	impudent	cheeky	crafty	insolent
15.	to reflect	to brag	to vaunt	to boast
16.	to try	to choose	to experiment	to test
17.	to fight	to thrash	to howl	to beat
18.	to mistreat	to torture	to torment	to train
19.	to retaliate	to crush	to avenge	to repay
20.	frequently	repeatedly	often	always

(Answers in Figure 28)

Numerical abilities

Many of us have had game partners, or opponents, who are particularly fast or infallible in calculating scores. Similarly, we have probably also encountered those who are slow or make frequent mistakes. In short, some players always seem to keep score; it is hardly surprising they are the ones who possess a numerical aptitude.

Of course the importance of numerical skills extends beyond the world of games to many areas where general intelligence is needed, and needless to say, such skills have a myriad practical and professional appli-cations. In Figure 10, we propose an unusual way of working with figures: You can work against the clock to see how many correct calculations you can do in the ninety seconds allowed, or you can compete against friends. Precision with figures, accuracy and speed are required in Figure 11; Figure 12 tests one's capac-ity to grasp the arithmetical operations and the prin-ciple behind them.

Visual-spatial abilities

An ability to discriminate between shapes and colours, to see relationships between diverse elements and to

Fig. 9   **Reconstructing Sentences**

Construct ten intelligible sentences by taking one phrase from each of the three columns. To make things easier, we have given the punctuation.

1. If you want to pull a friend out of the mud

2. Business is like a wheelbarrow;

3. Don't try skipping rungs,

4. You grow old by the grace of God,

5. Public opinion is not always right;

6. Intelligence is the art

7. Many people don't worry about their money

8. If you are tempted

9. When you have enough experience,

10. It's better to be worn out

A. doesn't run.

B. others act the same way with their time.

C. it doesn't move

D. with work

E. my words are worthless.

F. the crowd does not make fewer mistakes

G. of getting dirty too.

H. that you can draw the right conclusions.

I. you are too old

J. but staying young

a. is the art of the ego.

b. you mustn't be afraid

c. of seeing things in such a way

d. than the individual.

e. than rust.

f. unless you push it.

g. until they are nearly broke;

h. to praise me,

i. to enjoy it.

j. anyone who has a long road before him

(Answers in Figure 28)

Fig. 10   **Unusual Arithmetic**

In this exercise, the normal arithmetical signs have a different meaning, i.e.:

: = add
× = subtract
− = divide
+ = multiply

You have one minute and thirty seconds to perform the operations.

$4 \div 2 =$	$12 - 4 =$	$15 \times 5 =$	$33 - 11 =$
$3 + 7 =$	$16 - 4 =$	$12 \div 2 =$	$18 \times 6 =$
$16 \times 4 =$	$21 \div 7 =$	$17 \times 4 =$	$15 - 3 =$
$9 - 3 =$	$7 + 7 =$	$6 + 6 =$	$36 \div 12 =$
$8 + 5 =$	$64 - 16 =$	$72 - 12 =$	$12 - 4 =$
$9 \div 3 =$	$48 \div 24 =$	$18 \div 3 =$	$5 + 7 =$
$18 - 6 =$	$13 + 3 =$	$22 \times 2 =$	$35 \times 5 =$
$9 \times 2 =$	$21 - 7 =$	$4 + 7 =$	$25 \div 5 =$
$36 - 6 =$	$72 \div 16 =$	$80 - 20 =$	$4 + 12 =$
$24 \div 8 =$	$18 - 2 =$	$14 \div 7 =$	$14 \times 2 =$

Fig. 11 — Choose and Add

Add the numbers in those circles that are directly connected by the dotted line - - - - - -
Total: a)
Do the same with the numbers in the diamonds that are directly connected by the dotted line ......
Total: b)
Each number should be added only once.
You have one minute and thirty seconds.

(Answers in Figure 28)

Fig. 12 — The Hidden Sequence

In this exercise we propose several series of numbers, each of which has its own sequence. You have to identify the sequences and continue the series accordingly. Here are some examples to make the process clearer:

$$3 \overset{+2}{} 5 \overset{+2}{} 7 \overset{+2}{} 9 \overset{+2}{} 11 \overset{+2}{} 13 \quad \underline{\mathbf{15}} \quad \underline{\mathbf{17}} \quad \underline{\mathbf{19}}$$

Here we can see that each number is 2 more than the previous number, so the sequence in this series is +2.

$$2 \overset{2}{} 4 \overset{-1}{} 3 \overset{3}{} 9 \overset{-1}{} 8 \overset{2}{} 16 \overset{-1}{} 15 \overset{3}{} 45 \quad \underline{\mathbf{44}} \quad \underline{\mathbf{88}} \quad \underline{\mathbf{87}}$$

This sequence is also easy to spot: ×2, −1, ×3, −1, ×2, −1, ×3 . . .

Complete the following series.

1. **2 4 6 8** ___ ___ ___

2. **14 12 10 8** ___ ___ ___

3. **3 4 6 7 9** ___ ___ ___

4. **4 6 5 7 6** ___ ___ ___

5. **2 4 6 5 7 9 8** ___ ___ ___

6. **1 2 4 7** ___ ___ ___

7. **1 1 2 2 4 4** ___ ___ ___

(Answers in Figure 28)

isolate the essential features of a geometric, plastic or figurative structure is very important in a number of professional activities. The architect needs this ability, as does the painter, the pilot or electrician. Then too, shape and colour are automatically associated with beauty—a canvas by Caravaggio or Constable, a study by Da Vinci, a statue by Michelangelo or Moore, a facade by Bernini, are all structures expressing a harmony of tone, volume, light and shade, and an appreciation of the essence of line as well as the decorative effect. Among the predecessors of modern research into visual perception we can include Johann Wolfgang von Goethe (1749–1832), the poet, thinker and scientist. His approach was more than just inter-

disciplinary. He adopted a humanist or, more accurately, a psychological perspective, one attentive to the subjective moment.

The somewhat fanciful question he is thought to have asked, "What use is mathematics when you are judging light or colour?" is symptomatic of this approach.

Studies in perception, both past and present, have played an important part in psychological research in general, and many go beyond our area of concern, which is the ability to grasp visual detail, to perceive the similarities or differences between subjects and the relationships between shapes. Figures 13, 14 and 15 give interesting examples of this skill.

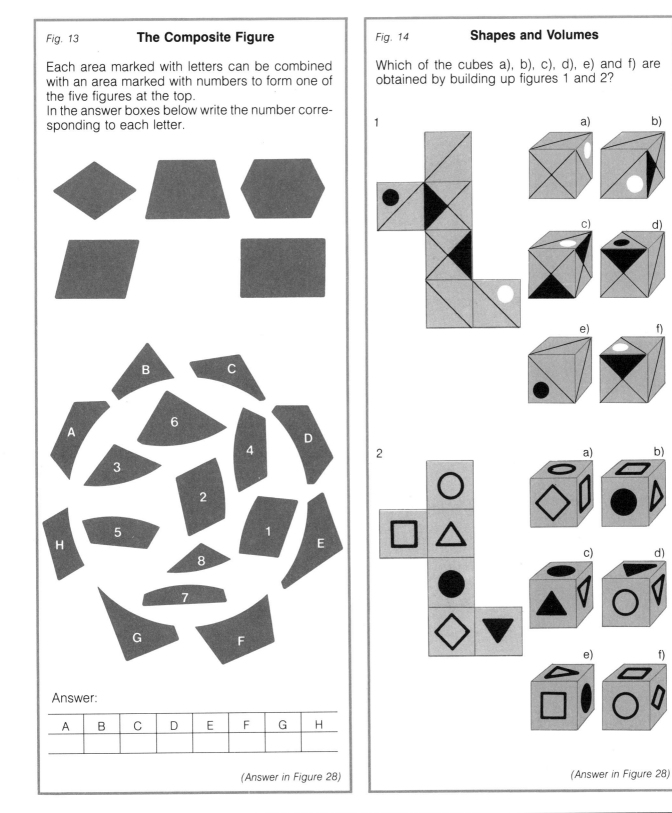

Fig. 13 — The Composite Figure

Each area marked with letters can be combined with an area marked with numbers to form one of the five figures at the top.
In the answer boxes below write the number corresponding to each letter.

Answer:

A	B	C	D	E	F	G	H

(Answer in Figure 28)

Fig. 14 — Shapes and Volumes

Which of the cubes a), b), c), d), e) and f) are obtained by building up figures 1 and 2?

1

a) b)
c) d)
e) f)

2

a) b)
c) d)
e) f)

(Answer in Figure 28)

Fig. 15

Match the Vases

You have three minutes to spot the three pairs of vases that are identical except for minute differences (after all, they are handmade). If you can't spot them, don't worry, the answer is given in Figure 28.

On one hand, the psychology of perception is connected to the senses themselves (sight, hearing, etc.), and on the other hand to the sensory data received—the constancy and repetitiveness of stimuli, the way they are presented and their reciprocal relationships are perceived to different degrees by the sensory organs. Each individual learns about the world through these organs, but what we discern also depends on our experiences, our needs and desires.

The things around us create spheres of stimuli to which we react as a whole, often without considering the component parts. For example, we perceive a picture or a melody, not flecks of colour or individual notes. Similarly, we place our experiences within a framework of time and space, so it is natural for us to accept the cause-and-effect relationship between our pressing a switch and a light coming on. Perceptual identification develops in a child precisely through this constancy and repetition of events which is responsible for our awareness of the permanent qualities and functions of individual objects.

We acquire our perception of the world intellectually. Hence, when we turn our attention from one thing to another, we believe that what we were just looking at stays where it is, or, if it was moving, that it continues to move; in other words that the object "behaves" as we think it should. This phenomenon involves both memory and reason. If we limit our attention to the visual sphere, we perceive an object as stable and permanent. As E. R. Hilgard observed: "When an object has been constituted perceptually as a permanent and stable thing...the tendency to see it as of normal color regardless of light and shadow is called *brightness* and color *constancy*. The tendency to see it as of standard shape regardless of viewing angle is called *shape constancy*. The tendency to see it as its usual measurable size regardless of distance is called *size constancy*. Finally the fact that objects retain their 'same' positions, even as we move about, is known as *location constancy*. The word 'constancy' is an exaggeration, but it dramatizes our relatively stable perception of objects. Object constancy is made up, then, of these five constancies of brightness, color, shape, size and location." Occasionally, the integration of what our sense organs register with our previous experience can lead to ambiguity (Figures 16 and 17), jumping to conclusions (Figure 18), or perceptual illusions (Figures 19 and 20).

In conclusion, therefore, we can say that both the action of our sense organs and our assumptions regarding the objects in question are of considerable importance in the process of perception. Our assumptions are based on information from our sensory

Fig. 16 **Reversible Figure and Background**

Notice how both the light and the dark areas can be seen as figures on a background.

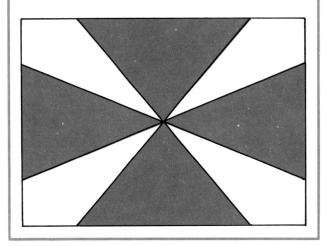

Fig. 17 **Ambiguous Stimuli**

This is an ambiguous drawing that can be seen either as an attractive young woman ("the wife") or as an old hag (jokingly known as the "mother-in-law").

Fig. 18   Patterning and Perceptual Grouping

The proximity of pairs of lines leads us to see three pairs with an extra line on the right.

The same lines as above, but the extensions at the top and bottom lead to the opposite pairing: We see three broken squares with an extra line on the left.

Fig. 19   An Impossible Drawing

The arch in this drawing appears to be supported by three columns at the bottom, but at the top it has only two columns.

Fig. 20

A. An Illusion Based on Relative Size. The central circles are the same size, but the one on the left looks bigger.

B. and C. Illusions Based on Intersecting Lines. The horizontal lines in B and C are parallel.

D. Ponzo's Illusion. The two horizontal lines are the same length, but the upper one appears to be larger.

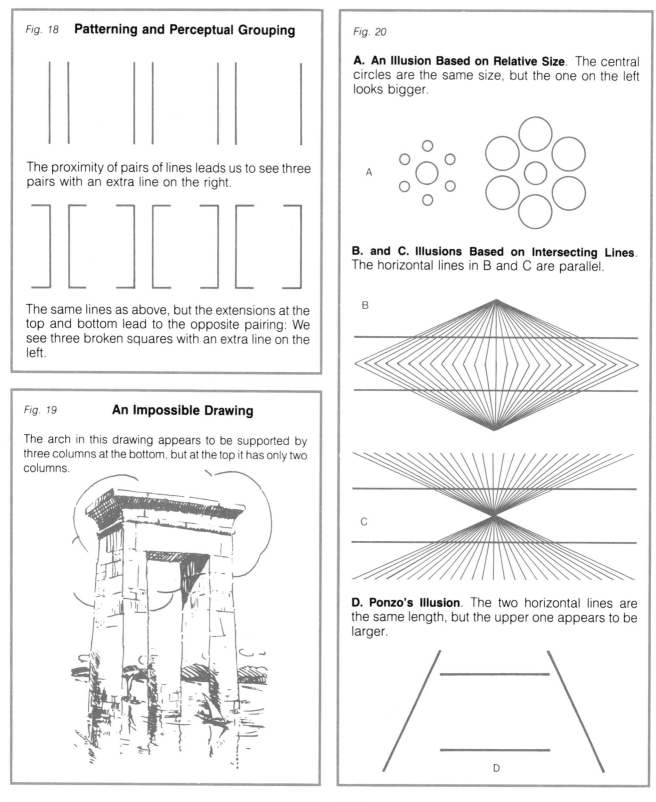

organs and on our previous experience. They are also based on our individual needs and wishes, which means we are more aware of some elements than others (our attention levels also differ).

Controversy is rife between those who support the theory that perception is an innate phenomenon and those who claim it is a result of our experiences.

Those who argue it is innate attach much weight to the fact that we are "built" to perceive things in particular ways. Our sensory equipment is inherited and our eyes are equipped for stereoscopic vision: Various experiments with young chicks show they can use this kind of vision even though their eyes have been bandaged from birth. The implications of Figure 21 are especially suggestive, as the photograph reveals that even in infancy when the child has yet to be influenced by the learning process, he is capable of making perfectly appropriate judgements on the basis of what he perceives.

On the other hand, those who favour the theory of experience emphasize the importance of what we know. According to this view, size, shape and dimension constancy are associated with a familiarity that is progressively established between the subject and his surroundings, a familiarity that will direct, guide and anticipate the way in which he perceives.

As in many instances, these opposing ideas can be reconciled by a synthesis of the two theories: It cannot be denied that our perception depends on the structure of our sensory organs; it is equally true, however, that various factors, such as what we have learned and our degree of sensitivity to our surroundings, are also determining factors.

Reason and memory

"Elementary, my dear Watson!" This is the famous phrase always used by Sherlock Holmes to conclude some flawless piece of reasoning, leaving Watson, his friend, assistant and companion, in a state of acute frustration. The strength of our fictitious sleuth's reasoning lay in his ability to draw logical conclusions from certain basic premises (a process known as deduction), and to make brilliant generalizations on the basis of specific details (induction).

It is no easy task to dissect the ways in which logical reasoning is expressed—be it by Holmes or anyone else. Here, we shall confine ourselves to measuring our abilities to isolate the general criteria that govern the continuation of logical sequences (Figures 22 and 23), and to working out solutions to problems such as those given in Figures 24 and 25. One way to make the "Four on a bench" puzzle particularly difficult is to try

Fig. 21 **The Visual Cliff**

No sooner can infants and young animals move about than they show an ability to perceive depths. The visual cliff consists of two surfaces made of the same material and with the same pattern, covered by a sheet of thick glass. One surface is directly under the glass while the other surface is at least twelve inches below it. When placed on the central area, the infant refuses to cross to the deep side, but will readily crawl to the shallow side.

and solve it from memory, without noting down each person's position; however, to avoid unnecessary aggravation only try it if your results in Figure 26 are excellent.

While the research on the nature of the *linguistic, cognitive representation,* and the *formal* theories is of major consequence, an in-depth review of it is beyond the scope of this book, as is a detailed review of the research on memory. Hence, in the game we have included, we have confined ourselves to assessing logical memorization, that is, the capacity to learn the message, plot or events contained in a passage. This is different from the following categories listed by Hilgard:

continued on page 54

Fig. 22   **Spot the Sequence**

All the exercises of this type consist of two series: the problem series and the answer series. The problem series follows a certain sequence which you have to identify. You must then decide which of the figures in the answer series is the logical continuation of the sequence.
Look carefully at the following example:

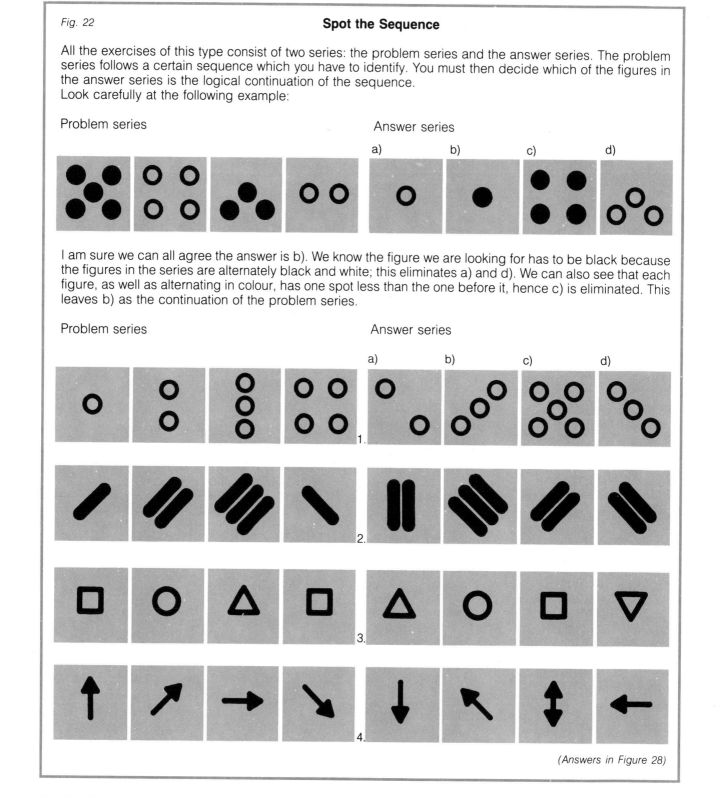

Problem series   Answer series

I am sure we can all agree the answer is b). We know the figure we are looking for has to be black because the figures in the series are alternately black and white; this eliminates a) and d). We can also see that each figure, as well as alternating in colour, has one spot less than the one before it, hence c) is eliminated. This leaves b) as the continuation of the problem series.

Problem series   Answer series

(Answers in Figure 28)

More Sequences

Fig. 23

Which of the four possible figures continues the problem series?

Problem series　　　　　　　　Answer series

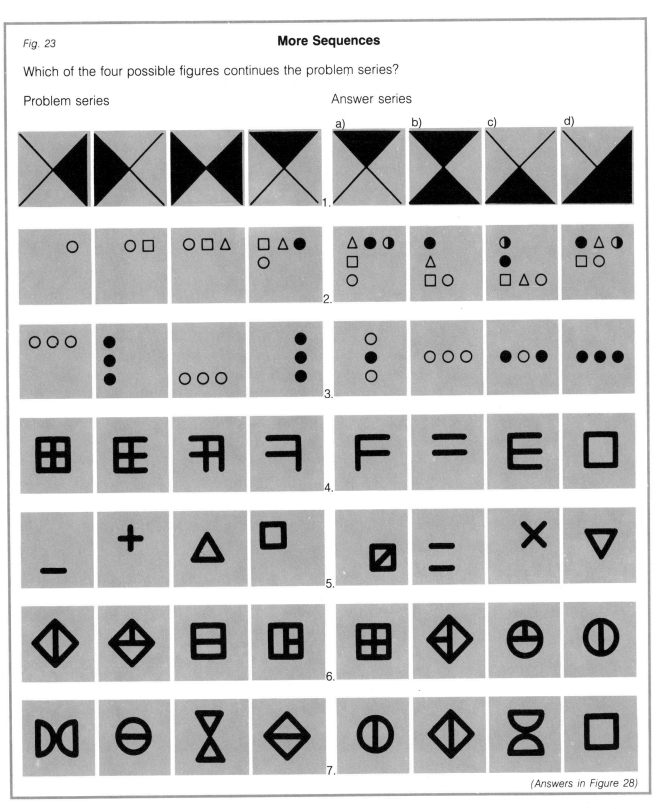

(Answers in Figure 28)

Fig. 24 The Merchants and Their Servants

Three merchants were travelling with their three servants. The merchants were very rich and feared their servants would attack them as soon as they could outnumber them.

They came to a river where the only ferry was one small boat which could carry only two people.

The merchants had to be very careful not to put themselves in a position where any of them could be outnumbered by their servants.

In what order then should they cross the river?

(Answer in Figure 28)

Fig. 26 Grand Celebration in Leeds

You have two minutes to read the following text, then turn to Figure 28.

"Yesterday, Friday the 23rd, there was a grand celebration in the district of Morton in Leeds, near St. Martin's Cathedral. Important civil and religious figures were there: Mr. Taylor, the Mayor, Mr. Harrison, the County Council Representative, and Archbishop Maguire. They spoke to a crowd of over 25,000 people. The reason for the celebration was the completion of restoration work on the statue of St. Joseph which is to be moved to the crypt of St. Martin's Cathedral. The cost of the restoration work totalled nearly $200,000, 25 percent of which was supplied by the local council, 40 percent by the county council and the remaining 35 percent by the diocese and local parishes."

(Answer in Figure 28)

Fig. 25 Four on a Bench

Four men are sitting on a bench. Their names are Curt, Abel, Simon and Burger. Each has a different marital status. By profession they are: a painter, a forester, a chauffeur and a bus driver. Given the information below, what is the chauffeur's name and what is Curt's job?

a) The forester is sitting next to the bachelor.
b) All the others are sitting on Curt's right.
c) The married man is younger than the widower. The fianceé is younger than the married man. The bachelor is the youngest of them all.
d) The youngest is also sitting at one end.
e) The forester is not engaged.
f) Simon is sitting next to the second in age.
g) The painter, who is sitting between two younger men, is older than Abel.
h) Curt is not a chauffeur.
i) Neither Abel nor the bus driver is the youngest.

(Answer in Figure 28)

Fig. 27 Six in a Car

There are six men in a six-seat car, three in the front and three in the back. By profession they are an architect, a doctor, a teacher, an engineer, a businessman and a building contractor. Their respective ages are, 43, 52, 40, 46, 36, and 42. Their hobbies are skiing, hunting, stamp collecting, tennis, swimming and running. The car has a left-hand drive.
Given the information below, work out: What is the doctor's hobby? How old is the one who likes running?

1. The architect is behind the wheel.
2. The man on the right of the back seat collects stamps.
3. The engineer is talking to the building contractor diagonally behind him.
4. The tennis player is talking to the man on his left about skiing.
5. The businessman is sitting between the teacher and the building contractor.
6. The 40-year-old is sitting in front of the teacher.
7. The 42-year-old is in the front seat.
8. The man sitting on the right, in front of the businessman, is 46.
9. The skiier is sitting next to the engineer.
10. The swimmer is sitting on the right behind the skiier.
11. The 36-year-old is sitting next to the stamp collector who is the oldest of the group.
12. The runner is talking to the man in front of him.

(Answer in Figure 28)

Fig. 28:   **Answers**

Figs. 6 & 7: **The New Word** 1, fish; 2, piece; 3, head; 4, ware; 5, man; 6, house; 7, note; 8, way; 9, bank; 10, bomb; 11, check; 12, net; 13, side; 14, shot; 15, neck; 16, arm.

Fig. 8: **The Dictionary and You** 1, b; 2, d; 3, b; 4, b; 5, c; 6, b; 7, d; 8, c; 9, b; 10, a; 11, b; 12, a; 13, b; 14, c; 15, a; 16, b; 17, c; 18, d; 19, b; 20, d.

Fig. 9: **Reconstructing Sentences** 1bG; 2Cf; 3jA (after Paula Modersohn-Becker; 4Ja; 5Fd; 6cH; 7gB (after Johann Wolfgang von Goethe); 8hE; 9Ii (after Somerset Maugham); 10De.

Fig. 11: **Choose and Add** a) 43; b) 28.

Fig. 12: **The Hidden Sequence**

1. $2 \overset{+2}{} 4 \overset{+2}{} 6 \overset{+2}{} 8 \overset{+2}{}$ **10 12 14**

2. $14 \overset{-2}{} 12 \overset{-2}{} 10 \overset{-2}{} 8 \overset{-2}{}$ **6 4 2**

3. $3 \overset{+1}{} 4 \overset{+2}{} 6 \overset{+1}{} 7 \overset{+2}{} 9 \overset{+1}{}$ **10 12 13**

4. $4 \overset{+2}{} 6 \overset{-1}{} 5 \overset{+2}{} 7 \overset{-1}{} 6 \overset{+2}{} \mathbf{8} \overset{\mathbf{-1}}{} \mathbf{7} \overset{\mathbf{+2}}{} \mathbf{9}$

5. $2 \overset{+2}{} 4 \overset{+2}{} 6 \overset{-1}{} 5 \overset{+2}{} 7 \overset{+2}{} 9 \overset{-1}{} 8 \overset{+2}{} \mathbf{10} \overset{\mathbf{+2}}{} \mathbf{12} \overset{\mathbf{-1}}{} \mathbf{11}$

6. $1 \overset{+1}{} 2 \overset{+2}{} 4 \overset{+3}{} 7 \overset{+4}{} \mathbf{11} \overset{\mathbf{+5}}{} \mathbf{16} \overset{\mathbf{+6}}{} \mathbf{22}$

7. $1 \overset{\times 1}{} 1 \overset{\times 2}{} 2 \overset{\times 1}{} 2 \overset{\times 2}{} 4 \overset{\times 2}{} \mathbf{8} \overset{\mathbf{\times 1}}{} \mathbf{8} \overset{\mathbf{\times 2}}{} \mathbf{16}$

Fig. 13: **The Composite Figure:** A4; B2; C8; D5; E3; F7; G6; H1.

Fig. 14: **Shapes and Volumes:** 1b; 1c; 1f; 2a; 2f.

Fig. 15: **Match the Vases** 1 & 9; 4 & 8; 5 & 12; the secret lies in checking the position of the eyes and the tentacles.

Fig. 22: **Spot the Sequence:** 1c; 2d; 3b; 4a.

Fig. 23: **More Sequences:** 1c; 2a; 3b; 4b; 5a; 6d; 7c.

Fig. 24: **The Merchants and Their Servants** 1. Two servants cross to the other side; 2. one servant comes back; 3. two servants row over to the other side; 4. one servant comes back; 5. two merchants cross over; 6. one merchant and one servant come back; 7. two merchants cross over; 8. one servant comes back and makes two trips to take the servants to the other side.

Fig. 25: **Four on a Bench** The chauffeur is named Burger, and Curt is a bus driver.

Fig. 26: **Grand Celebration in Leeds** Based on what you read in Figure 26, complete the story by filling in the blanks. When you finish, compare the two texts to see how much you remembered.

"Yesterday, ... 23rd., there was a grand celebration in the. . . . . of . . . . in Leeds, near . . . . Cathedral. Important civil and religious figures were there: Mr. Taylor, the . . . . , Mr. Harrison, the . . . . and . . . . .Maguire. They spoke to a crowd of over . . . . people. The reason for the celebration was the completion of restoration work on the . . . . .of St. Joseph, which is to be moved to the. . . . . .of . . . . Cathedral. The cost of the restoration work totalled nearly . . . . , ... of which was supplied by the diocese and local parishes."

Fig. 27: **Six in a Car** The doctor's hobby is hunting; the runner is 43 years old.

Fig. 31: **The Swinging Koala**

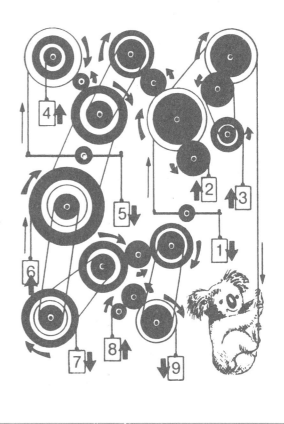

"Recognition.—That form of remembering indicated by a feeling of familiarity when something previously encountered is again perceived.

Redintegrative memory.—Remembering the whole of an earlier experience on the basis of partial cues; recollection of events in the personal history of the subject, with their attendant circumstances. . .

Rote memorization.—Verbatim learning as in learning a poem "by heart". . .

Serial memorization.—That form of rote memorization in which a list of items, or a passage of prose or poetry, is learned in sequence from beginning to end, so that each item or word is a cue to the one that follows it. . ."

Such faculties as those above indicate the complex nature of intelligence. And, of course, factors like motivation, interest and anxiety play an important role in determining how these faculties operate, just as personal and environmental characteristics do in influencing test performances.

Our games give you the chance to become aware of your intellectual skills and to gain a rough evaluation of your capacities for verbal, numerical, and visual-spatial logic, and for memorization and reasoning. Their purpose is to provide you with a better understanding of certain aspects of yourself so you can smile at your own and other people's strengths and failings. Now, let's try the last tests in this section. Do not be alarmed if they seem too demanding. If, on the other hand, they seem too easy, follow the advice given above and try to work out the answers using just your memory, without drawing diagrams or writing anything down.

Intelligence as a synthesis of abilities

This somewhat general review of the faculties that constitute intelligence has followed Thurstone's theories; other structural features which certain authors consider characteristic of intellectual faculties will be discussed later. At this point, an overview is called for. This is possible thanks to the work of H. J. Eysenck, the noted psychologist born in Berlin in 1916, who is currently Professor of Psychology at London University, and is also an authoritative exponent of the inheritability of intelligence (this too, will be discussed later). We have included two separate tests, each consisting of a number of items and each designed to furnish an overall assessment of intelligence. Their degree of difficulty is very similiar, so the scores should be roughly the same. Good luck.

Evaluating our Intelligence (I)

Instructions
The test consists of forty items and you have thirty minutes in which to solve them. The score is equal to the number of correct answers you get in that time without looking up the answers. Do not spend too long on any one item; go back if you have time at the end.

---

①

Insert the missing number.

25   20   15   10

---

②

Underline the word that does not belong.

coach   car   bus   wagon   sleigh

---

③

Insert the missing number.

3   7   16   35   -

---

④

Underline the animal that does not belong.

ant   spider   bee   moth   gnat

---

⑤

The names of the following animals have been re-arranged. Underline which animal is the smallest.

NOBIS
TCA
HPESE
USMOE
IRGAFFE

---

(6)

Write in a word with a meaning in common with the words on either side of the brackets.

remainder (　　) repose.

---

(7)

Which of the six numbered figures completes the series? (Write the number in the box.)

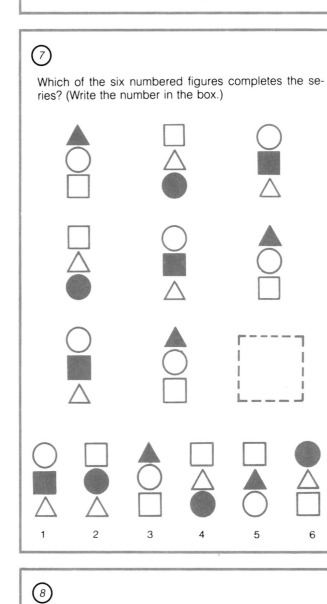

---

(8)

What word completes the first word and begins the second?

CH (...) IC

---

(9)

Which of the six numbered figures completes the series? (Write the number in the box.)

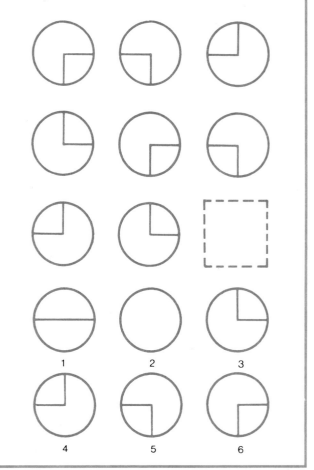

---

(10)

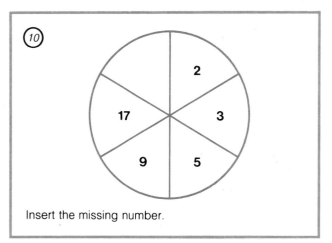

Insert the missing number.

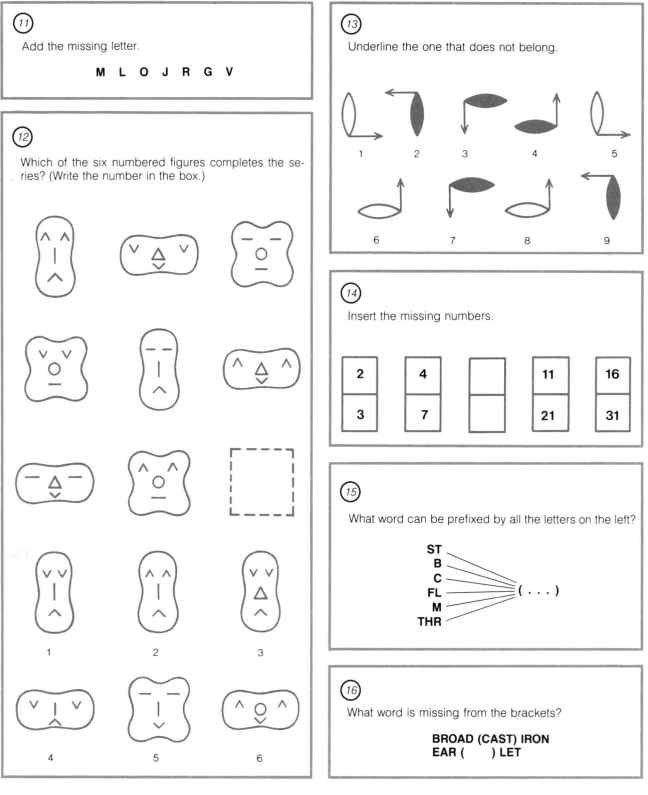

(11)

Add the missing letter.

M L O J R G V

(12)

Which of the six numbered figures completes the series? (Write the number in the box.)

1 2 3

4 5 6

(13)

Underline the one that does not belong.

1 2 3 4 5

6 7 8 9

(14)

Insert the missing numbers.

2	4		11	16
3	7		21	31

(15)

What word can be prefixed by all the letters on the left?

ST
B
C
FL
M
THR

(. . .)

(16)

What word is missing from the brackets?

BROAD (CAST) IRON
EAR ( ) LET

(17) Insert the missing number.

14   9   5

21   8   13

28   9   [ ]

(18) Underline the word that does not belong.

**opulent   deterrent   station
hilarity   ability   police**

(19) Insert the word missing in the brackets that will complete the first word and begin the second.

CO(....)AL

(20) Underline which of the following is not a boy's name.

**TEBORR
DIBENETC
AILIWLM
SUVEN**

(21) Insert the missing word in the brackets.

**supper (pure) German
moment (....) delivery**

(22) Insert the missing number.

(23) Write in a word with a meaning in common with the words on either side of the brackets.

line (....) noise

(24) Underline the face that does not belong.

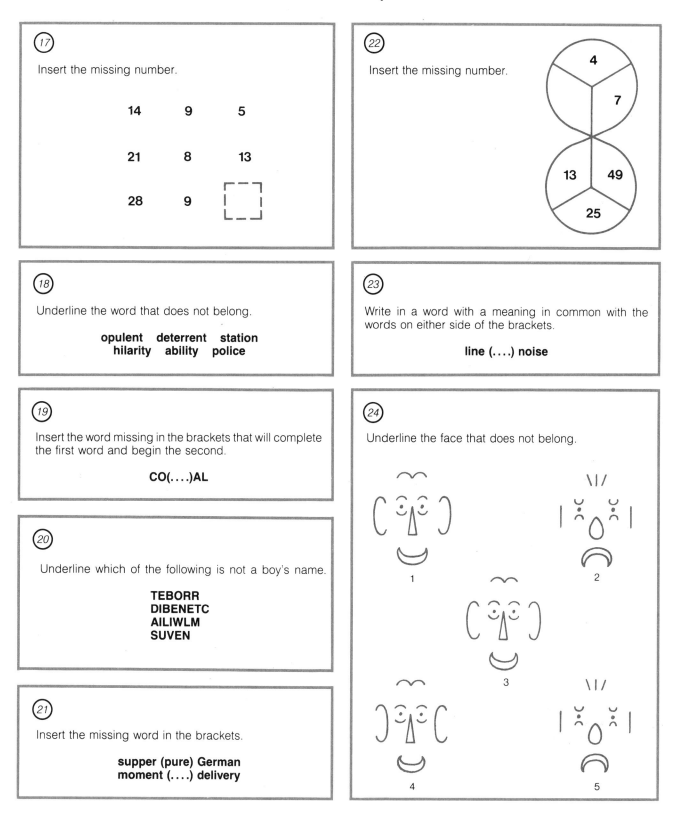

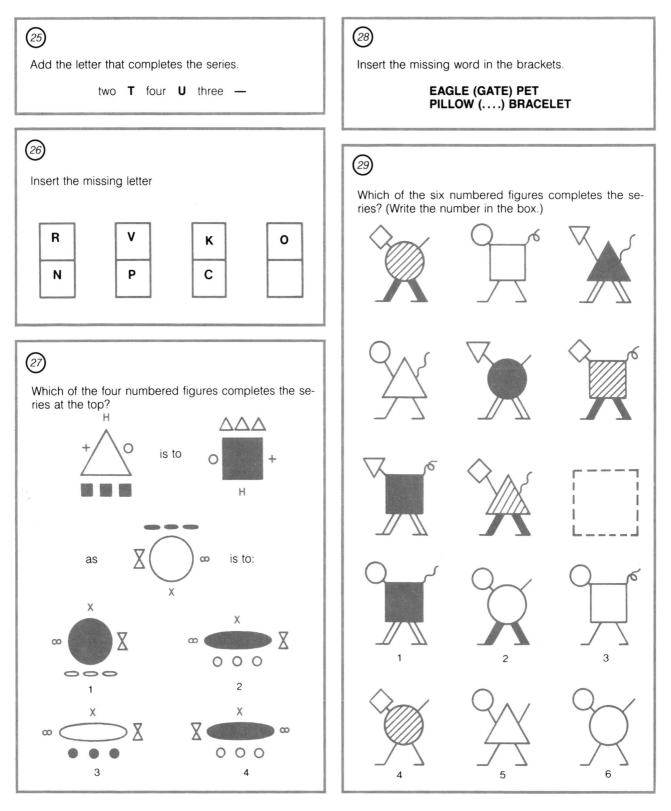

25

Add the letter that completes the series.

two **T** four **U** three —

26

Insert the missing letter

R		V		K		O
N		P		C		

27

Which of the four numbered figures completes the series at the top?

28

Insert the missing word in the brackets.

EAGLE (GATE) PET
PILLOW (....) BRACELET

29

Which of the six numbered figures completes the series? (Write the number in the box.)

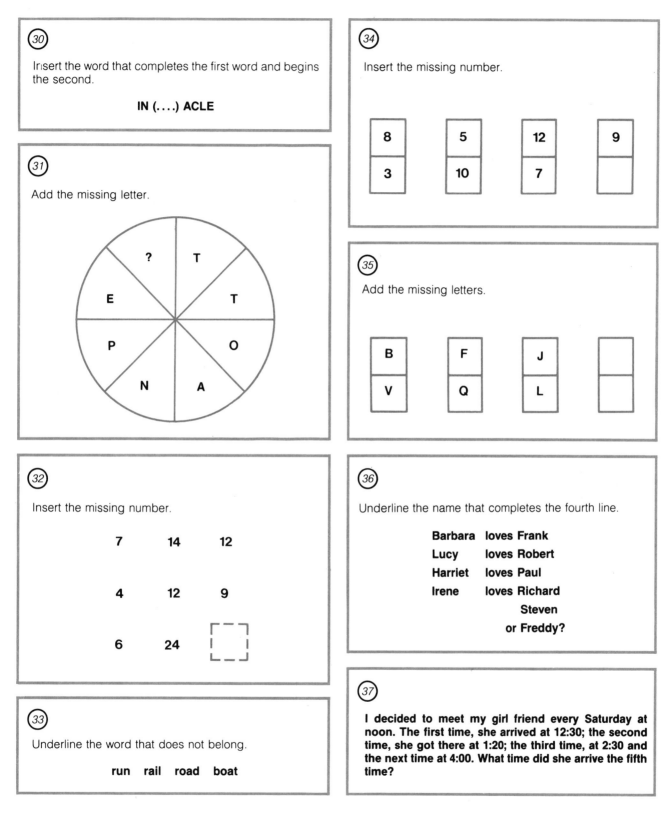

30

Insert the word that completes the first word and begins the second.

IN (. . . .) ACLE

31

Add the missing letter.

32

Insert the missing number.

7   14   12

4   12   9

6   24

33

Underline the word that does not belong.

run   rail   road   boat

34

Insert the missing number.

8		5		12		9
3		10		7		

35

Add the missing letters.

B		F		J		
V		Q		L		

36

Underline the name that completes the fourth line.

Barbara   loves Frank
Lucy   loves Robert
Harriet   loves Paul
Irene   loves Richard
Steven
or Freddy?

37

I decided to meet my girl friend every Saturday at noon. The first time, she arrived at 12:30; the second time, she got there at 1:20; the third time, at 2:30 and the next time at 4:00. What time did she arrive the fifth time?

(38)

Which of the six numbered figures completes the series? Underline the answer.

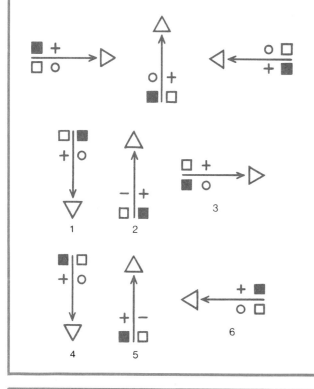

(39)

Underline the word that does not belong.

AZEETRIULOS
IHNUEIRAMCUEIS
NIVOERINUURSIS
REALOPPOOSILILOO

(40)

Insert the missing numbers.

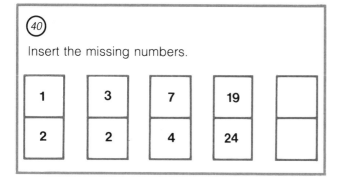

Answers

1. 5   (The numbers decrease by five each time.)

2. Sleigh   (It has no wheels.)

3. 74   (Each number is double the previous ones plus 1, 2, 3 and 4; hence $35 \times 2 + 4 = 74$.)

4. Spider   (It has eight legs, the others have six.)

5. Mouse   (The other animals are bison, cat, sheep, giraffe.)

6. Rest   (Remainder means the same as rest, and rest also means repose.)

7. 4   (Three shapes—a circle, a square and a triangle—appear in each of the three positions; one is black, the others are white.)

8. Ant

9. 6   (The sector rotates 90 degrees counterclockwise in each column and clockwise in each line.)

10. 33   (Each number is double the previous number minus one, hence $17 \times 2 = 34 - 1 = 33$.)

11. C   (There are two alternate series; in the first series, you skip one, two, three, etc. letters forward; in the second series, you skip one, two, three, etc. letters backward. If you skip three letters back from G, you get C.)

12. 1   (There are three head shapes, three nose, mouth and eyebrow shapes; each of these occurs only once in each line and in each column.)

13. 4   (The white ovals are attached to arrows pointing up or to the right; the black ovals have arrows pointing down or to the left. Oval four is black, but has an arrow pointing up.)

14. 7 + 13   (The numbers at the top increase by 2, 3, 4 and 5; those on the bottom increase by double those amounts, 4, 6, 8, 10.)

15. OAT

16. Ring   (The bracketed word forms a bridge between the words outside the brackets; it completes the first word and begins the second.)

17. 19   (To obtain the third number in each row, subtract the second number from the first.)

18. Police   (In all the other words, the first two letters are alphabetically consecutive; in police they are in reverse order.)

19. MET

20. Venus   (The boy's names are Robert, Benedict and William.)

21. MOLE   (The word in brackets is formed by putting the second and third letters of the words outside the brackets in reverse order.)

22. 97 (The series begins with 4 and follows the contours of the figure eight: each number is double the previous number minus one: $49 \times 2 = 98 - 1 = 97$.)

23. Row

24. 4 (Faces 1 and 3 are identical, so are 2 and 5.)

25. H (T is the first letter of "two," U is the third letter of "four" and H is the second letter of "three." Consequently the number of the letter in each of the words is one less than the number indicated by the word itself.)

26. E (The letters at the bottom precede the letters at the top by 4, 6, 8 and 10 letters in alphabetical order.)

27. 2 (The three small squares under the big triangle become three equal, small triangles above the big square. The three small figures on the right, the left and on top of the big triangle, change position. The geometric figures in the first drawing, which are either white or black, remain the same colour in the second drawing.)

28. LIAR (The word in brackets is formed by putting the second and third letters of the words outside the brackets in reverse order.)

29. 6 (In each row and each column, there are three body types—round, square and triangular—three head types—round, square and triangular—three tail types—straight, wavy or curly—and three leg types—a single line, black or white. Also, the bodies are black, white or striped. The missing animal must therefore be number 6.)

30. TENT

31. E (The letters, when read alternately and clockwise, spell the words "tone" and "tape.")

32. 20 (The number in the last column is obtained by subtracting X from the number in the second column, where X = the number by which that in the first column must be multiplied to obtain that in the second column, as in $6 \times 4 = 24$; $24 - 4 = 20$.)

33. Boat (The others can be followed by the word "way"; boat cannot.)

34. 14 (There are two series, one of odd numbers and the other of even numbers. Both increase by two each time and change position each time, moving up or down.)

35. N and G (The letters on the top row move forward in alphabetical order, skipping three letters each time. The letters on the bottom line move in the opposite direction, skipping four letters each time.)

36. Steven (The first letters of the names of the lovers are separated by three, five and seven letters. Irene and Steven continue the series because I is separated from S by nine letters.)

37. 5:50 (The first time she was 30 minutes late; the second time, 30 + 50 minutes late; the third time she was 30 + 50 + 70 minutes late; the fourth time 30 + 50 + 70 + 90 minutes late; finally, the fifth time, she was 30 + 50 + 70 + 90 + 110 minutes late.)

38. 1 (The arrow, the triangle and the white and black squares rotate 90 degrees each time. The cross and the circle do the same, but trade places.)

39. NIVOERINUURSIS (Zeus, Hermes and Apollo were Greek gods. Venus was a Roman goddess. The names are hidden in the letters and can be found by extracting only those letters that follow a vowel.)

40. 115 and 576 (The series begins with one-half. For the following values, add 1, 2, 3 and 4 respectively. Divide each result by 1×1, 1×2, $1 \times 2 \times 3$, $1 \times 2 \times 3 \times 4$.)

To determine your IQ, mark your score on the graph shown in Figure 29 (one point for every correct answer). Draw a vertical line from your score to meet the diagonal and at the point where they meet, draw a horizontal line to cross the vertical IQ axis. Your IQ is indicated at the point where the parallel line and the IQ axis meet.

Difficult? Perhaps it is more difficult to explain than to do, but there is an example on the graph for you to follow. If you have a score of nine (nine correct answers), you IQ is 100. Once you have calculated your IQ, you may feel pleased if it is high, or disheartened (which is unnecessary as this is just a book of games) if it is not as good as you thought it would be. If you want to compare your score with a general average, you can either refer to Figure 30—

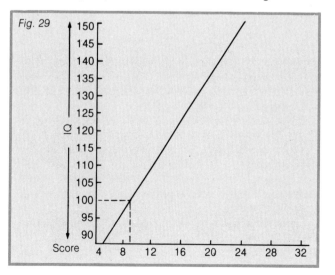

Fig. 30 — Average IQs of Various Professions in the U.S.

Profession	IQ	Category
Accountants	128	
Lawyers	128	
Managerial executives	125	
Journalists	124	Conceptual professions
Office managers	124	
Teachers	122	
Draftsmen	122	
Chemists	120	
Librarians	120	
Craftsmen	112	
Specialized technicians	110	
Shop foremen	110	
Aeronautical technicians	109	Skilled manual trades
Electricians	109	
Turners/lathe operators	108	
Press operators	108	
Technicians/mechanics	106	
Welders	104	
Painters and decorators	98	
Cooks and bakers	97	
Truck drivers	96	Unskilled manual work
Laborers	96	
Foresters	95	
Farmers	91	
Miners	91	

Evaluating our Intelligence (II)

Instructions

There are forty problems in this test and you have thirty minutes to solve them. The score is equal to the number of correct answers you get in that time without looking up the answers. Do not spend too long on any single item; go back only if you have time at the end.

1 Insert the missing number.

36   30   24   18

2 Underline the one who does not belong.

Auden   Eliot   Shakespeare   Dickens   Wordsworth

3 Which of the six numbered figures completes the series? (Write the answer in the box.)

remember that the data, which refers to the American population, is not very recent—or to Figure 46 in the next chapter (where we discuss various aspects and problems of IQ testing).

You should remember too, that the IQ levels given in Figure 29 refer to the British population which, of course, has its own particular linguistic, educational and cultural heritage (this also applies to the next test, *Evaluating our Intelligence II*), hence, at best, these values are only indicative when they are applied to other nationalities.

It is a good idea to take a day off between tests, otherwise not only might you be tired but you will have had too much practice solving problems that are similar.

4

Insert the missing number.

4   9   17   35   -   139

5

Underline the city that does not belong.

**Shanghai   Lhasa   Delhi
Cairo   New Orleans   Quebec**

6

One of the following is not a football team. Underline it.

**ESDGODR
KEYNASE
XRSEOD
ILCASADRN
SDTOIIETRNOL**

7

Insert the missing word in the brackets.

**hoop (band) group
money (....) invent**

8

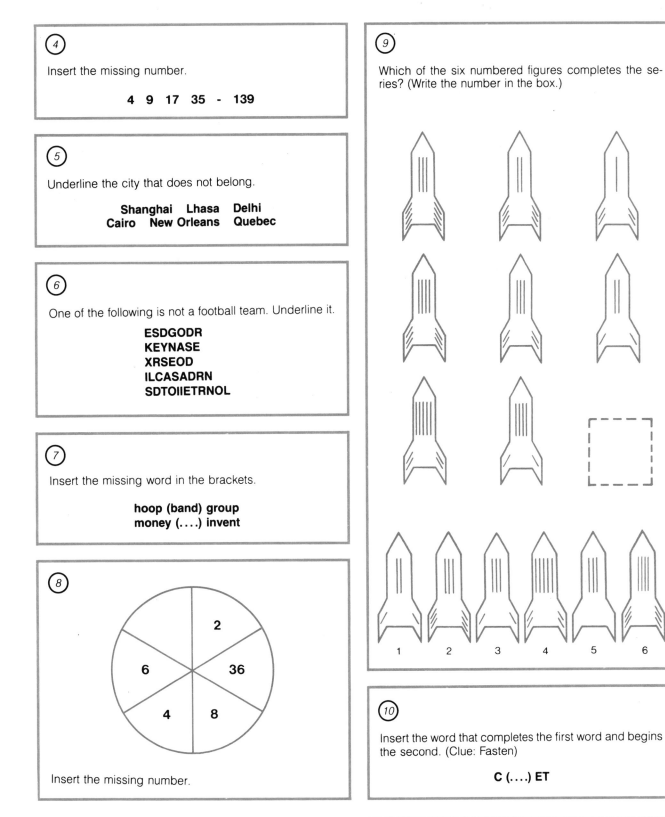

Insert the missing number.

9

Which of the six numbered figures completes the series? (Write the number in the box.)

10

Insert the word that completes the first word and begins the second. (Clue: Fasten)

C (....) ET

(11)

Underline the figures that do not make a pair.

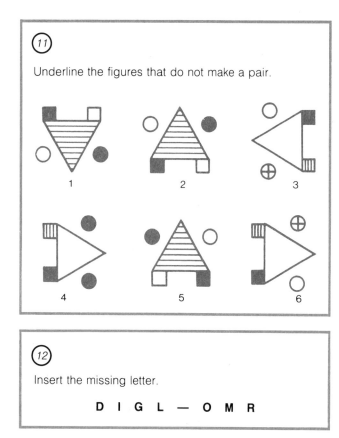

1   2   3

4   5   6

(12)

Insert the missing letter.

D I G L — O M R

(13)

Insert the missing number.

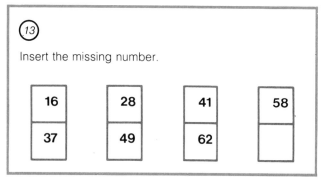

16	28	41	58
37	49	62	

(14)

Insert the word in the brackets that can be prefixed by all the letters on the left.

T
P
TR   (. . . .)
F
IMP

Kim was a half-Indian, half-English boy being trained for service in Afghanistan where Russia was making its presence felt. Kim's creator, Rudyard Kipling (1856–1936), famed for his writing about India, the jungle and the British Empire, described several of the exercises for memorizing large numbers of objects and their relative positions, that were part of Kim's training for the "big game." Kim sat cross-legged on the floor in front of a low table covered with a cloth while the instructor skillfully arranged semiprecious stones, beads, and small and large objects of both everyday and unusual use and of various colours, shapes and sizes on the cloth. After a short while, he covered everything and asked the boy to tell him exactly what he had seen and the position of each item in relation to the others. A common variation of this was to send the boy out of the room, change the arrangement of the objects, remove some of them, replace them with similar objects, and then ask him to enumerate the changes. The objects in the photograph opposite are all familiar and there are not an inordinate number of them, so it should not be too daunting to attempt the same exercise. Take five minutes to study the photograph carefully then turn the page and identify the items that are missing or have been changed in the second picture (continue reading only if you have finished the experiment or if you are not going to try it).

A useful tip is not to take the most obvious looking things for granted. It is a known fact that optical illusions are based on the "normal" way our minds work (see the caption on p. 78 about the way in which we perceive transparency and surfaces that seem to vary in size). In fact our minds "want" to see things as simply as possible, and with just a few indications we will work out the whole picture to our satisfaction, even if, from the physical point of view, the indications are insufficient. As a result, the picture we see actually may not be a faithful representation of reality. An example of this, known as amodal perception, is seen in the photographs on pp. 127 and 128 (the girl covered with the sheet and with the sheet removed).

Returning to the game at hand, in the first picture we see, for example, a glass at the top left of the picture. We have to remember that it is there, its shape and that it is upside down. In the next photograph, the glass is right side up. Normally, at home for instance, we would notice the first two variables—whether there is a glass and what its shape is, but the third variable is usually irrelevant, so we could easily make a mistake on this point.

The capacity to learn and remember is significant in this game (see pp. 49 and 54 on the subject of recognition and memorization). Our perception of the world is, in fact, acquired intellectually through a combination of memory and reason as well as through our sense organs and through supposition. In a game, this is deliberately complicated even further.

15

Find the words that have the same meaning as those in the brackets.

P + (fortune) = (pick)

16

Insert the missing number.

9	4	20
8	5	12
7	6	

17

Underline the word that does not belong.

**companions camp pain moans
canon money snoop scamp**

18

Insert the word that completes the first word and begins the second. (Clue: Drops)

ST (. . . .) BOW

19

One of the following is not a girl's name. Underline it.

**EAROTBR
DALNI
TEEMILCNEN
IPRGE**

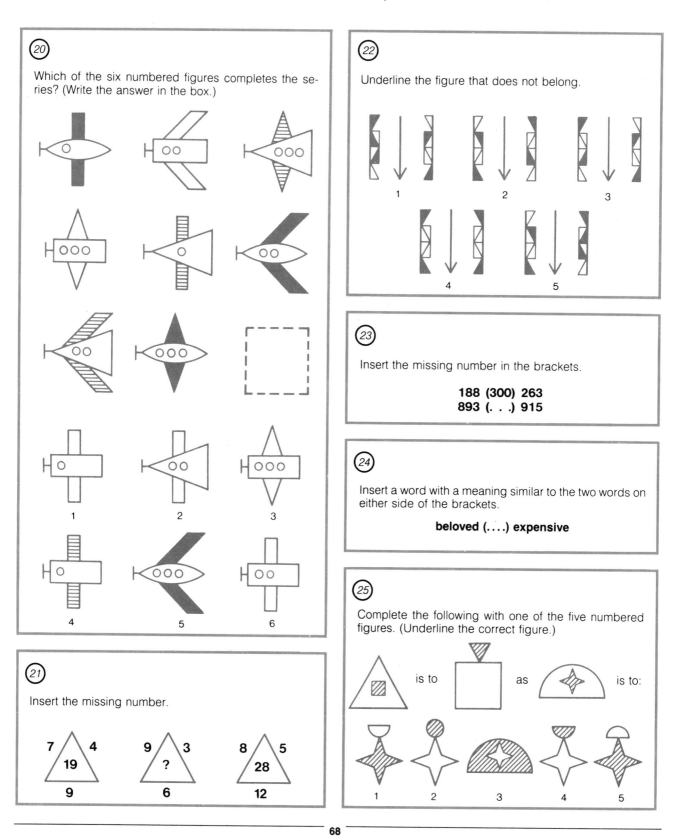

20 Which of the six numbered figures completes the series? (Write the answer in the box.)

21 Insert the missing number.

22 Underline the figure that does not belong.

23 Insert the missing number in the brackets.

188 (300) 263
893 (. . .) 915

24 Insert a word with a meaning similar to the two words on either side of the brackets.

beloved (....) expensive

25 Complete the following with one of the five numbered figures. (Underline the correct figure.)

26

One of these is not a film star. Underline it.

BALEG
NORLE
OROPEC
RCOEIC
DABTOR

27

Which of the six numbered figures completes the series? (Write the number in the box.)

28

Add the missing letter.

S   P   L

M   I   D

U   P

29

Insert the missing number in the brackets.

347 (418) 489
643 (. . .) 721

30

Which of the six numbered figures completes the series? (Underline the correct figure.)

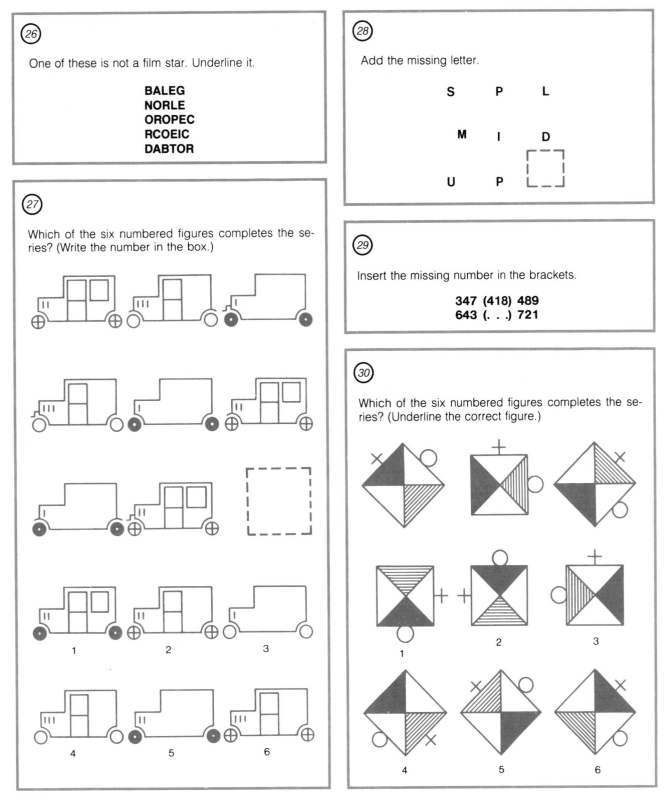

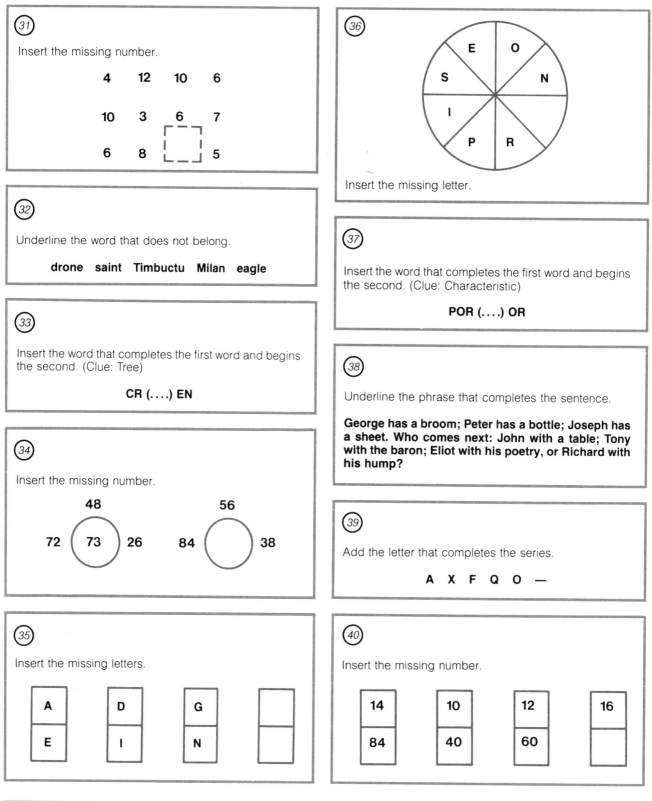

31

Insert the missing number.

4   12   10   6

10   3   6   7

6   8   [ ]   5

32

Underline the word that does not belong.

drone   saint   Timbuctu   Milan   eagle

33

Insert the word that completes the first word and begins the second. (Clue: Tree)

CR (....) EN

34

Insert the missing number.

48   56

72   73   26   84   ( )   38

35

Insert the missing letters.

A	D	G	
E	I	N	

36

E   O
S   N
I
P   R

Insert the missing letter.

37

Insert the word that completes the first word and begins the second. (Clue: Characteristic)

POR (....) OR

38

Underline the phrase that completes the sentence.

George has a broom; Peter has a bottle; Joseph has a sheet. Who comes next: John with a table; Tony with the baron; Eliot with his poetry, or Richard with his hump?

39

Add the letter that completes the series.

A   X   F   Q   O   —

40

Insert the missing number.

14	10	12	16
84	40	60	

Answers

1. 12 (The numbers decrease by six each time.)

2. Dickens (He was not a poet.)

3. 5 (In each line and each column there is: a man with his arms up, his arms stretching out, and his arms down, a black head, a white head, and a striped one.)

4. 69 (Each number is double the previous number, to which one is then alternately added or subtracted, therefore $2 \times 35 = 70 - 1 = 69$.)

5. Quebec (All the other cities are on approximately the same latitude; Quebec is much further north.)

6. Detroit Lions (The Lions are a football team. The Dodgers, Yankees, Red Sox and Cardinals are baseball teams.)

7. Coin (Coin can refer to a piece of money or mean to invent.)

8. 64 (The numbers diagonally opposite each other are the number and its square; the square of 8 is 74.)

9. 5 (The number of lines in each rocket gradually decreases as does the number of lines in the wings.)

10. LOCK

11. 2 and 4 (1 & 5 and 3 & 6 are pairs: You get one of the figures by turning the other figure 180 degrees. This is not the case with 2 and 4.)

12. J (There are two alternating series of letters; in each series you skip two letters from one to the next. If you skip H and I after G, you obtain J.)

13. 79 (The difference between the two numbers in each rectangle is always 21; the lower number is always the greater, therefore $58 + 21 = 79$.)

14. ACT

15. Luck and pluck (P + luck = pluck.)

16. 4 (In each line, subtract the second number from the first and multiply by 4: $7 - 6 = 1 \times 4 = 4$.)

17. Money (All the other words are formed with letters from the word "companions.")

18. RAIN

19. Gripe (Roberta, Linda and Clementine are the girls' names.)

20. 1 (There are three body shapes, three wing shapes and one, two or three rings on the body; the wings are black, white or striped. Each of these elements occurs only once in each line and column.)

21. 21 (Multiply the two numbers at the top of the triangle and subtract the number at the bottom of the triangle, hence $9 \times 3 = 27 - 6 = 21$.)

22. 4 (In Figs. 1 and 5 and Figs. 2 and 3, the triangles at the top and the bottom are complementary—black in one figure, white in the other. Fig. 4 does not follow the pattern. Similarly the two sides of the figures—to the left and right of the arrows—are complementary, whereas in Fig. 4 they are identical.)

23. 88 (The number inside the brackets is the difference between the numbers outside the brackets multiplied by four.)

24. DEAR

25. 4 (The larger shape turns upside down and rests on top of the smaller figure; the smaller figure becomes larger and the larger one smaller; the striped surface becomes white and vice versa.)

26. Cicero (The actors are Gable, Loren, Cooper and Bardot.)

27. 4 (Each line and each column contains a car with black wheels, one with white wheels and another with a cross on the wheels; there are one, two or three vents on the hood. There can be a door and a window, just a door, or neither. There can be a starting crank, a bumper, or neither. The answer must follow this pattern.)

28. J (The letters in the second column are formed by working backward alphabetically from the letters in the first column, skipping two, three and four places respectively. Those in the third column are formed by working backward from the letters in the second column and skipping three, four and five places respectively. The letter preceding P by six places is J.)

29. 682 (The bracketed number is one-half the sum of the numbers outside the brackets.)

30. 1 (The large square turns 45 degrees counterclockwise each time. The cross and the circle also turn 45 degrees, but clockwise.)

31. 9 (The numbers in the third column are obtained by adding together those in the first two columns and then subtracting the number in the last column. Therefore, $(6 + 8) - 5 = 9$.)

32. Eagle (In all the other words, the first and last letters are in alphabetical order; in eagle, the first and last letters are the same.)

33. OAK

34. 89 (Divide each of the numbers outside the circle by two and then add the resulting numbers together.)

35. J and T (In the top line, two letters are skipped between the letters; in the bottom line, three, four and five letters are skipped.)

36. R (When read clockwise, the letters spell the word "prisoner.")

37. TRAIT

38. Eliot with his poetry (The names contain six, five and six letters respectively, therefore the next name must have five letters. The things contain five, six and five letters respectively, hence the next thing must have six letters. Only Eliot (five letters) and poetry (six letters) follow the pattern.)

39. Each letter in the series corresponds to its numerical place in the alphabet. The sequence is determined by alternately working from the beginning and the end of the alphabet, starting with 1, which corresponds to A, and then adding 2, 3, 4, 5 and 6. Thus:

A corresponds to	1 from the beginning				
X	"	"	3	"	" end	+2
F	"	"	6	"	" beginning	+3
Q	"	"	10	"	" end	+4
O	"	"	15	"	" beginning	+5
F	"	"	21	"	" end	+6

40. 112 (In each rectangle, the bottom number is obtained by squaring the top number, dividing the square by two, then subtracting the top number. Thus, $16^2 = 256$; $256 \div 2 = 128$; $128 - 16 = 112$.)

The graph in Figure 29 can also be used here to determine an IQ score. Follow the method explained on p. 61. Your score on the second test should approximate that on the first test. If it does not, it could be for one of several reasons: You paid more or less attention to individual items, or to the test as a whole; you were too motivated, or not enough so; your concentration was disturbed by other factors (noisy atmosphere, tiredness, etc.)—or a number of other variables.

One reason why scores are often better on the second test is that you come to it in training, so to speak; as we have pointed out, the tests share essentially similar items.

Bear in mind too, that Eysenck, who conceived these tests, considers IQ scores obtained with nine to twenty-one correct answers to be sufficiently valid and reliable. This produces an IQ range of 100 to 130. Higher or lower scores are not differentiated to the same degree, hence, in the case of very high scores, it could be that thirty or more correct answers will not be adequately represented on the IQ graph in Figure 29. This could lead to discrepancies: Quite different scores might yield relatively similar IQs, for instance, or vice versa. It is time then to take leave of rigid classifications and many of the statistical procedures commonly used in these tests, and move into a "frontier" zone. We do just that with the tests at the end of this chapter.

Exercises for "Intellectual Giants"

The results of these tests cannot be converted into IQ scores. You are very good if you can manage to complete an entire exercise in one evening. Indeed the average person will probably not be able to solve more than one or two problems.

We should point out that tests of this level of difficulty do not lend themselves to more precise evaluations. Why, then, do we include them? Simply to give those who would like to try their hand at them a chance to do so. Work at them if you wish, but do not attempt to calculate your IQ from the results.

Exercise 1

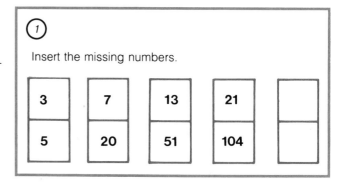

① Insert the missing numbers.

3	7	13	21	
5	20	51	104	

② **UNUSUAL** is to **UNPREPOSSESSING** as **UNDULATING** is to ?

DUBIOUS   PREPONDERANCE   INSOLUBLE CONTINUOUS   ROUNDABOUT

③ Insert the missing number.

118   199   226   235   -

④ If **GIBE – FADE = 81,** then **DICE – CEDE = ?**

⑤

REPUBLICAN = 108
DEMOCRAT = ?

⑥

LOUSE is to **SCALP**
as **HOUND** is to ?

PIXIE   ACTOR   GUSTO   HOURS   SHAFT

⑦

Insert the missing number.

7   10   -   94   463

⑧

GENERATION = 95
TELEVISION = ?

⑨

Insert the missing letter.

B   C   E   J   -

⑩

HOLY is to **SLOB**
as **LOW** is to ?

ONE   OLD   GLOW   BOW   SOW

⑪

Insert the missing number.

0   2   8   18   -

⑫

Insert the missing number standing up.*

$8 \frac{2}{3}$ $11 \frac{3}{4}$ **?** $12 \frac{2}{5}$

*Clue: Pretend your birthplace is England and that you are a faithful subject of Her Majesty the Queen.

⑬

Continue the series:

1   1   2   3   5   8   13   21   -

There are two ways to find the answer, one easy and the other hard. See if you can find both.

⑭

Insert the missing number.

ARID = 80   DEAR = 89   RAID = 63   READ = ?

⑮

Insert the missing number.

2   20   42   68   -

⑯

REWARDED = 80
COORDINATE = 75
OPINIONATED = ?

⑰

Find the one that does not belong.

**SUPERCILIOUSNESS   CONSCIOUSLY
INIMITABLE   EXTERMINATORY
SEPARATED**

(18) Insert the missing number.

CAGE	BEG	BIDE
+ FAD	− HID	− FADE
= 2227	= 563	= ?200

(19) **BAROMETER** is to **GASOMETER** as **PUGILISM** is to ?

LIGHTNING   PROTECTIONISM
CRUISING   BIMETALLISM

(20) Insert the four missing numbers.

         (172   4   327   628)   (67   4   19)
(4)   (147   84   403   403   147   28)
              (-   -   -   -)

Exercise 2

(1) Insert the missing number.

$3\frac{1}{2}$ 4   7   14   49   -

(2) If **CARUSO = 84** and **GIGLI = 56,** how much is **CROSBY** worth?

(3) Insert the missing number.

8   10   16   34   -

(4)
DRIVER = 7
PEDESTRIAN = 11
ACCIDENT = ?

(5) **EVE − ADAM = JOAN − ?**

BILL
DON
JOHN
MIKE
ART

(6) **PASTICHE = PESTILENCE = ?**

LASCIVIOUS   PISTACHIO
SENTIMENT   PUMPERNICKEL

(7) Insert the missing letter.

E   N   S   J   -

(8) Insert the missing number.

REMBRANDT = 83
CEZANNE = 48
CONSTABLE = ?

(9) Find the one that does not belong.

JOT   FED   DIN   GUT   FOX

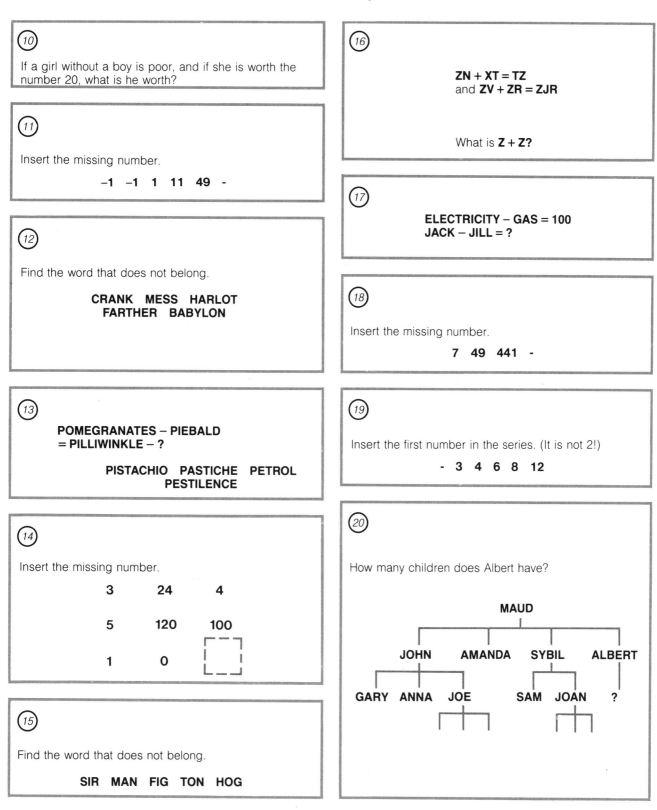

(10) If a girl without a boy is poor, and if she is worth the number 20, what is he worth?

(11) Insert the missing number.

−1 −1 1 11 49 -

(12) Find the word that does not belong.

**CRANK   MESS   HARLOT
FARTHER   BABYLON**

(13) **POMEGRANATES – PIEBALD
= PILLIWINKLE – ?**

**PISTACHIO   PASTICHE   PETROL
PESTILENCE**

(14) Insert the missing number.

3	24	4
5	120	100
1	0	

(15) Find the word that does not belong.

SIR   MAN   FIG   TON   HOG

(16) **ZN + XT = TZ
and ZV + ZR = ZJR**

What is **Z + Z?**

(17) **ELECTRICITY – GAS = 100
JACK – JILL = ?**

(18) Insert the missing number.

7 49 441 -

(19) Insert the first number in the series. (It is not 2!)

- 3 4 6 8 12

(20) How many children does Albert have?

MAUD

JOHN   AMANDA   SYBIL   ALBERT

GARY   ANNA   JOE   SAM   JOAN   ?

Answers: Exercise 1

1. 31 and 185   (To obtain the top number in each rectangle, take the numbers 2, 3, 4, 5 and 6 and square each of them, then subtract 1, 2, 3, 4 and 5 respectively. To obtain the bottom number, take the cube of 2, 3, 4, 5 and 6 and subtract the top number.)

2. INSOLUBLE   (Give the vowels the following values: $A = 1$, $E = 2$, $I = 3$, $O = 4$, $U = 5$. When the values of the vowels in each word are added, the pair must be equal.

$$5 + 5 + 5 + 1 = 16$$
$$5 + 2 + 4 + 2 + 3 = 16$$
$$5 + 5 + 1 + 3 = 14$$
$$\text{thus: } 3 + 4 + 5 + 2 = 14$$

The vowels in the other words do not add up to 14.)

3. 238   (Divide the differences between the consecutive numbers by 3 and add to the previous term to get the next number.)

4. 56   (Give the letters their numerical place in the alphabet, square each and add the squares together. Subtract the sums of the squares to get the answer.

As: GIBE − FADE
       (7925) − (6145)
square $(49 + 81 + 4 + 25)$ − $(36 + 1 + 16 + 25)$
sum   159   − 78   = 81)

5. 84   (There are two series. One assigns the following values to the vowels: $A = 1$, $E = 2$, $I = 3$, $O = 4$, $U = 5$. The other is the numerical position of the letters (excluding the vowels) in reverse alphabetical order. Thus: $B = 25$, $C = 24$, to $Z = 1$.)

6. ACTOR   (Substitute numbers for letters, alternately taking A as 1, B as 2, etc., and Z as 1, Y as 2, etc. Thus, LOUISE adds up to 58, SCALP to 75, HOUND to 58; of the other words only ACTOR adds up to 75.)

7. 25   (Take the first number, multiply it by 2 and subtract 4; then multiply by 3 and subtract 5; then multiply by 4 and subtract 6, etc.)

8. 89   (The letters are alternately assigned their corresponding numbers in proper alphabetical order, and in reverse alphabetical order: $Z = 1$ to $A = 26$ in other words. Starting in reverse alphabetical order with $G = 20$, and continuing in reverse order, $E = 5$, and so on until we reach the total 95.)

9. X   (B is the second letter of the alphabet; multiply 2 by 3 and then subtract 3; this yields 3. C is the third letter of the alphabet; multiply 3 by 3, and subtract 4; this yields 5. E is the fifth letter of the alphabet, etc.)

10. OLD   (H is the eighth letter of the alphabet, and, in reverse, S is the eighth letter of the alphabet. All the letters in each pair of words correspond in the same manner.)

11. 32   (Square the numbers 0, 1, 2, 3, 4 respectively and multiply by 2 each time.

$$\text{Thus: } 0^2 \times 2 = 0$$
$$1^2 \times 2 = 2$$
$$2^2 \times 2 = 8$$
$$3^2 \times 2 = 18$$
$$4^2 \times 2 = 32.)$$

12. 11   (Start with the sentence GOD SAVE THE QUEEN. Assign each letter its appropriate number in the alphabet. Add the numbers for each word and divide the sum by the number of letters in the word.

$$\text{Thus GOD} = \frac{7 + 15 + 4}{3} = \frac{26}{3} = 8\frac{2}{3}$$
$$\text{and THE} = \frac{20 + 8 + 5}{3} = \frac{33}{3} = 11.)$$

13. 34   (Easy. Each number is obtained by adding the preceding two numbers: $13 + 21 = 34$, hence the missing one is 34.
Difficult. The square of any number differs by one from the product of the numbers to the right and left of it. $21^2 = 441$; $13 \times 34 = 442$.)

14. 47   (Give each letter its appropriate number in the alphabet's order, and multiply by the number denoting its position in the word, that is 1, 2, 3 or 4.)

15. 98   (Take the series:

8	10	12	14	16
Square each:	64	100	144	196	256
Divide by 2:	32	50	72	98	128
Subtract 30:	2	20	42	68	98.)

16. 87   (There are two series. One is $A = 5$, $E = 4$, $I = 3$, $O = 2$, $U = 1$; the other is the number of the letter (other than the vowels) in the alphabet's order. The two series are combined and the values of the letters added, as, REWARDED $= 18 + 4 + 23 + 5 + 18 + 4 + 4 + 4 = 80$.)

17. CONSCIOUSLY   (Code the vowels $A = 5$, $E = 4$, $I = 3$, $O = 2$, $U = 1$. Add the numerical values of the vowels in each word. All come to 18 except those in CONSCIOUSLY which come to 8.)

18. 2   (The letters stand for numbers: $A = 4$, $B = 9$, $C = 1$, $D = 5$, $E = 2$, $F = 7$, $G = 8$, $H = 3$, $I = 6$.)

19. CRUISING   (Call the vowels $A = 1$, $E = 2$, $I = 3$, $O = 4$, $U = 5$. Total the values of the vowels in the word and you obtain: 9 is to 9 as 11 is to ? Only CRUISING adds up to 11.)

20. 147 4 172 7 (Give the letters of the alphabet the usual numbers, A = 1 to Z = 26. The sentence reads: MARY HAD A LITTLE LAMB. The numbers of the letters, however, are each squared and 3 is added each time.

Thus: MARY = $(13^2 + 3)$ $1^2 + 3$ $(18^2 + 3)$ $25^2 + 3$
= 169 + 3 1 + 3 324 + 3 625 + 3
= 172 4 327 628

etc.)

Answers: Exercise 2

1. 343 (Multiply each number by the preceding one and divide by 2.)

2. 39 (Determine the numerical values of the letters going up and down in alphabetical order, starting alternately with A and Z.)

3. 88 (Multiply each number by 3 and subtract 14. 3 × 34 = 102, 102 − 14 = 88.)

4. 9 (Count the number of letters in each word and add one.)

5. MIKE (The numerical value of the letters in the male names follows the alphabetical order; the value of the letters in the female names corresponds with the reverse alphabetical order: Z = 1, Y = 2, etc. EVE − ADAM = 30, JOAN − MIKE = 30.)

6. PUMPERNICKEL (The letters are given their appropriate numbers, alternately using the alphabet forward and backward:

P = 16 forward, U = 6 backward, etc.

PASTICHE and PESTILENCE add up to 131; of the others only PUMPERNICKEL also does.)

7. X (Assign each letter its number in the reverse alphabetical order, that is 22, 13, 8, 5. Each number is derived from the preceding one by adding 4, 3, 2, 1 and then halving: 22 + 4 = 26, 26 ÷ 2 = 13; 5 + 1 = 6, 6 ÷ 2 = 3. The third letter in the inverted alphabet is X.)

8. 44 (Give the letters the appropriate numbers in the alphabet; starting with the first letter, add each alternate letter.)

9. GUT (The two consonants in the other words are separated from the vowel by an equal number of letters: J comes five letters before O, and T comes five letters after O.)

10. 13 (Assign appropriate numbers to the letters: GIRL (5267) and BOY (931). POOR (4336) is the result of 5267 less 931. 20 is the sum of the figures in girl, and 13 is the sum of the figures in boy.)

11. 179 (Consider a series of numbers starting with 1, in which each number is formed by multiplying the previous number by 3: 1, 3, 9, 27, 81, etc. Consider another series starting with 2: 2, 4, 8, 16, 32, etc. Subtract the latter from the former and you obtain the series given here. Thus 243 − 64 = 179.)

12. HARLOT (The number of letters in the alphabet's order that separate the first and last letters of each word is the same as double the number of letters in the word between its first and last letters, plus one.
CRANK, for instance, has three letters between C and K. Twice 3 plus 1 is 7, and there are seven letters separating C and K in the alphabet: D E F G H I J
HARLOT is the one that does not belong.)

13. PETROL (Substitute numbers for letters in each word, alternately counting from the beginning and the end of the alphabet. Only PETROL completes the equation properly.)

14. 0 (To obtain the second number in each row, calculate the cube of the first number and subtract the first number, as, $3^3 = 27$, 27 − 3 = 24. To obtain the third number, divide the second number by 12 and then square it.)

15. TON (In all the other words, the consonants are next to one another in the alphabet: S and R, M and N, F and G, H and G.)

16. X (Letters are assigned a particular value Z = 1, X = 2, V = 3, T = 4, R = 5, P = 6, N = 7, L = 8, and J = 9, by starting at the end of the alphabet and skipping one letter each time.)

17. 0 (Give each letter its number in the alphabet, alternating between the proper and reverse alphabetical order. Total the numbers in each word.)

18. 441 (Multiply each number by the last figure in the number to obtain the succeeding number.)

19. 4/3 (Multiply two successive numbers and divide by 1, 2, 3 and 4 respectively to get the next term:

$$\frac{4/3 \times 3}{1} \qquad \frac{3 \times 4}{2} \qquad \frac{4 \times 6}{3} \qquad \frac{6 \times 8}{4}$$

20. 1 (Assign the vowels the following values: A = 0, E = 1, I = 2, O = 3, U = 4. Totalling the figures in each name produces the number of children. Maud = 0 + 4 = 4; John = 3, etc.)

To conclude the chapter, we offer a compromise between perceptual abilities and the worlds of nature and imagination; a small, cuddly Koala bear is playing with a contraption labelled with a series of numbers (Figure 31). This game uses visual-spatial abilities— the capacity to grasp the connection between various parts; to assess which parts are essential to the sequence of movements and the extent to which they affect it; and to predict the result of the movement of each wheel. Let's see what happens. Good luck and, above all, have fun!

Fig. 31   **The Swinging Koala**

When the koala pulls the cord towards himself, all the gears start moving. Try to discover in which direction the numbered gears move.

The solution is found in figure 28: with 9 correct answers your judgment is excellent; with 7 good; with 5 fair.

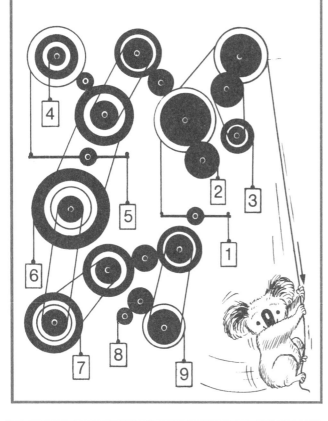

If we look at Fig. 3 in the illustration opposite, we would probably agree that it shows a transparent oval on top of an opaque oval. Actually, the large oval is not transparent as the image was made of cardboard which does not permit light to pass through. The card was cut as shown in Fig. 2 and arranged in such a way that the complete mosaic created the image seen in Fig. 3. This could be considered a trick to make something look transparent when in fact it is not. Fig. 1 could also be described as an illusion, but of the opposite kind, as the small oval looks opaque. Indeed, in this case, a sheet of coloured plastic was used, which permits a good deal of light to filter through.

It could be said that our system of perception follows rules by which we perceive things as transparent or not. The perception of transparency, therefore, is not an arbitrary illusion but is subject to precise conditions which fall into two basic categories. The first category is figurative: An element has to clearly protrude beyond the outline of the other element (which is the case in Fig. 3, for example, but not in Fig. 1) and the outline of the object should be continuous (which it is not in Figs. 9 and 5). The second category concerns the colour relationship between the different areas: The overlapping area must be an intermediate colour between those of the other areas, otherwise we do not perceive transparency (Fig. 6). Of course these categories consist of quite distinct elements which have been experimentally proven in a number of ways. For example, in Fig. 7, one of the ovals seems to be transparent both with respect to the background and the other oval.

The illustration on the following page is also an example of what might be called illusion, although the term could be misleading. In the accepted sense of the word, we experience "illusion" when what we perceive does not correspond to the actual physical reality (as it is defined by science). Thus we tend to believe that sometimes human perception works in a distorted fashion. In truth, it is never wrong. It merely follows rules that are different from those we would expect. To study perception means to study, and use, these rules, which could, in turn, lead to evaluations that are mistaken from the physical point of view.

Returning to the concept of illusions and bearing in mind the above, we can see that some of the nine rectangles appear wider than others, making it particularly hard for us to accept the fact that they are all the same size. To explain this kind of illusion, we need to know the mechanisms that determine how we perceive things, that is how we derive our immediate impressions of the world. In the example of the rectangles, the blue and white stripes in each affect different retina cells and cortical neurons, depending on the width (i.e.,the frequency) of the stripes. These cells also interconnect to differing degrees depending on how far the stripes are from the edges. We could say then, that the impression of width is created by the various combinations of the two effects. For instance, Fig. 3 (where the figures are numbered from left to right and top to bottom) looks narrower than Fig. 2, whereas Fig. 5 looks wider than Fig. 3, and, in general, despite the fact that the size is the same, the figures with their stripes set close together look wider than those that are all white or all blue. There is, therefore, a physiological explanation for this phenomenon which, far from being subject to the arbitrary "judgement" of the observer, is actually constant and produces a form of perception that is, on the whole, universal.

4

6

7

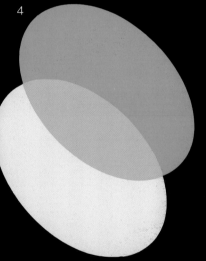
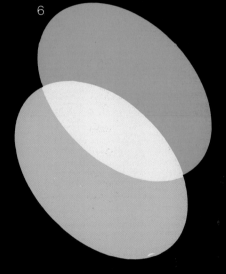
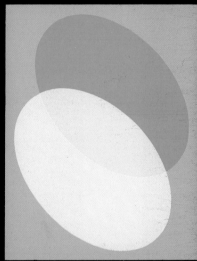

5

8

9

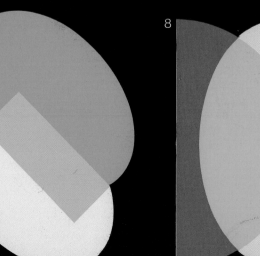
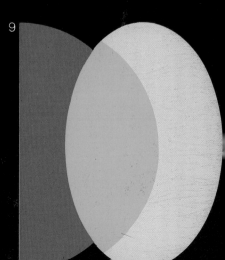

Tests of intelligence, aptitude and interest

"...of those to whom much is given, much is required."
(John F. Kennedy)

Heredity or environment?

Whether our intelligence depends largely on what we inherit from our parents or comes from the environment in which we are educated, live and work is a dispute of long-standing, and one given impetus by A. Jensen's article in the *Harvard Educational Review* some fifteen years ago. The controversy continues to rage, finding outlets in scientific journals, popular books, the daily papers and magazines.

Indeed, Jensen's article seemed designed to inflame its readers. Reporting on a series of studies on the genetic nature of intelligence, Jensen concluded that it was but a vain exercise to try to make up for differences in aptitude through education, as the environment could do very little to counteract the innate predispositions that determine the level of intelligence.

Quite apart from the question of the scientific validity of such a claim, it would be most surprising if the subject did not become an emotional one, given its vast existential, ethical, social and political implications. The two sides (the geneticists and the environmentalists) support their respective cases by drawing upon specific arguments. We will summarize them briefly.

Our summary is accompanied by a series of tables which appear to add weight to one or the other of the two theories.

Parents and children

Those in support of the heredity theory generally cite a number of studies comparing parental IQs to those of their children.

Figure 32 reveals a much higher correlation between the intellectual performance of children and their natural parents than between children and their adoptive parents. In this context, the coefficient of correlation (r), varies from 0 (no correlation) to 1 (maximum correlation).

Studies involving twins are particularly interesting. Research on the relationship between heredity and environment is made less difficult by the presence of identical twins (monozygotic or MZ) who are genetically identical because they develop from a single egg (they are therefore of the same sex, except in those rare instances where they are of opposite sexes as a result of Turner's syndrome). Let us consider, for example, family likeness with regard to height (Figure 33). Siblings of the same parents present a certain degree of similarity, represented by a correlation factor of r = 0.60. Fraternal twins (dizygytic or DZ) do not present more genetic similarities than siblings born separately, as the former develop from separate eggs and, hence are not necessarily of the same sex, nor do they necessarily look alike. However, it is possible that the effects of the common intrauterine environment

Fig. 32	The Correlations Between Parents' and Childrens' IQs	
	The correlation for children examined between 10 and 18 years of age (average age 13) using the Stanford-Binet IQ.*	
	No. of cases	Correlation coefficient (r)
Natural parents with whom the children have lived		
IQ of the natural mother and IQ of the child	63	0.44
Years of education of the mother and IQ of the child	92	0.32
Years of education of the father and IQ of the child**	60	0.40
Adoptive parents with whom the children have lived at least ten years		
Cultural level of the adoptive mother and IQ of the child	100	0.02
Cultural level of the adoptive father and IQ of the child	100	0.00

* All the children were adopted before they were six months old.
** Not supplied by the authors, but calculated on the basis of data available. The cultural level of the natural father was not known for the other 40 cases in the sample of 100.

and similar treatment and feeding after birth may make fraternal twins slightly more alike than their brothers and sisters; when this occurs in its most marked form it is apt to slightly exceed a correlation factor of $r = 0.64$. The highest degree of similarity is found with identical twins, $r = 0.93$.

Findings regarding IQs are analogous. The greatest similarities are seen among identical twins, followed by fraternal twins, and lastly, ordinary siblings (Figure 34). Research involving identical twins who have been raised separately is quite interesting, particularly in those cases where there has been a marked difference in the two environments; the high correlation between the IQs of the twins can only support the theory of hereditability of intelligence (we are referring to groups of subjects, of course; there are always exceptions in the case of individual subjects). Figure 33 shows how for a number of identical twins brought up in separate environments there continues to be a high degree of correlation between their IQs.

From school to the family

On the other hand, supporters of the environmental theory point to research equally worthy of attention.

First of all, various studies have shown that an improvement in environment leads to a corresponding rise in scores. Studies on children brought up in orphanages and children placed with stable families at the age of two or three, reveal that, in time, the two groups were notably different: At about nineteen years of age, those in the first group had an average IQ of approximately 64, while those in the second group had an average IQ of 96 at six years of age; as adults they led completely normal lives and their children had average IQs of 105.

In addition, although most environmentalists accept the data in Figure 32 (which shows a higher degree of correlation between the IQs of natural parents and their children than found between adoptive parents and adopted children), many studies have shown that the intelligence level of adopted children was generally of a higher average than would be expected on the basis of the IQs of their natural parents.

The need for synthesis

In view of the profound ethical and social implications of these two theories, it is clear that a solution which would put this unproductive dispute to rest, could only prove beneficial.

a)—There is no doubt that intelligence contains a genetic element: All living beings and all their functions are linked to organisms and activities that preceded

Fig. 33   The Similarity in Height of Children Born of the Same Parents

Pairs of children	No. of pairs	Correlation coefficient (r)
Siblings (pairs of the same sex)	52	0.60
Dizygotic twins (of the same sex)	52	0.64
Monozygotic twins	50	0.93

Fig. 34   The Similarity in IQ (Binet) Between Children of the Same Parents

Pairs of children	No. of pairs	Correlation coefficient (r)
Siblings*	384	0.53
Dizygotic twins (of the same sex)**	482	0.63
Monozygotic twins**	687	0.87

* From McNemar (1942)
**From Nichols (1965)

Fig. 35   The Correlation in Intelligence Tests Taken by Monozygotic Twins Brought up Separately

Test	No. of pairs	Correlation coefficient (r)
Stanford-Binet*	19	0.77
Vocabulary test and progressive matrices**	37	0.77
Stanford-Binet (British version)***	53	0.86

* From Newman, Freman & Holzinger (1937)
**From Shields (1962)
***From Burt (1966)

them in the evolutionary process; what is more, given that all individuals have specific characteristics connected to their genetic makeup, there is no reason to suppose that the latter would not be reflected in intellectual and behavioural aspects as well.

It is also worth noting that it is very difficult to study what is innate in man and what is acquired; genetic differences rapidly become fused with the environment. However, it is equally difficult to accept the notion that environment alone was responsible for the genius of Mozart which showed itself when he was a child, or for the fact that Pauli wrote a seminal work on relativity at the age of eighteen. On the other hand, even children brought up in the same family reveal marked differences in temperament, talent, disposition and intelligence.

b)— Certainly, it cannot be denied that in large measure, the environment influences the development of every individual. Human beings who have grown up in the wild—"wolf children"—show no marked improvements after attempts are made to educate them; the lack of a human cultural context in early childhood

Fig. 36   Correlations and Averages

Great differences of opinion have divided psychologists regarding the interpretation of data on heredity and environment, particularly in respect to the research on adoptive families, as reviewed above. On reexamination of the facts, it becomes clear that, given the same data, interpretations based on the *correlation coefficient* and those based on *average values,* can yield different results. As a general rule, the correlation coefficient leads to results supporting the theory of heritability (based on inferences drawn from the correlations), whereas the average scores favour the environmental interpretation. Consequently, in past debates, psychologists tended to support the statistical method that produced data in keeping with their own particular views.

The fact that correlations and averages consider two separate aspects of the data is evident when you compare the work of Burks (1928) and Leahy (1935). If you consider only the correlations, the results of the two studies are similar; they both indicate a lower correlation between the intelligence of adoptive parents and their children than between natural parents and their children.

However, when you examine the averages, the results are different. In Burks' study, adopted children showed a lower IQ than natural children, while in Leahy's study their IQ was equal to that of natural children. Hence, studies that agree on correlations do not necessarily agree on average values. These differences are not coincidental. In point of fact, to achieve a full understanding of the data, both correlations and averages must be taken into account.

seriously limits the possibility of their developing acceptably articulate speech, despite the efforts of their teachers. They are, of course, extreme examples, but numerous studies have shown that certain disadvantages in early life resulting from a lack of environmental stimuli are particularly unyielding.

How, then, do we resolve the conflict between a) and b)?

Although we recognize the importance of inherited attributes, once these are formed it is impossible to change them.

It may be that genetic engineering will lead to results totally undreamt of today, but this will not happen in the near future. In the meantime, if we limit ourselves to a consideration of only the inherited aspects of intelligence we render ourselves powerless. But if we move to act, and act positively, on the environment, we can help people to realize their intellectual and human potential to its fullest. In this way, our efforts will not be wasted, but will contribute to improving individuals and society; in the proper environment, many children and adults have been helped to overcome slight, and at times seemingly insurmountable difficulties and have reached worthwhile goals.

But what is intelligence?

There is yet another source of controversy and it emerges from the fact that greater value is placed on the IQ than it is due; at times, we too have implied that the term IQ is synonymous with intelligence, however when such is the case, we use the word intelligence to mean the ability to face and solve certain problems. Hence the evaluations of intelligence that we have discussed so far are valid only in this very limited sense.

It does happen, though, that the IQ is often thought of as a general measure of human ability, particularly by the layman. Unfortunately this leads to a distorted view of the exceedingly complex and fascinating phenomenon of the human character, as well as to unnecessary anxieties.

People with high IQs are particularly good at solving the very tests by which the level is measured, but this does not mean they are more gifted in absolute terms than those with lower scores. Many people excel in a variety of activities, despite the fact that their intellectual level is not particularly high. Why? Because they are gifted in terms of creativity, common sense or tenacity. We will come back to this later, but for the moment, it might be interesting to get a clearer idea of the verbal, mathematical and visual-spatial aspects of our intelligence by doing the following tests.

Verbal ability

Instructions
You have thirty minutes to solve the problems. The score is equal to the number of correct answers obtained within that time without looking up the answers. Do not linger on any single item. Go back at the end if you have time.

① Insert the word similar in meaning to the words outside the brackets.

NEW (....) TALE

② Insert the word that completes the first word and begins the second (Clue: Boy)

BAL (....) DER

③ Find the one that does not belong in these anagrams.

SCHAMOT
LABLOTOF
CEXTIRC
SNINET

④ Find the word ending that can be prefixed by the following letters:

S
SL
PR
TR
L
BR
(...)

⑤ Insert the word that has a meaning in common with the words outside the brackets.

PUSH (....) NEWSPAPERS

⑥ Insert the word that completes the first word and begins the second. (Clue: Finish)

TR (....) IVE

⑦ Find the one that does not belong.

TIRANAS
TINLOM
RYBOCS
RYLESEP

⑧ Insert the word that can precede the three words to the right of the brackets.

(....) ——— **BIRD**
——— **BALL**
——— **MAIL**

⑨ Insert the word that has a meaning in common with the words outside the brackets.

FRIEND (....) JOIN

⑩ Insert the word that completes the first word and begins the second.

EX (....) ACLE

⑪ Find the one that does not belong.

ILAM   DRIOA   PENOH   DREAGN

⑫ Insert the word that can precede the three words to the right of the brackets.

(....) ——— **TREE**
——— **HORN**
——— **LACE**

⑬ Find the word that can be prefixed by the following letters:

S
R
H
CL
D
F
G   (....)
B
N
P
T
W

⑭ Insert the word that completes the first word and begins the second.

SP (....) CH

(15)

Insert the word that has a meaning in common with the words outside the brackets.

CUT (....) OPENING

(16)

Find the one that does not belong.

TRACROS
TEADS
LEPAPS
RESHICER
BABECAGS

(17)

Insert the word that completes the first word and begins the second.

ST (....) PLE

(18)

Find the word that can be prefixed by all the following:

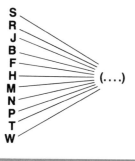

(19)

Insert the word that has a meaning in common with the words outside the brackets.

PUNISH (....) NICE

(20)

Find the one that does not belong.

HARCI
NOPEY
PYPOP
CUTREBPUT
LIPUT

(21)

Insert the word that completes the first word and begins the second.

APR (....) ION

(22)

Find the one that does not belong.

REETIRR
STALANIA
XEBOR
LUNTAW

(23)

Insert the word that has a meaning in common with the words outside the brackets.

FLAME (....) SHOOT

(24)

Find the word ending that can be prefixed by all the following:

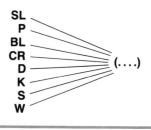

(25) Insert the word that completes the first word and begins the second.

ST (....) ER

(26) Find the one that does not belong.

RUYERS   SEEXS   NOLLWARC   AROLFID

(27) Insert the word that has a meaning in common with the words outside the brackets.

CROWD (....) NEWSPAPERS

(28) Insert the word that completes the first word and begins the second.

A (....) Y

(29) Find the one that does not belong.

OCIRA   OKOTY   OOTRONT   REBLAGED

(30) Find the word ending that can be prefixed by all the following:

FL
TH
R
K
P
S
W
ST

(....)

(31) Find the word ending that can be prefixed by all the following:

R
T
B
C
D
G
K
L
S
V

(....)

(32) Insert the word that has a meaning in common with the words outside the brackets.

SHAPE (....) CLASS

(33) Insert the word that completes the first word and begins the second.

HAM (....) ENT

(34) Find the one that does not belong.

LEEGA
WARPSOR
RALK
LAHEW

(35) Insert the word that completes the first word and begins the second.

S (....) GET

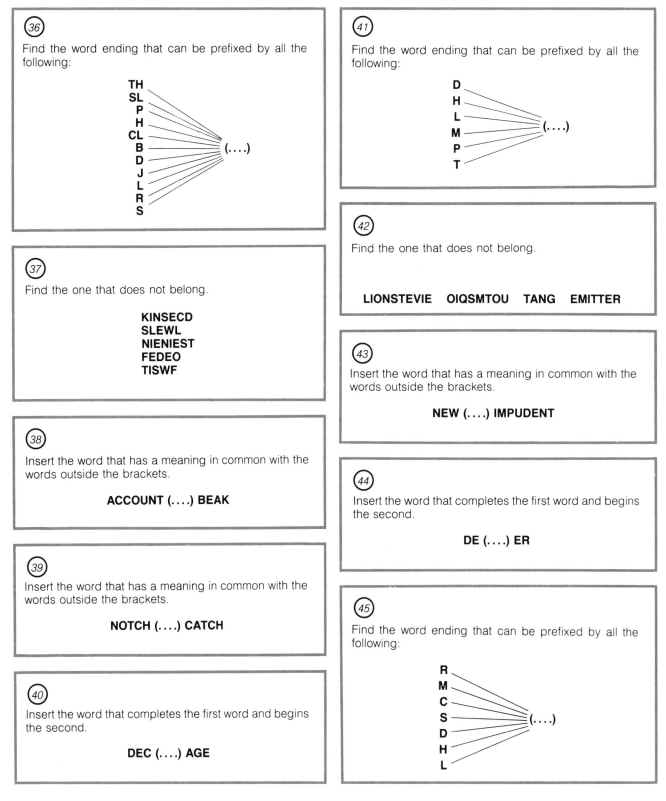

36 Find the word ending that can be prefixed by all the following:

TH
SL
P
H
CL
B
D
J
L
R
S

(....)

37 Find the one that does not belong.

KINSECD
SLEWL
NIENIEST
FEDEO
TISWF

38 Insert the word that has a meaning in common with the words outside the brackets.

ACCOUNT (....) BEAK

39 Insert the word that has a meaning in common with the words outside the brackets.

NOTCH (....) CATCH

40 Insert the word that completes the first word and begins the second.

DEC (....) AGE

41 Find the word ending that can be prefixed by all the following:

D
H
L
M
P
T

(....)

42 Find the one that does not belong.

LIONSTEVIE   OIQSMTOU   TANG   EMITTER

43 Insert the word that has a meaning in common with the words outside the brackets.

NEW (....) IMPUDENT

44 Insert the word that completes the first word and begins the second.

DE (....) ER

45 Find the word ending that can be prefixed by all the following:

R
M
C
S
D
H
L

(....)

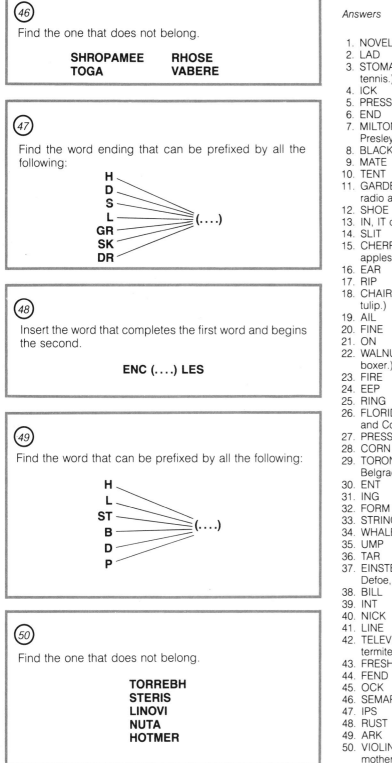

(46)

Find the one that does not belong.

**SHROPAMEE   RHOSE
TOGA   VABERE**

(47)

Find the word ending that can be prefixed by all the following:

H
D
S
L   (....)
GR
SK
DR

(48)

Insert the word that completes the first word and begins the second.

ENC (....) LES

(49)

Find the word that can be prefixed by all the following:

H
L
ST
B   (....)
D
P

(50)

Find the one that does not belong.

**TORREBH
STERIS
LINOVI
NUTA
HOTMER**

Answers

1. NOVEL
2. LAD
3. STOMACH   (All the others are ball games: football, cricket and tennis.)
4. ICK
5. PRESS
6. END
7. MILTON   (All the others are singers: Crosby, Sinatra and Presley.)
8. BLACK
9. MATE
10. TENT
11. GARDEN   (All the others are means of communication: mail, radio and phone.)
12. SHOE
13. IN, IT or AR.
14. SLIT
15. CHERRIES   (All the other words have A in them: carrots, dates, apples and cabbages.)
16. EAR
17. RIP
18. CHAIR   (All the others are flowers: peony, poppy, buttercup, tulip.)
19. AIL
20. FINE
21. ON
22. WALNUT   (All the others are breeds of dog: terrier, alsatian and boxer.)
23. FIRE
24. EEP
25. RING
26. FLORIDA   (All the others are English counties: Surrey, Essex and Cornwall.)
27. PRESS
28. CORN
29. TORONTO   (All the others are capitals: Cairo, Tokyo and Belgrade.)
30. ENT
31. ING
32. FORM
33. STRING
34. WHALE   (All the others are birds: eagle, sparrow and lark.)
35. UMP
36. TAR
37. EINSTEIN   (All the others are famous writers: Dickens, Wells, Defoe, Swift.)
38. BILL
39. INT
40. NICK
41. LINE
42. TELEVISION   (All the others are insects: mosquito, gnat, termite.)
43. FRESH
44. FEND
45. OCK
46. SEMAPHORE   (All the others are animals: goat, horse, beaver.)
47. IPS
48. RUST
49. ARK
50. VIOLIN   (All the others are relatives: brother, sister, aunt and mother.)

Numerical Ability

Instructions
You have thirty minutes to solve the following problems. The score is equal to the number of correct answers you get within the time limit without looking up the answers. Do not spend too long on any one item. If you have time at the end, go back.

1

Insert the missing number.

      18 20 24 32 -

2

Insert the missing number.

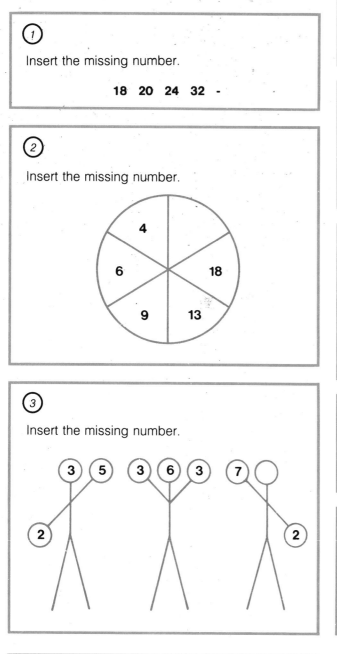

3

Insert the missing number.

4

Insert the missing number.

    212 179 146 113 -

5

Insert the missing number.

    6 8 10 11 14 14

6

Insert the missing number.

    17 (112) 39

    28 (   ) 49

7

Insert the missing number.

    3   9   3

    5   7   1

    7   1   □

8

Insert the missing number.

    7 13 24 45 -

9

Insert the missing number.

    234 (333) 567

    345 (   ) 678

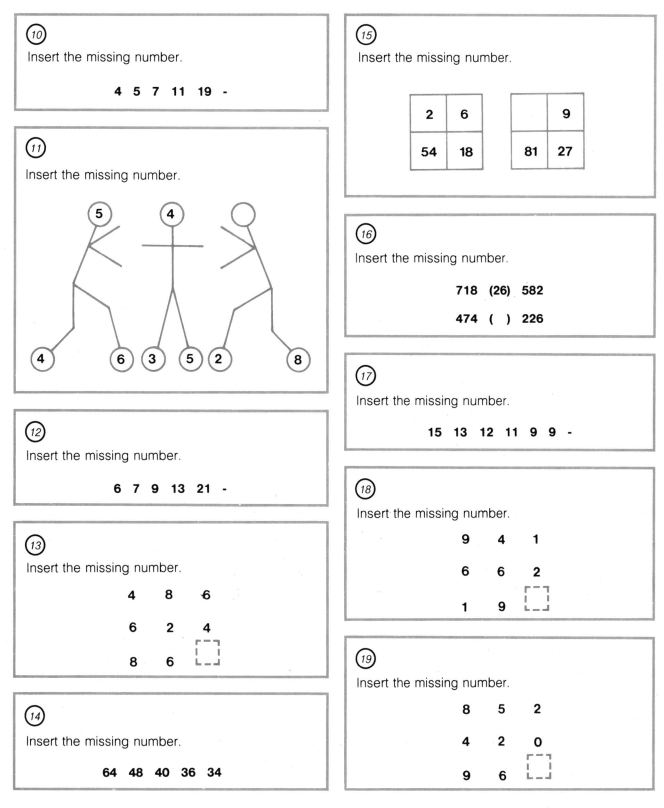

(10) Insert the missing number.

4 5 7 11 19 -

(11) Insert the missing number.

(12) Insert the missing number.

6 7 9 13 21 -

(13) Insert the missing number.

4   8   6

6   2   4

8   6   ☐

(14) Insert the missing number.

64 48 40 36 34

(15) Insert the missing number.

2	6
54	18

	9
81	27

(16) Insert the missing number.

718 (26) 582

474 ( ) 226

(17) Insert the missing number.

15 13 12 11 9 9 -

(18) Insert the missing number.

9   4   1

6   6   2

1   9   ☐

(19) Insert the missing number.

8   5   2

4   2   0

9   6   ☐

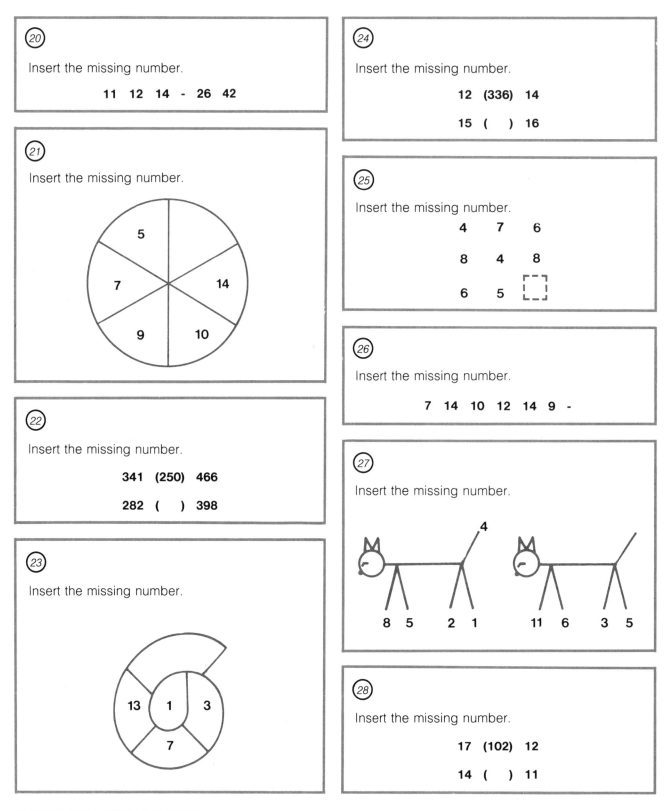

(20)

Insert the missing number.

11 12 14 - 26 42

(21)

Insert the missing number.

5

7   14

9   10

(22)

Insert the missing number.

341 (250) 466

282 (   ) 398

(23)

Insert the missing number.

13   1   3

7

(24)

Insert the missing number.

12 (336) 14

15 (   ) 16

(25)

Insert the missing number.

4   7   6

8   4   8

6   5

(26)

Insert the missing number.

7 14 10 12 14 9 -

(27)

Insert the missing number.

8 5   2 1   11 6   3 5

4

(28)

Insert the missing number.

17 (102) 12

14 (   ) 11

29

Insert the missing number.

172   84   40   18   -

30

Insert the missing number.

1   5   13   29   -

31

Insert the missing number.

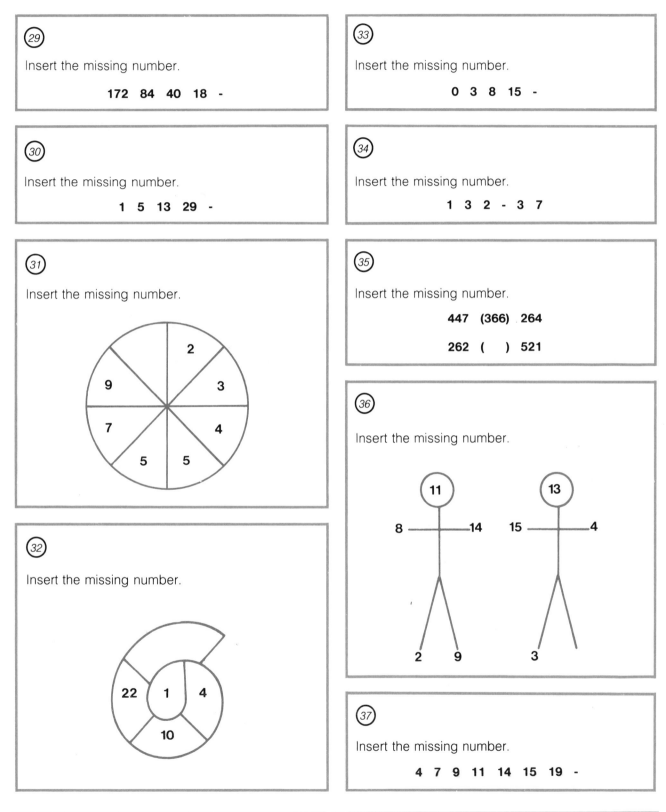

32

Insert the missing number.

33

Insert the missing number.

0   3   8   15   -

34

Insert the missing number.

1   3   2   -   3   7

35

Insert the missing number.

447   (366)   264

262   (   )   521

36

Insert the missing number.

37

Insert the missing number.

4   7   9   11   14   15   19   -

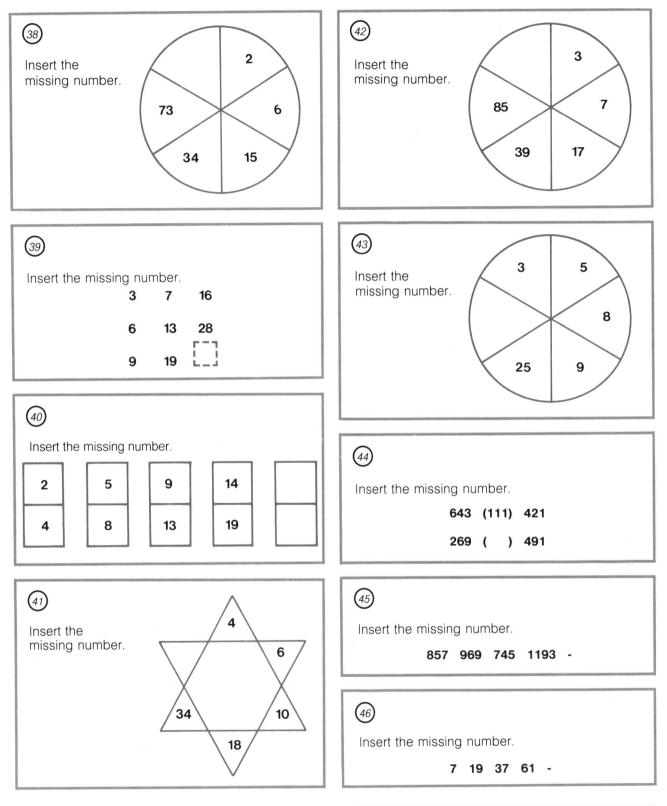

38

Insert the missing number.

2

73   6

34   15

39

Insert the missing number.

3   7   16

6   13   28

9   19   [ ]

40

Insert the missing number.

2	5	9	14	
4	8	13	19	

41

Insert the missing number.

4

6

34   10

18

42

Insert the missing number.

3

85   7

39   17

43

Insert the missing number.

3   5

8

25   9

44

Insert the missing number.

643 (111) 421

269 (   ) 491

45

Insert the missing number.

857 969 745 1193 -

46

Insert the missing number.

7 19 37 61 -

(47)

Insert the missing number.

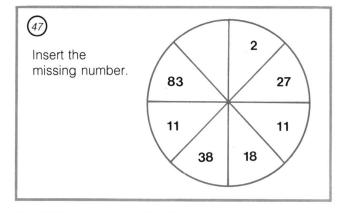

(48)

Insert the missing number.

9 (45) 81

8 (36) 64

10 (–) ⌐ ⌐
        ⌐_⌐

(49)

Insert the missing number.

5 41 149 329 -

(50)

Insert the missing number.

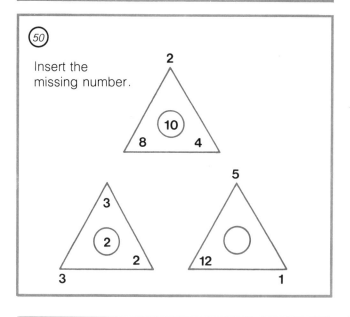

Answers

1. 48 (Add 2, 4, 8 and finally 16.)

2. 24 (Going counterclockwise, the numbers increase by 2, 3, 4, 5, 6.)

3. 5 (To obtain the number on the head, the numbers on the arms pointing up are added and the ones on the arms pointing down are subtracted.)

4. 80 (Subtract 33 for each number.)

5. 18 (There are two alternating series, one increasing by 4 steps, the other by 3 steps.)

6. 154 (Add the numbers outside the brackets and multiply by 2.)

7. 3 (Take the difference between the numbers in the first two columns and divide by 2.)

8. 86 (Double the number and then subtract 1, 2, 3 and 4.)

9. 333 (Subtract the left-hand number from the right-hand number to get the number in the brackets.)

10. 35 (The series increases by 1, 2, 4, 8 and 16 steps.)

11. 5 (The number in the head is one-half of the total of the numbers in the feet.)

12. 37 (Double each number and subtract 5 to obtain the next number.)

13. 7 (The numbers in the third column are one-half the total of the numbers in the other two columns.)

14. 33 (The series descends by 16, 8, 4, 2 and 1.)

15. 3 (Going round the square clockwise, multiply by 3.)

16. 14 (Add the numbers outside the brackets and divide by 50 to obtain the number inside the brackets.)

17. 6 (There are two alternating series; one descends by 3, the other by 2.)

18. 4 (Each row adds up to 14.)

19. 3 (The numbers decrease by equal steps, 3 in the first row, 2 in the second and 3 in the third.)

20. 18 (Doubling each term and subtracting 10 produces the next.)

21. 18 (The larger numbers are twice the numbers diagonally opposite them.)

22. 232 (Subtract the left-hand side from the right-hand side and double the answer.)

23. 21 (The numbers increase by intervals of 2, 4, 6 and 8.)

24. 480 (The number inside the brackets is twice the product of the numbers outside the brackets.)

25. 2 (The third column is twice the difference between the first and second columns.)

26. 19 (There are two series, one increases by intervals of 3, 4 and 5; the other decreases by intervals of 2 and 3.)

27. 3 (Subtract the sum of the second and fourth paws from the sum of the first and third paws to obtain the number at the end of the tail.)

28. 77 (The number in the brackets is one-half the product of the numbers outside the brackets.)

29. 7 (Halve each number and subtract 2 to get the next number.)

30. 61 (Add twice the difference between successive numbers to get the next one. Thus, $5 - 1 = 4$; $2 \times 4 = 8$; $8 + 5 = 13$; etc.)

31. 11 (Double each number and add 1 to obtain the number in the section diagonally opposite.)

32. 46 (Add 1 to each number and then double it to produce the next number.)

33. 24 (The series increases by 3, 5, 7 and 9.)

34. 5 (There are two alternating series, one increasing by 2 each time, the other by 1 each time.)

35. 518 (The number inside the brackets is twice the difference between the numbers outside the brackets.)

36. 3 (Subtract the total of the numbers on the legs from the total of the numbers on the arms to obtain the number on the head.)

37. 19 (There are two alternating series; one ascending by 5, the other ascending by 4.)

38. 152 (Working clockwise, double each number and add 2, 3, 4, 5 and 6.)

39. 40 (The numbers in the second column are formed by doubling the numbers in the first column and adding 1; those in the third column by doubling the numbers in the second column and adding 2. Thus, $(2 \times 19) + 2 = 40$.)

40. 20 and 26 (The numerators increase by 3, 4, 5 and 6; the denominators increase by 4, 5, 6 and 7.)

41. 66 (Working clockwise, double each preceding number and subtract 2.)

42. 179 (Each figure is obtained by doubling the preceding one and adding 1, 3, 5, 7 and finally 9.)

43. 64 (3, 5 and 8 are squared to produce the numbers in the sections diagonally opposite.)

44. 111 (The number inside the brackets is one-half the difference of the numbers outside the brackets.)

45. 297 (The difference between two consecutive terms is doubled each time, and alternately added and subtracted from the second number to produce the following one.)

46. 91 (Add 1 to the first number $(7 + 1 = 8)$, then add the sum to the second number $(8 + 19 = 27)$ and so on until you get (125 + the missing number = ?). The sums obtained so far make the series 1, 8, 27, 64, 125, which are the cubes of numbers 1, 2, 3, 4 and 5. To complete the series, take the cube of 6 ($=216$) so you reach ($125 + ? = 216$) and the answer is 91.)

47. 6 (There are two alternating series. Each one is squared and a constant 2 added.

The first is	:	0	3	6	9,
square	:	0	9	36	81,
add 2	:	2	11	38	83.
The second is	:	5	4	3 hence 2,	
square	:	25	16	9 hence 4,	
add 2	:	27	18	11 hence 6.)	

48. 55 and 100 (The number to the right of the brackets is the square of the number to the left of the brackets. The number inside the brackets is one-half the total of the numbers outside the brackets.)

49. 581 (Start with the series

	:	0	2	4	6 hence 8,
multiply by 3	:	0	6	12	18 hence 24,
square	:	0	36	144	324 hence 576,
add 5	:	5	41	149	329 hence 581.)

50. 6 (In each triangle, add all numbers inside the triangle and subtract the numbers outside the triangle; this produces the number in the circle.)

Visual-Spatial Ability

Instructions
You have thirty minutes to solve the problems. The score is equal to the number of correct answers you get within the time limit without looking up the answers. Do not spend too long on any one problem. Go back if you have time at the end.

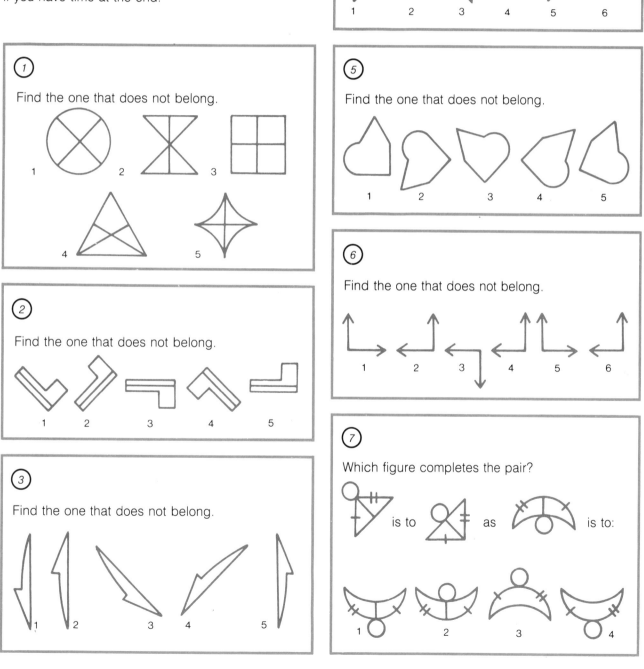

1 Find the one that does not belong.

2 Find the one that does not belong.

3 Find the one that does not belong.

4 Find the one that does not belong.

5 Find the one that does not belong.

6 Find the one that does not belong.

7 Which figure completes the pair?

... is to ... as ... is to:

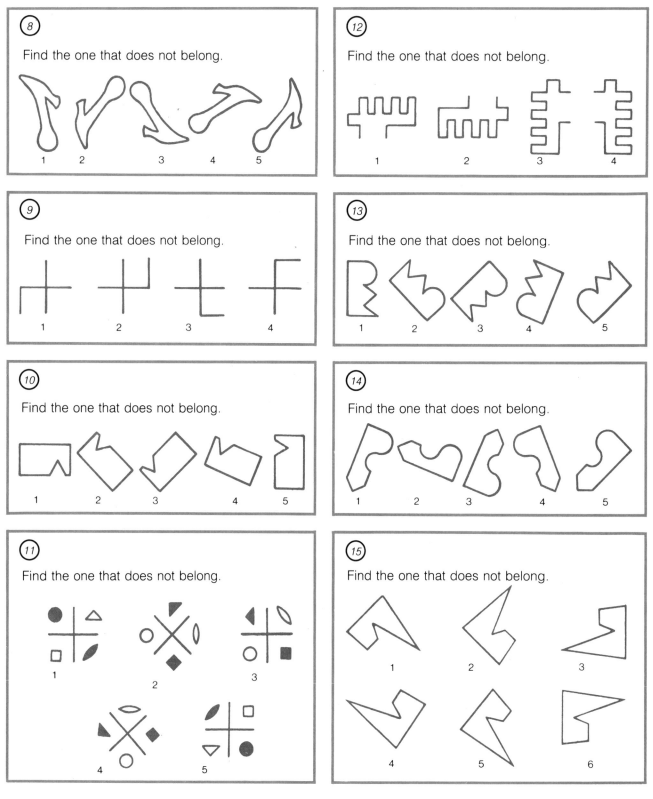

8 Find the one that does not belong.

1   2   3   4   5

9 Find the one that does not belong.

1   2   3   4

10 Find the one that does not belong.

1   2   3   4   5

11 Find the one that does not belong.

1   2   3   4   5

12 Find the one that does not belong.

1   2   3   4

13 Find the one that does not belong.

1   2   3   4   5

14 Find the one that does not belong.

1   2   3   4   5

15 Find the one that does not belong.

1   2   3   4   5   6

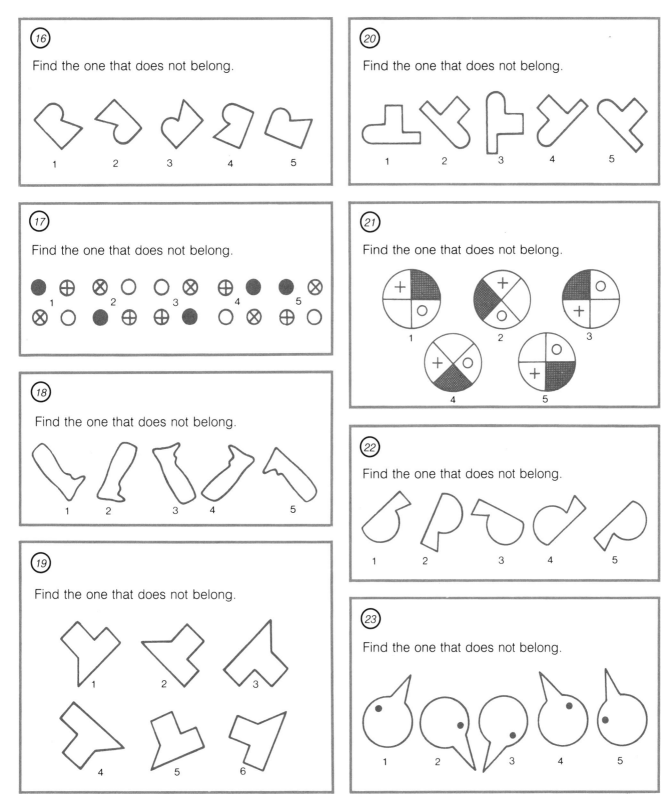

16

Find the one that does not belong.

1   2   3   4   5

17

Find the one that does not belong.

18

Find the one that does not belong.

1   2   3   4   5

19

Find the one that does not belong.

1   2   3

4   5   6

20

Find the one that does not belong.

1   2   3   4   5

21

Find the one that does not belong.

1   2   3

4   5

22

Find the one that does not belong.

1   2   3   4   5

23

Find the one that does not belong.

1   2   3   4   5

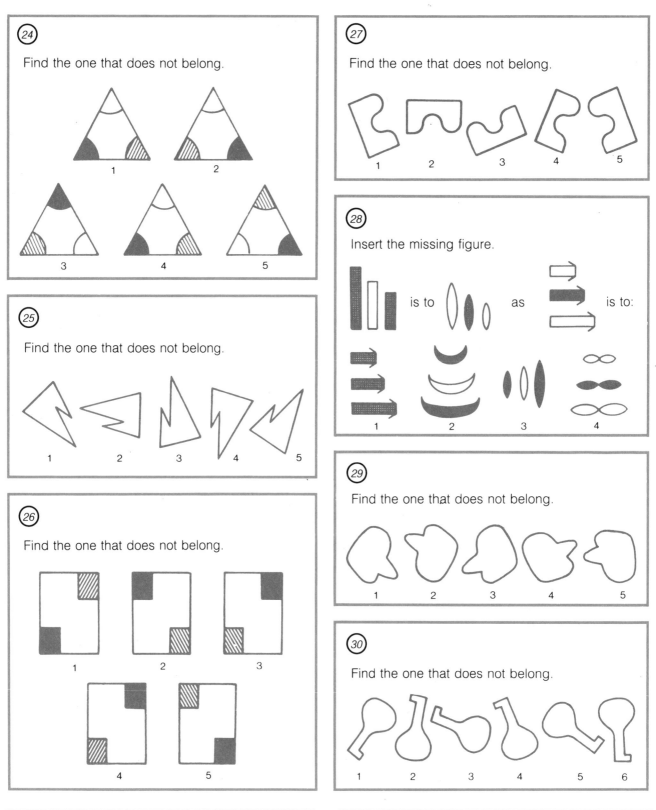

24 Find the one that does not belong.

1 2 3 4 5

25 Find the one that does not belong.

1 2 3 4 5

26 Find the one that does not belong.

1 2 3 4 5

27 Find the one that does not belong.

1 2 3 4 5

28 Insert the missing figure.

is to ... as ... is to:

1 2 3 4

29 Find the one that does not belong.

1 2 3 4 5

30 Find the one that does not belong.

1 2 3 4 5 6

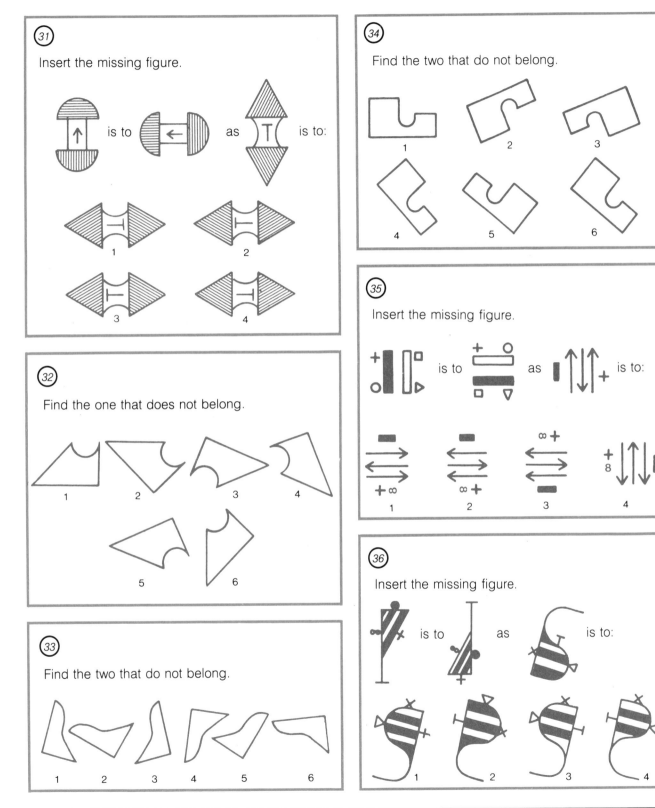

31 Insert the missing figure.

32 Find the one that does not belong.

33 Find the two that do not belong.

34 Find the two that do not belong.

35 Insert the missing figure.

36 Insert the missing figure.

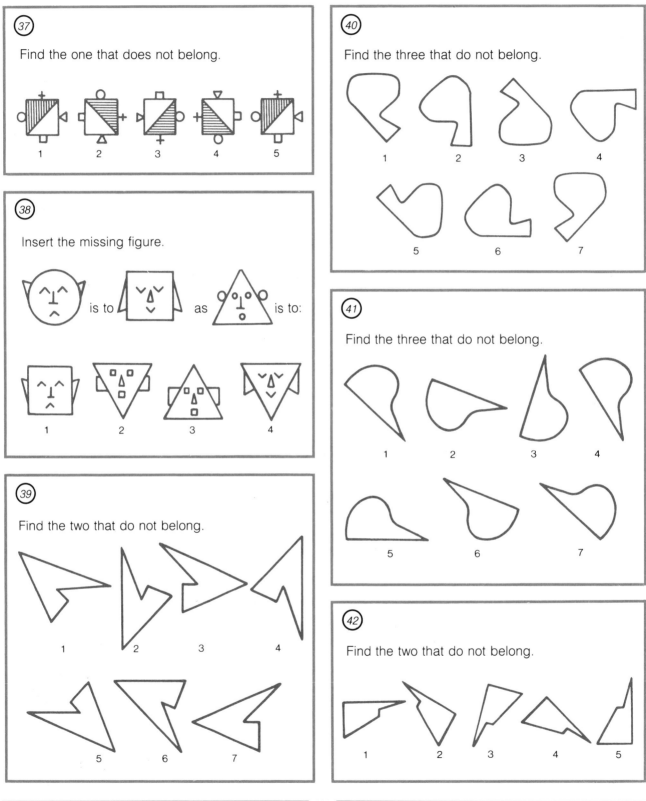

37 Find the one that does not belong.

1   2   3   4   5

38 Insert the missing figure.

is to ... as ... is to:

1   2   3   4

39 Find the two that do not belong.

1   2   3   4

5   6   7

40 Find the three that do not belong.

1   2   3   4

5   6   7

41 Find the three that do not belong.

1   2   3   4

5   6   7

42 Find the two that do not belong.

1   2   3   4   5

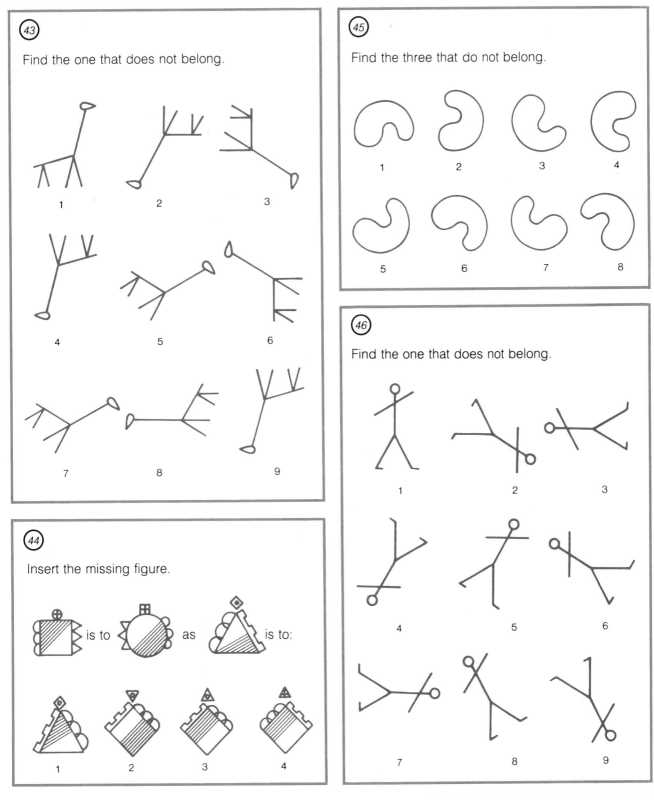

43

Find the one that does not belong.

1 2 3

4 5 6

7 8 9

44

Insert the missing figure.

is to ... as ... is to:

1 2 3 4

45

Find the three that do not belong.

1 2 3 4

5 6 7 8

46

Find the one that does not belong.

1 2 3

4 5 6

7 8 9

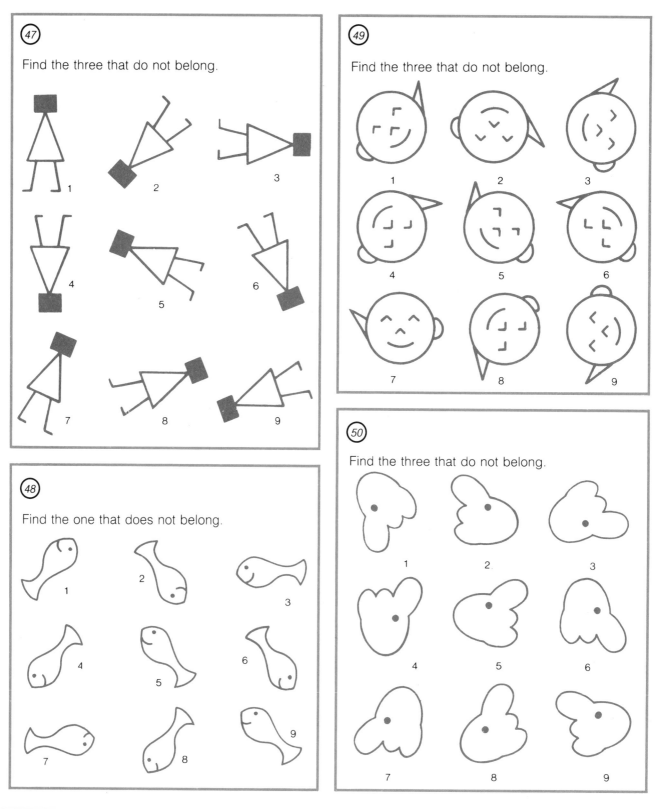

47 Find the three that do not belong.

48 Find the one that does not belong.

49 Find the three that do not belong.

50 Find the three that do not belong.

Answers

1. 4 (All the other drawings can be turned upside down without it making any difference.)

2. 3 (All the other figures can be rotated so they coincide.)

3. 2 (All the other figures can be rotated so they coincide.)

4. 4 (The figure is turned 90 degrees counterclockwise each time, except for no. 4 which is turned clockwise.)

5. 1 (All the other figures can be rotated so they coincide.)

6. 4 (The figure is turned 90 degrees counterclockwise each time, except for no. 4 which is turned clockwise.)

7. 1 (The figure is turned over and the circle is transferred to the other side.)

8. 4 (All the other figures can be rotated so they coincide.)

9. 4 (All the other figures can be rotated so they coincide.)

10. 5 (All the other figures can be rotated so they coincide.)

11. 3 (The figure rotates counterclockwise 45 degrees and the black shading rotates one position further, except in no. 3 which therefore does not belong.)

12. 3 (The other three show a *right* hand rotated into various positions; 3 is a *left* hand!)

13. 2 (All the other figures can be rotated so they coincide.)

14. 1 (All the other figures can be rotated so they coincide.)

15. 5 (All the other figures can be rotated so they coincide.)

16. 4 (All the other figures can be rotated so they coincide.)

17. 5 (The black circle is turned 90 degrees each time. In no. 5, the cross and X are also in different places; in the other figures, the cross is in the same row as the black circle.)

18. 3 (All the other figures can be rotated so they coincide.)

19. 6 (All the other figures can be rotated so they coincide.)

20. 2 (All the other figures can be rotated so they coincide.)

21. 5 (1 and 3, and 2 and 4 are pairs; they can be rotated one-quarter turn so they coincide. If no. 5 were rotated by the same amount it would not coincide with any of the others because the cross and circle would be in the wrong place.)

22. 1 (All the other figures can be rotated so they coincide.)

23. 4 (All the other figures can be rotated so they coincide.)

24. 2 (All the other figures can be rotated so they coincide.)

25. 4 (All the other figures can be rotated so they coincide.)

26. 3 (1 and 4, and 2 and 5 are pairs. In each pair the black and the shaded portions change places. The shading of no. 3 goes the wrong way.)

27. 5 (All the other figures can be rotated so they coincide.)

28. 2 (Shading is transferred from the outer figures to the inner figures and vice versa; the position, upright or horizontal, remains constant.)

29. 3 (All the other figures can be rotated so they coincide.)

30. 3 (All the other figures can be rotated so they coincide.)

31. 3 (The figure rotates clockwise, the arrow counterclockwise.)

32. 5 (All the other figures can be rotated so they coincide.)

33. 1 and 2 (All the other figures can be rotated so they coincide.)

34. 2 and 5 (The other four figures can be rotated so they coincide; nos. 2 and 5 cannot.)

35. 2 (The figure is turned counterclockwise 90 degrees and then the small side figures are interchanged; i.e., those at the top go to the bottom, those at the bottom go to the top.)

36. 3 (The figure is turned 180 degrees (upside down), the three black bands become two and the three small figures move counterclockwise by one position.)

37. 3 (Each of the other drawings follows the rule that the entire drawing is rotated 90 degrees each time; in no. 3 the shading goes the wrong way.)

38. 2 (What is round in the first figure becomes square; what points up, points down.)

39. 3 and 6 (The other five figures can be rotated so they coincide.)

40. 1, 3 and 6 (The other four figures can be rotated so they coincide.)

41. 2, 3 and 7 (The other four figures can be rotated so they coincide.)

42. 1 and 4 (The other figures can be rotated so they coincide.)

43. 8 (All the other figures can be rotated so they coincide.)

44. 3 (The bottom shape and the top shape change places; the figure inside the top shape remains, but the shaded and unshaded areas in the bottom shape change places. The decorations on the right and left of the main figure change places.)

45. 1, 6 and 7 (The other five figures can be rotated so they coincide.)

46. 7 (All the other figures can be rotated so they coincide.)

47. 2, 6 and 7   (The other six figures can be rotated so they coincide.)

48. 6   (All the other figures can be rotated so they coincide.)

49. 1, 6 and 8   (The other six figures can be rotated so they coincide.)

50. 5, 6 and 8   (The other six figures can be rotated so they coincide.)

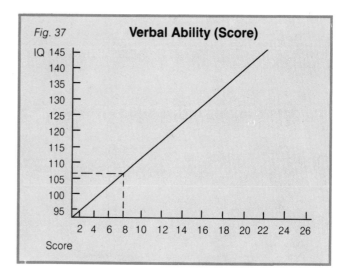

When you have totalled the number of correct answers to each of the above three tests of verbal, mathematical and visual-spatial intelligence, you can evaluate your IQ level by using Figures 37, 38 and 39. The method is the same as that used for Evaluating our Intellectual Level (I & II) in the previous chapter (which was based on Figure 29). Again, the IQ levels are only fully reliable in the range between 100 and 130.

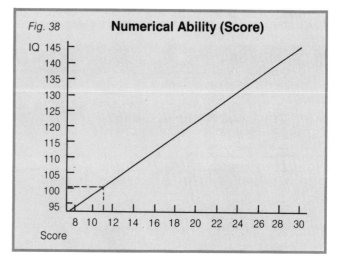

Aptitudes

What does an individual need in order to carry out a particular activity satisfactorily? What aptitudes are necessary in what situations? Teachers, businessmen, trainers, psychologists, coaches—generally all those whose jobs involve improving the performance of others—have been trying to answer these questions for years.

Obviously a person's IQ level is a useful indication of his or her potential. If, for example, you score well on the verbal, numerical and visual-spatial tests, you might expect a reasonable success in, respectively, the literary, logical-formal and figurative-geometric disciplines. Naturally, these are only expectations and, like all expectations, not always realized.

However, if we want more specific information, what material can we use? In addition to the tests which evaluate the intellectual factors mentioned above (called the primary abilities), there is a group of tests commonly referred to as the "multiple aptitude test batteries for special programs" which are used in educational and vocational counselling, although not as frequently today as in the past; current theories of intelligence are more fully developed than were Thurstone's and there is also a tendency now to limit the use of tests which might prove to be highly selective.

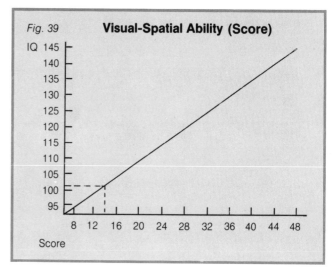

An interesting example of these test batteries—compiled on the basis of factorial analysis—is the General Aptitude Test Battery (GATB), developed by the United States' Employment Service for career guidance and widely used in the 1950s and 1960s. The following factors were included in the GATB:

1. Intelligence [G]. Found by adding the scores on the three tests used to measure the basic factors (vocabulary, arithmetical reasoning, three-dimensional space).
2. Verbal aptitude [V]. Measured by a vocabulary test requiring the examinee to indicate which two words in a set have either the same or opposite meanings.
3. Numerical aptitude [N]. Measured by computation and arithmetical reasoning tests.
4. Spatial aptitude [S]. Measured by three-dimensional space tests involving the ability to comprehend a two-dimensional representation of a three-dimensional object, and to visualize the effects of movement in three dimensions.
5. Form perception [P]. Measured by two tests, one requiring the examinee to match identical drawings of tools, and the other to match geometric forms.
6. Clerical perception [Q]. Similar to P, but requiring the matching of names rather than pictures or forms.
7. Motor coordination [K]. Measured by a simple "paper and pencil" test requiring the examinee to make specified pencil marks in a series of squares.
8. Finger dexterity [F]. Two tests requiring the assembling and disassembling, respectively, of rivets and washers.
9. Manual dexterity [M]. Two tests requiring the examinee to transfer and reverse pegs in a board.

This kind of analysis can be extended and used to measure the special aptitudes needed for very particular activities, such as certain office or workshop tasks for which specific skills are essential. In turn, these "specific aptitudes" can be broken down even further by sensory discrimination tests (relating to colours, names, shapes, touch, taste, etc.), and tests of manual dexterity, limb coordination and reaction speed. They can then be combined in a variety of ways according to specific requirements.

continued on page 122

Fig. 40   **The Fourth Word**

Instructions

The words before and after the equal sign are related. Identify the missing fourth word (?) and circle the correct answer. The following example illustrates the principle underlying the exercises:

Summer : rain = winter : ?
  a) heater
  b) snow
  c) spring
  d) Christmas
  e) white

In this case, the answer is, of course, b. You have six minutes for the twelve exercises.

(*Answers in Figure 45*)

Example:

①

Car : road = train : ?
  a) dyke
  b) bridge
  c) tracks
  d) station
  e) points

②

Machine : metal = man : ?
  a) soul
  b) spirit
  c) baby
  d) flesh
  e) hands

(3)

Pot : wheel = car : ?
    a) road
    b) assembly line
    c) workshop
    d) gas station
    e) ramp

(4)

Son : family = city : ?
    a) borough
    b) citizens
    c) county
    d) village
    e) state

(5)

Nature : virgin forest = cultivation : ?
    a) axe
    b) field
    c) protected forest
    d) roads
    e) farmers

(6)

Chair : armchair = garden : ?
    a) park
    b) wood
    c) meadow
    d) bench
    e) fence

(7)

Eye : picture = ear : ?
    a) noise
    b) song
    c) melody
    d) note
    e) sound

The clues you get in detective novels can produce their own puzzles, some more complex than others. Agatha Christie (1891–1976), the undisputed queen of the detective novel, dropped her clues sparingly in the course of her tales. Indeed, finding them, putting them in order, and finally interpreting them is something of a challenge for her readers. Difficult, yes, but, as she always said with typical British aplomb, quite possible.

Political strategies too, can incorporate seemingly unconnected elements which, once joined, can produce the desired results, or so it is hoped. A stateman's skill lies in his being able to recognize what issues and conditions are the most important at a given moment in history, and then to accurately predict their development. To do this, it is essential to be able to see the whole picture, assessing each element and assigning it its proper place.

With the video game "Labyrinth," the approach is somewhat different, for it consists of finding your way into a geometric structure which you are shown in full at the beginning. The problem is then to remember the original layout, which is essential if you are not going to lose your way along the different paths which come up in rapid succession on the screen.

The word puzzle is used to describe a variety of problems and enigmas; it is also used in reference to jigsaws, with which you reconstruct a picture. Starting with all the fragments jumbled, you have to rebuild the original picture, and that can be just about anything from an autumn landscape to the Mona Lisa, to the latest sports car. It is a test of both your patience and skill.

In reconstructing an image (as in the illustration on the facing page), spatial and perceptual faculties are the most consequential, that is being able to visualize the relationships between the different shapes as one must in drawing a pattern from memory, and to identify visual details, and similarities or differences between the various parts. Of course, depending on the task, more specific aptitudes and characteristics, which vary from person to person, also come to the fore, such as dexterity, indecision, calmness or irritability.

The reconstruction of images is a worthy exercise in structuring reality, teaching you to give meaning to individual elements within a wider framework. In fact, the individual pieces have no significance if they are not seen in relation to the complete composition, just as individual notes only take on substance when placed within the framework of a melody. In this sense, much more is tested than simply single faculties, for highly complex processes of analysis and synthesis are demanded.

It has been shown that perceptual experiences not only engage one's senses (in the case of a jigsaw, the arrangement of the pieces and their relationship to each other), but also draw upon an individual's expectations and accumulated experiences. In effect, a jigsaw puzzle can stimulate the entire personality.

Our perception of movement relies on the same mechanisms we now know from our discussion of transparency, varying surface dimension and amodal completion (see pp. 126-9), in other words the combination of specific decoding processes in perceptual activity. The phenomenon of amodal completion in dynamic situations draws particular attention to these processes. It has been observed that if you throw a ball behind a screen, the path of the ball is imagined from the moment it disappears until it reappears. In much the same fashion, we "see" the route of a car when it goes behind a building (and so moves out of our line of vision) and reappears a few seconds later.

In effect, all events are not only located in space, but also in time; actions then, have both a spatial and a temporal dimension. However, there is a tendency toward perceptual stability: In our mind's eye, an object remains constant and does not change from the instant we last "saw" it until it reappears in a new situation. The way our eyes function contributes to this impression, for they do not perceive individual stages of movement (which are seen in the breakdown in the photograph opposite). "In a classical experiment," wrote E.R. Hilgard, "a subject wore reversing lenses, so that he saw the world upside down. At first the perceived world swirled by as he looked around. One of his first adaptations to the way of perceiving the world was a decrease in this movement as constancy of location was regained. Another sign of regained constancy of location was that the fire was again heard to crackle in the fireplace where it was seen, a harmony of location that was at first lost because only the eyes, and not the ears were perceiving in reverse..." Hilgard went on to say that in the case of coloured lenses, the distortion consisted only in the fact that everything had a blue cast when the subject looked to the left, and a yellow cast when he looked to the right. At first he reported an intensification of the yellow when he looked from left to right, but this disappeared after using the glasses for a few days. However, it reappeared when he removed the glasses. It was as though the experience of chromatic modification in itself—resulting from moving his eyes—led him to see yellow on his right and blue on his left even without the coloured lenses. Quite interesting phenomena generate from what is known as illusion of movement, in other words, the perception of motion when there is no basis in fact for it. These illusions have been studied in depth by the Gestalt psychologists (a theory to which we referred earlier); one of the most common illusions occurs when you are on a moving train. If you keep your eyes fixed on the third rail you get the impression the rail is moving in the opposite direction. Then too, everyone has probably experienced the feeling that the train you are on is moving when, in fact, the train on the opposite track is the one that is moving. In these and similar situations, our perceptual system adapts to a frame of reference which is characterized by the fact that we are in motion. Another example of apparent motion is a TV cartoon which is actually separate pictures blending together in continuous succession, as is the case with the frames of any film.

(8)

Flame : candle = cancer : ?
- a) water
- b) tumour
- c) bacteria
- d) sea
- e) tissue

(9)

Creation : annihilation = production : ?
- a) construction
- b) destruction
- c) disintegration
- d) confusion
- e) combustion

(10)

Clock : time = thermometer : ?
- a) sun
- b) fever
- c) ice
- d) temperature
- e) season

(11)

To fly : to plummet = to swim : ?
- a) to drown
- b) to drift
- c) to sink
- d) to suffocate
- e) to dive

(12)

Sky : cloud = earth : ?
- a) wood
- b) meadow
- c) house
- d) men
- e) sea

Fig. 41 **Opposites**

Instructions
Of the five words suggested, choose the one that is closest to the opposite meaning of the word given.

Example:

To learn

    a) to inform
    b) to cram
    c) to study
    d) to repeat
    e) to forget

The correct answer is e: to forget. You have nine minutes to answer the following twenty-two exercises.

(Answers in Figure 45)

---

③ To move
    a) to stop
    b) to sit
    c) to run
    d) to be still
    e) to dance

④ Pleasure
    a) suffering
    b) anxiety
    c) pain
    d) discomfort
    e) sorrow

① Vendetta
    a) pardon
    b) atonement
    c) satisfaction
    d) justice
    e) reprisal

② Convex
    a) arched
    b) spherical
    c) concave
    d) circular
    e) curved

⑦ Time
    a) past
    b) future
    c) universe
    d) eternity
    e) space

⑧ Career advancement
    a) professional rise
    b) success
    c) failure
    d) professional decline
    e) censure

⑤ To fall
    a) to get up
    b) to arise
    c) to walk
    d) to seize
    e) to emerge

⑥ To imprison
    a) to escape
    b) to flee
    c) to run
    d) to resist
    e) to set free

⑨ Sensitive
    a) indelicate
    b) obstinate
    c) insensitive
    d) inflexible
    e) sentimental

⑩ Egotism
    a) cordiality
    b) humility
    c) affability
    d) altruism
    e) meekness

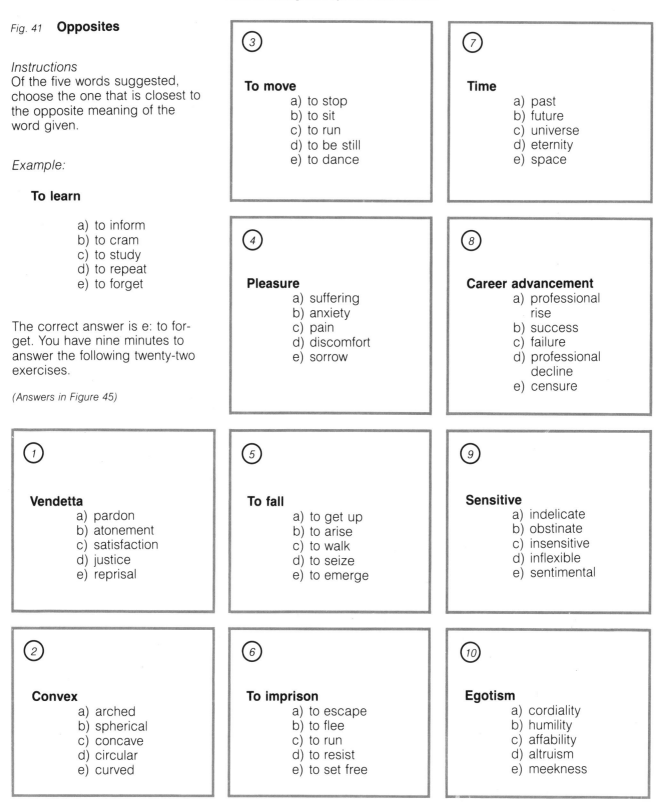

(11)

Unsteady
a) resolute
b) proud
c) controlled
d) fragile
e) stable

(15)

Shame
a) honour
b) praise
c) pride
d) forgiveness
e) repentance

(19)

Avarice
a) richness
b) generosity
c) poverty
d) magnanimity
e) patronage

(12)

Slack
a) solid
b) taut
c) bound
d) complete
e) stable

(16)

To speak
a) to sing
b) to converse
c) to be quiet
d) to mutter
e) to laugh

(20)

Evolution
a) revolution
b) regression
c) restriction
d) recession
e) repression

(13)

Cowardice
a) heroism
b) combat
c) audacity
d) courage
e) fury

(17)

Movement
a) pause
b) immobility
c) tranquillity
d) stability
e) speed

(21)

Insecurity
a) confidence
b) ingenuousness
c) trust
d) courage
e) boldness

(14)

To dominate
a) to work
b) to serve
c) to carry out
d) to conform
e) to harmonize

(18)

Concrete
a) ambiguous
b) abstract
c) imprecise
d) absurd
e) deviant

(22)

Province
a) city
b) region
c) metropolis
d) village
e) colony

Fig. 42 **Work Out
the Processes**

Instructions
Each of these exercises presents a mechanical, technical or physical process. Of the possibilities given, mark the one you think is correct. If an exercise seems too difficult, move to the next rather than trying to guess.

You have a total of twenty-six minutes for the twenty-three exercises.

(Answers in Figure 45)

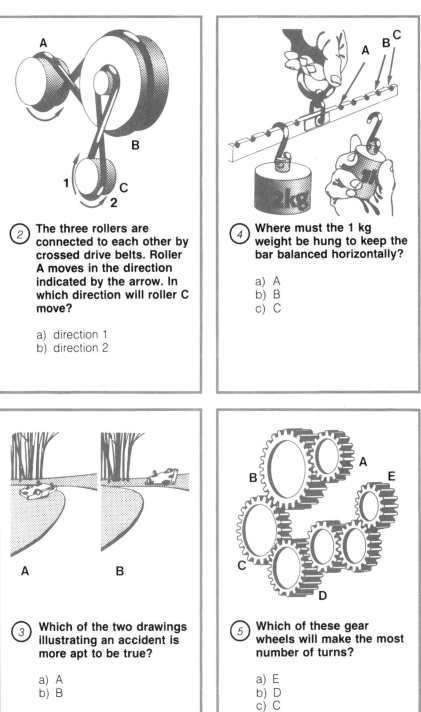

② The three rollers are connected to each other by crossed drive belts. Roller A moves in the direction indicated by the arrow. In which direction will roller C move?

a) direction 1
b) direction 2

④ Where must the 1 kg weight be hung to keep the bar balanced horizontally?

a) A
b) B
c) C

① The glass parallelepiped is resting on a horizontal base. Its center of gravity is marked with a cross. Will it fall over in this position?

a) yes
b) no

③ Which of the two drawings illustrating an accident is more apt to be true?

a) A
b) B

⑤ Which of these gear wheels will make the most number of turns?

a) E
b) D
c) C
d) B
e) A
f) they will all turn at the same speed

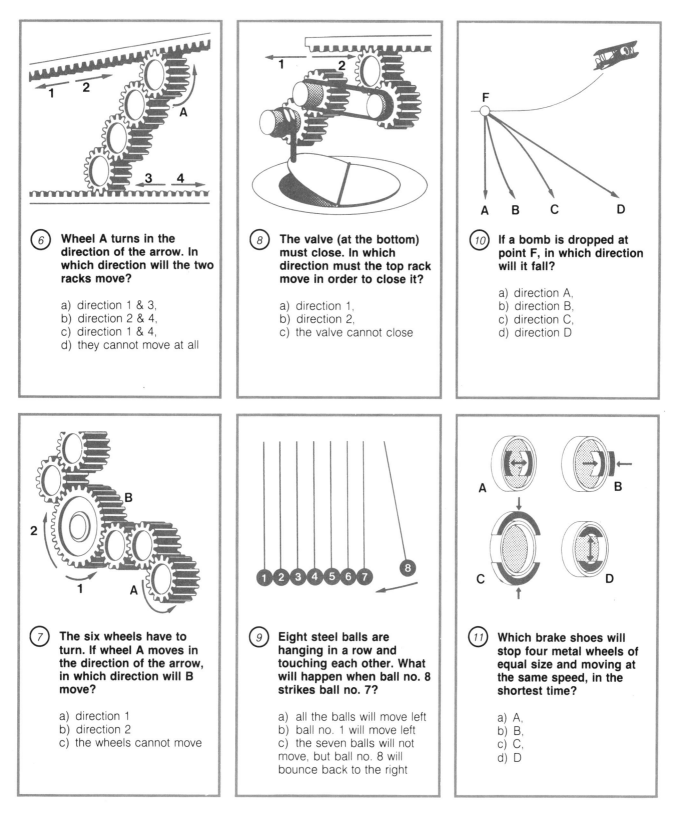

6 Wheel A turns in the direction of the arrow. In which direction will the two racks move?

a) direction 1 & 3,
b) direction 2 & 4,
c) direction 1 & 4,
d) they cannot move at all

8 The valve (at the bottom) must close. In which direction must the top rack move in order to close it?

a) direction 1,
b) direction 2,
c) the valve cannot close

10 If a bomb is dropped at point F, in which direction will it fall?

a) direction A,
b) direction B,
c) direction C,
d) direction D

7 The six wheels have to turn. If wheel A moves in the direction of the arrow, in which direction will B move?

a) direction 1
b) direction 2
c) the wheels cannot move

9 Eight steel balls are hanging in a row and touching each other. What will happen when ball no. 8 strikes ball no. 7?

a) all the balls will move left
b) ball no. 1 will move left
c) the seven balls will not move, but ball no. 8 will bounce back to the right

11 Which brake shoes will stop four metal wheels of equal size and moving at the same speed, in the shortest time?

a) A,
b) B,
c) C,
d) D

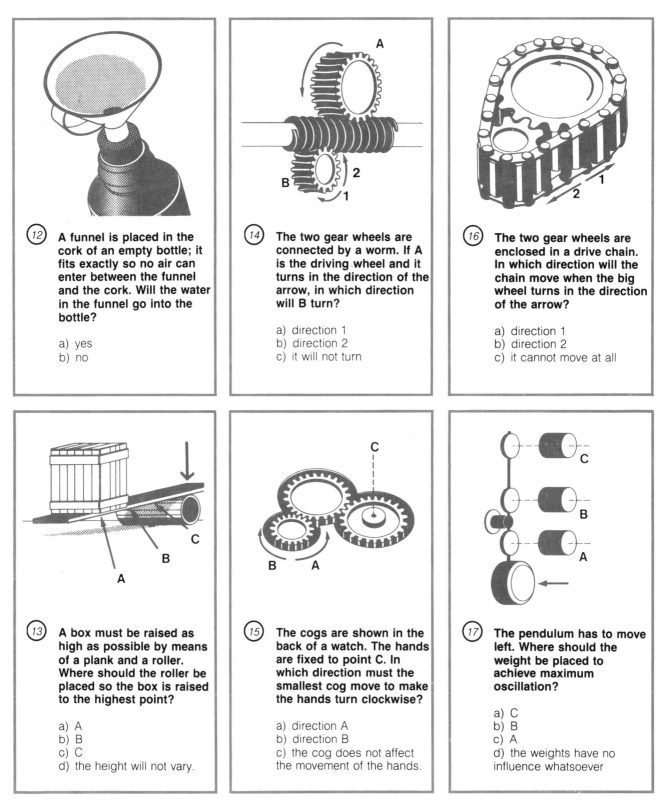

12 A funnel is placed in the cork of an empty bottle; it fits exactly so no air can enter between the funnel and the cork. Will the water in the funnel go into the bottle?

a) yes
b) no

14 The two gear wheels are connected by a worm. If A is the driving wheel and it turns in the direction of the arrow, in which direction will B turn?

a) direction 1
b) direction 2
c) it will not turn

16 The two gear wheels are enclosed in a drive chain. In which direction will the chain move when the big wheel turns in the direction of the arrow?

a) direction 1
b) direction 2
c) it cannot move at all

13 A box must be raised as high as possible by means of a plank and a roller. Where should the roller be placed so the box is raised to the highest point?

a) A
b) B
c) C
d) the height will not vary.

15 The cogs are shown in the back of a watch. The hands are fixed to point C. In which direction must the smallest cog move to make the hands turn clockwise?

a) direction A
b) direction B
c) the cog does not affect the movement of the hands.

17 The pendulum has to move left. Where should the weight be placed to achieve maximum oscillation?

a) C
b) B
c) A
d) the weights have no influence whatsoever

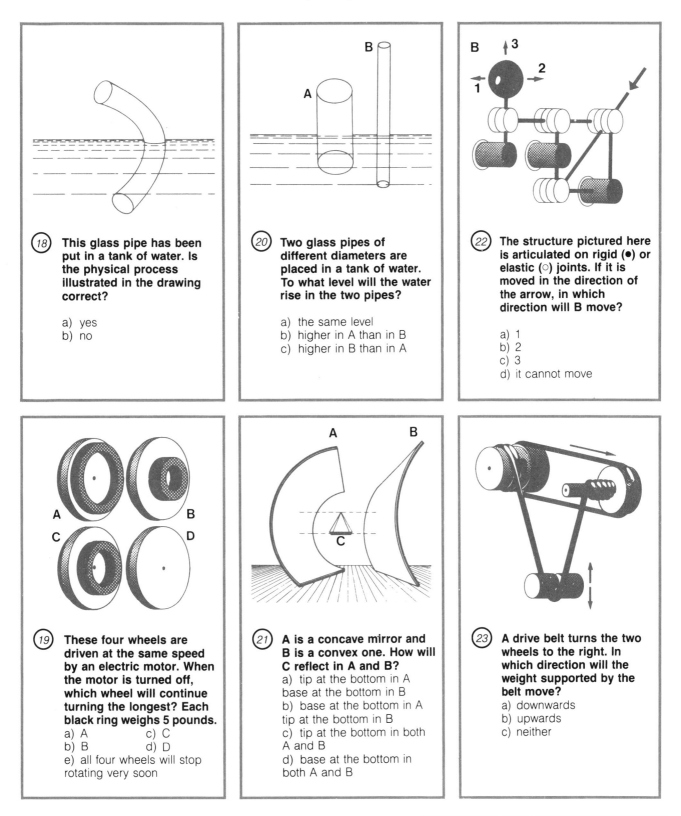

(18) **This glass pipe has been put in a tank of water. Is the physical process illustrated in the drawing correct?**

a) yes
b) no

(20) **Two glass pipes of different diameters are placed in a tank of water. To what level will the water rise in the two pipes?**

a) the same level
b) higher in A than in B
c) higher in B than in A

(22) **The structure pictured here is articulated on rigid (●) or elastic (○) joints. If it is moved in the direction of the arrow, in which direction will B move?**

a) 1
b) 2
c) 3
d) it cannot move

(19) **These four wheels are driven at the same speed by an electric motor. When the motor is turned off, which wheel will continue turning the longest? Each black ring weighs 5 pounds.**

a) A   c) C
b) B   d) D
e) all four wheels will stop rotating very soon

(21) **A is a concave mirror and B is a convex one. How will C reflect in A and B?**
a) tip at the bottom in A base at the bottom in B
b) base at the bottom in A tip at the bottom in B
c) tip at the bottom in both A and B
d) base at the bottom in both A and B

(23) **A drive belt turns the two wheels to the right. In which direction will the weight supported by the belt move?**
a) downwards
b) upwards
c) neither

Fig. 43 **Practical Calculation**

Instructions
Although the following seventeen exercises do not require any more than an elementary knowledge of math, only a few people will be able to do all of them with the same ease; some of them, in fact, are quite complicated. Use a separate sheet of paper to make calculations and approximate the answers to two decimal points.

You have sixty minutes for the seventeen questions.

(Answers in Figure 45)

② **If you divide a number by 3.4 and the answer is 9.2, what is the number?**

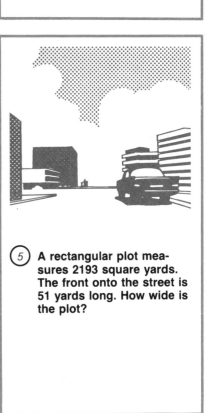

④ **A sum of money is divided between four people so A gets 1/4, B gets 1/5, C 3/10 and D the rest ($25). How much does each one get?**

A . . .
B . . .
C . . .

① **A bartender draws the following amounts of beer in three days: 3 gallons, 4.6 gallons and 9.2 gallons. For each glass (0.1 gallon) he gets $1.50. At the end, how much money will he have in the cash register if the register was empty when he started?**

③ **The director is three times as old as the apprentice and twice as old as his secretary. The ages of all three together add up to 88. How old is each one?**

director:
secretary:
apprentice:

⑤ **A rectangular plot measures 2193 square yards. The front onto the street is 51 yards long. How wide is the plot?**

6. Fifty labourers work 142 days to dig a ditch. How long would thirty workers have to work to dig the same ditch?

8. A teacher multiplies one-half a number by one-third of the number and gets 24. He then asks his students: "What was the original number?"

10. A driver's reaction speed is 1 second. If he is driving at 96 kilometers per hour, how many meters forward will the car move between the time a danger appears and the driver applies the brakes.

7. An old car is sold with a discount of $750, which is 18 percent of the original sale price. What was the original price and what is the selling price?

9. In the end-of-season sale, a shop sells a pair of socks originally priced at $1.45 for 87 cents. How much of a discount was given?

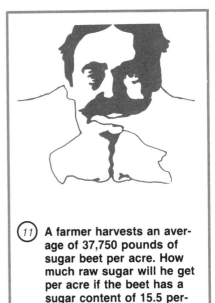

11. A farmer harvests an average of 37,750 pounds of sugar beet per acre. How much raw sugar will he get per acre if the beet has a sugar content of 15.5 percent?

12 In 1950, there were 1,570,400 horses in Germany. In 1967 there were only 283,200. By what percentage did the number of horses decrease?

14 The multiplication ratio of two gear wheels (Z1:Z2) is 3:5. Wheel Z1 does 225 rpm. How many revolutions per minute will Z2 do?

16 A boy sells pens to his schoolmates. He sells two pens for the price he paid for three. How much is his profit?

13 One-fifth of a sum of money is three dollars more than one-sixth of the same amount. How many dollars is the sum of money?

15 A number is multiplied by 3, divided by four, and the result is 3/10. What is the number?

17 Together a lion, a leopard and a jackal devour a zebra. Alone, the lion could finish the zebra in one hour but the leopard would take three hours, and the jackal six hours. How long does it take them to eat it together?

Fig. 44 **Approximate Calculation**

Instructions
The exercises on these pages are basically simple; the only problem is that very high numbers are involved and the time given is short. The exercise must be done by approximating the answers. Each exercise is followed by five possible answers. Mark the one you think is correct.

Remember that: multiplication (×) and division (÷) are done before addition (+) and subtraction (−). You have eight minutes to answer the questions.

(Answers in Figure 45)

②

314739
+
2058524
+
192573
+
98702
+
4072639

a   12 419 647
b   8 643 529
c   6 737 177
d   4 892 437
e   9 214 888

④

425248
−
138546
−
217489
−
16079

a   53 134
b   109 494
c   39 714
d   98 317
e   49 411

⑥

38315
×
539
−
7802
:
94

a   20 651 702
b   4 837 248
c   230 921 044
d   970 633 520
e   970 428

①

75239
−
12724
−
29846

a   49 437
b   32 669
c   24 319
d   18 024
e   51 006

③

72
+
240
+
28
+
100

a   700
b   350
c   435
d   440
e   850

⑤

250758
×
2073

a   500 177
b   419 234
c   519 821 334
d   104 329 494
e   4 398 523 474

⑦

52416
:
576
−
38269
:
781

a   15 748
b   9 502
c   1 211
d   814
e   42

Answers

Fig. 45

Fig. 40. The Fourth Word: 1c; 2d; 3b; 4e; 5c; 6a; 7b; 8e; 9b; 10d; 11c; 12e.

Total score:

Fig. 41. Opposites: 1a; 2c; 3d; 4c; 5a; 6e; 7d; 8d; 9c; 10d; 11e; 12b; 13d; 14b; 15a; 16c; 17b; 18b; 19b; 20b; 21a; 22c;

Total score:

Fig. 42. Work Out the Processes: 1a; 2b; 3b; 4b; 5a; 6a; 7b; 8b; 9b; 10c; 11c; 12b; 13c; 14c; 15a; 16c; 17a; 18b; 19a; 20c; 21a; 22d; 23a.

Total score:

Fig. 43. Practical Calculation: 1. $252; 2. 31.28; 3. apprentice 16, secretary 24, director 48; 4. A—$25, B—$20, C—$30; 5. 43 yards; 6. 236 2/3 days; 7. $4,166.66, $3,416.66; 8. 12; 9. 40 percent; 10. 26 2/3; 11. 5851.25 pounds; 12. 82 percent; 13. $90; 14. 375 rpm; 15. 2/5; 16. 50 percent; 17. 40 minutes.

Total score:

Fig. 44. Approximate Calculation: 1b; 2c; 3d; 4a; 5c; 6a; 7e.

Total score:

Fig. 50. The Mechanical Koala: see below

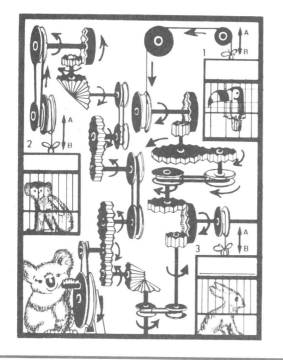

Evaluating our aptitudes

Rather than go into details about highly specialized exercises, this might be a good point to tackle a few tests.

Figures 40 and 41 allow you to evaluate your own and other people's verbal aptitude; Figure 42 tests technical-spatial abilities; Figures 43 and 44 evaluate your computation aptitude.

All the answers are given in Figure 45, at the end of the tests. By counting one point for each correct answer you will arrive at the total score for each test.

A comparative evaluation is also possible by likening your scores to those of others. Then too, it is interesting to look at people's scores in relation to their jobs, bearing in mind how satisfying they find their work, and their degree of success (or failure).

Age

One's performance on intelligence tests tends to stabilize in the late teens, however it remains customary to talk in terms of IQ despite the fact that any difference between the scores of a seventeen-year-old, say, and a nineteen-year-old is known to be due to their individual capacities rather than their age.

On the whole, the IQ levels to which we have referred so far (e.g., in Figure 29) observe the current practice and are based on a statistical process in which average scores are given a value of 100 and the range of scores follows a given distribution curve. Because this is a rather technical area and we will not be examining it, we refer you to A. Anastasi's *Psychological Testing*. However, we would like to point out that the classifications in Figure 46 are generally valid for IQs obtained in the different tests, even though they are not linked to chronological age.

It is also worth noting that as people get older, their performance in certain areas changes. Where the speed of response is important, Figure 47 shows how abilities, and hence scores, increase up to the age of thirty-five and then drop, while in tests that do not involve dexterity, a drop occurs only after the age of sixty.

Does this prove superiority of the young and indicate the elderly are unfit for positions of responsibility? Not at all! The decline in scores on certain intelligence tests does not mean that adults of middle years and beyond are less able to carry out their roles in society. Although new experiences are assimilated less quickly, much that is learned in the past is not forgotten.

Fig. 46			
	IQ	Verbal Description	Percentage of subjects in each group
	140 and over	Excellent	About 1 percent
	120–139	Very good	About 10 percent
	110–119	Good	About 20 percent
	90–109	Average	About 50 percent

If we consider *wisdom* the accumulation of past experiences and *intelligence* the ability to apply that wisdom to current problems, we understand how an older person can be more competent than someone younger who is faster perhaps, but lacks the other's experience. Intelligence tests place inordinate weight on items requiring ingenuity, speed and the ability to adapt to new situations, and not enough weight on the equally important accumulation of experience, for it is this that allows older people to effectively cope with many stiuations in their private and professional lives.

Arguments for and against the tests

While it is clear from what we have been saying, that undue consequence should not be attached to scores in these tests, there is the reverse problem, namely that it is quite common today to deny the validity of these tests, and indeed, to charge them with serious shortcomings. This merits some discussion.

The general criticism of psychological tests is that they are limited by bias and a circumscribed context and fail to make room for such factors as diverse cultural backgrounds, motivation, interests, etc.. Hence, they cannot yield accurate assessments. They are also seen as an invasion of privacy for the purpose of gaining information or worse still, as tools for discriminatory

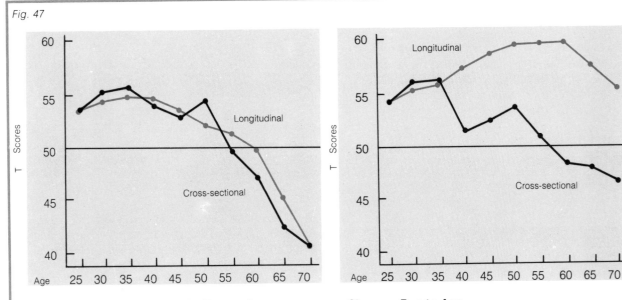

Changes in Intellectual Ability Due to Age

The scores are based on the results of a battery of tests in the five primary abilities. The battery is particularly weighted with tests of speed like the verbal fluency test. Both the longitudinal and cross-sectional data indicate that the peak of one's abilities is reached at about 35 years of age and drops rapidly after 50. The scores are expressed in units of standard deviation with an average of 50 and a standard deviation of 10. The average of 50 is based on a sample of 1000 adult subjects.

Changes Due to Age

The above graph is based on a combination of the scores from verbal comprehension and reasoning tests, neither of which involve a speed factor. Here, the cross-sectional and longitudinal data show markedly different results: The cross-sectional data indicates the peak is reached at age 35, whereas the longitudinal data shows the peak at 60. In both cases, the decline as a result of age is considerably less than what is shown in the graph on the left.

selection. Even the most innocuous of them are thought to be forms of classification administered by "experts" who are not held accountable for the manner in which they perform.

There is no denying a measure of truth in this criticism, but the flaw is that it mistakes what are actually peripheral problems regarding testing for central issues. Indeed, specialists today are particularly sensitive to these problems.

It is now generally accepted that the results from these tests are primarily useful as guidelines which help us to deepen our understanding of the human personality as much as possible: "Therefore, if psychotherapists who use quantification methods want to avoid simply classifying and producing statistical analyses of the data gathered from the experiments. . . they have to refer to theories, to formulate hypotheses about the ways in which the mental equipment works. . .in order to understand fully the results they obtain."

Tests can be very useful as a way of learning about your abilities, aptitudes, and motivation in the areas in which you now work, or in new areas of work which you might want to consider. Put in this context, the scores shed their "authoritative" character, and can be used to improve individual and collective well-being. In short, they are no longer regarded as invasive instruments but rather as stimuli to self-improvement.

Success

Who can say if a person with a particular score on an IQ test or on a visual-spatial aptitude test will do well in a job, or even in life for that matter? Success depends on a myriad imponderables, luck being not the least important.

A survey of various people included in those tomes of the illustrious, *Who's Who in America* and *American Men of Science,* indicates little difference between their IQs and those of "average" citizens.

Moreover, it is well-known that common sense, self-control, motivation, ambition and the ability to develop harmonious relationships are determinative in one's success in work. It is no coincidence that in large measure educational and vocational guidance is based on questionnaires such as "The Choice of Faculty," a self-evaluation questionnaire given to a group of university students, which we have reproduced below. It can be

continued on page 138

Choosing Your Major

Instructions for filling in the questionnaire and interpreting the results

Indicate your degree of personal interest, i.e., *how much* you are interested in each of the activities described below, by writing an X in the appropriate box.

For example: Indicate how much you are interested in the following activities:

	not at all	not much	quite	very
Making model airplanes	☐	☐	☐	☐
Reading modern poetry	☐	☐	☐	☐

Suppose you have no interest in making model planes, but are very interested in reading modern poetry; mark your choice with an X in the boxes as follows:

	not at all	not much	quite	very
Making model airplanes	☒	☐	☐	☐
Reading modern poetry	☐	☐	☐	☒

When you have answered all the questions, follow the indication given on the score grouping tables (p. 135) and transfer the Xs to the interpretation tables at the end of the questionnaire according to the rule below:

a) three Xs if you marked "very"

b) two Xs if you marked "quite"

c) one X if you marked "not much"

d) no X if you marked "not at all"

The highest percentages show you are suitable for the degree courses to which the scores refer.

Item	not at all	not much	quite	very

1. Understanding the atom, its constituent elements and the laws which govern its behaviour. ☐ ☐ ☐ ☐

2. Knowing which laws of physics govern the working of an engine. ☐ ☐ ☐ ☐

3. Reading literary magazines from cover to cover. ☐ ☐ ☐ ☐

4. Working with statistical control systems designed to improve output programs, cures, etc. ☐ ☐ ☐ ☐

5. Learning about the art of vine cultivation, the treatment of grapes, wine pressing and fermentation. ☐ ☐ ☐ ☐

6. Working in a bank. ☐ ☐ ☐ ☐

7. Dealing with work conditions and problems, national insurance, the protection and promotion of the work force. ☐ ☐ ☐ ☐

8. Understanding the technical terminology for marine and air navigation. ☐ ☐ ☐ ☐

9. Being able to judge the beauty of a building, product or any kind of object. ☐ ☐ ☐ ☐

10. Studying the interrelation of engineering and geology. ☐ ☐ ☐ ☐

11. Studying nuclear engineering and its countless applications. ☐ ☐ ☐ ☐

12. Taking the time to admire a plant and its individual parts. ☐ ☐ ☐ ☐

13. Analyzing past events to make reliable predictions about the future on the basis of reasoned calculations. ☐ ☐ ☐ ☐

14. Learning why some man-made satellites go out of orbit and fall. ☐ ☐ ☐ ☐

15. Learning about the preparation of food for astronauts. ☐ ☐ ☐ ☐

16. Visiting a cave. ☐ ☐ ☐ ☐

17. Studying the reasons for the structural modifications of early aircraft which led to today's supersonic planes. ☐ ☐ ☐ ☐

18. Examining the laws of several countries and comparing how they differ when they relate to the same situations. ☐ ☐ ☐ ☐

19. Analyzing your country's economy. ☐ ☐ ☐ ☐

20. Writing poetry or short stories. ☐ ☐ ☐ ☐

21. Helping to repair a car. ☐ ☐ ☐ ☐

22. Visiting a museum. ☐ ☐ ☐ ☐

23. Learning the basic principles of marine navigation. ☐ ☐ ☐ ☐

24. Applying data derived from abstract premises to concrete elements. ☐ ☐ ☐ ☐

25. Understanding and being able to cure animals in order to prevent their illnesses from spreading to their fellow creatures and to man. ☐ ☐ ☐ ☐

26. Spending your entire life studying the stars. ☐ ☐ ☐ ☐

27. Dedicating yourself to the problems of developing countries. ☐ ☐ ☐ ☐

28. Being able to identify microorganisms, bacilli and viruses under a microscope. ☐ ☐ ☐ ☐

29. Seeking opportunities to learn more about the history of aeronautics. ☐ ☐ ☐ ☐

30. Being able to understand and relive what an artist felt by looking at the artist's work. ☐ ☐ ☐ ☐

31. Finding imaginative uses for discarded pieces from an electronics laboratory. ☐ ☐ ☐ ☐

32. Spending an extended period in a space laboratory. ☐ ☐ ☐ ☐

33. Visiting a nuclear power plant. ☐ ☐ ☐ ☐

34. Being able to help someone who is injured. ☐ ☐ ☐ ☐

Item	not much	not at all	quite	very

35. Doing technical drawings using a ruler, set square and compass. ☐ ☐ ☐ ☐

36. Working on roads from a technical vantage point, i.e., planning their construction, and their links to other means of communication. ☐ ☐ ☐ ☐

37. Studying local politics. ☐ ☐ ☐ ☐

38. Understanding how a microcomputer, a transistor, or the control panel of a lift works. ☐ ☐ ☐ ☐

39. Being able to work out the result of a chemical process on your own before getting the answer from your teacher or a book. ☐ ☐ ☐ ☐

40. Defending the rights of a citizen accused of breaking the law. ☐ ☐ ☐ ☐

41. Knowing why, for instance, a particular canal was built where it is and not somewhere else. ☐ ☐ ☐ ☐

42. Understanding the laws that govern the life and movement of the stars, planets and galaxies. ☐ ☐ ☐ ☐

43. Raising chickens. ☐ ☐ ☐ ☐

44. Visiting a natural history museum. ☐ ☐ ☐ ☐

45. Studying the origins of a foreign language. ☐ ☐ ☐ ☐

46. Dealing with the public in a bank. ☐ ☐ ☐ ☐

47. Understanding the psychology of the society of which you are a part. ☐ ☐ ☐ ☐

48. Assisting in the technical improvement of radiotherapy equipment, such as X-ray machines. ☐ ☐ ☐ ☐

49. Studying microbes in depth, in order to identify them, discover their characteristics and isolate them. ☐ ☐ ☐ ☐

50. Collaborating, as an expert on the protection of the natural environment. ☐ ☐ ☐ ☐

51. Dedicating your life to the alleviation of

Albert Michotte (1881–1965), Baron van der Berek—psychologist, founder of the "Institut de Psychologie Appliquée et de Pédagogie" of the University of Louvain and of the Société Belge de Psychologie, and president of the International Union for Scientific Psychology until 1960—was responsible for some fundamental research on amodal completion. His experiments, conducted under the wide umbrella of causal perception, dealt with the influence one object can have on another in our perception, even in situations where no additional elements with their own shape, brightness or colour exist; there may be nothing linking one part to another that our senses can immediately perceive yet this does not prevent the incidence of marked integration phenomena. In Fig. a, below, for example, the presence of the dark transverse strip means we do not perceive two separate light figures, but rather a single large rectangle passing behind the dark rectangle.

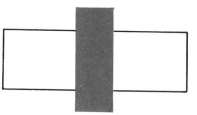

Similarly, in Fig. b, the four segments seem to join to form a cross, whereas in reality, should the dark rectangle which determines the amodal completion of the segment be removed, we might find a different formation, such as that in Fig. c.

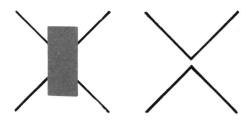

We could say, then, that the parts that do not immediately strike the eye are "seen," or perceived, as existing underneath what is seen. This form of perception is distinguished from modal perception which is based on the fact that direct stimuli coming from the object strike a sensory "pattern."

Michotte concentrated on experiments with moving and static objects: By throwing a ball behind a screen he demonstrated that a process of identification with an object could exist or not exist from the moment of the object's disappearance until the moment it reappeared, depending on the time lapse between the two. It is quite normal to see a car that passes behind a building and reappears seconds later on the other side, as one and the same. However, it could be that the car stopped out of the line of vision and a similar car appeared on the other side. The phenomenon of amodal perception is constant, provided the time interval is not too great. In static situations, the operative principles are those

illustrated by Figs. a, b and c. A book may cover part of a table, but we "see" the table's entire surface, even when some of it is under the book and thus, cannot directly stimulate our eyes. According to scholars who draw upon Gestalt theory—which interprets reality in terms of wholes, shapes and structures, maintaining that elements should not be considered in isolation but rather as parts of a wider and more global context—amodal completion is an underlying factor behind certain principles, such as the resemblance of two parts, contiguity of line, and similarity of outline. These principles help us to understand the impression created by the photograph on p. 127. There is no doubt whatsoever that a continuity exists between the parts of the girl that are visible on the two sides of the page. Here, as in similar situations, there is a tendency to simplify our perception as much as possible: Fig. b, which we discussed above, is "seen" as a cross,—that is, as simply as possible. In the same fashion and in keeping with the principle of perceptual "economy," the naked parts seen in the photograph tend to be completed as a nude figure. In other words, clothing would complicate the issue and this is precisely what we tend to avoid. Hence our surprise, and perhaps disappointment, when we see the following page.

Michotte was careful to distinguish amodal completion from imagination. We can, of course, imagine something behind another object, but in reality this does not happen. Instead we are inclined to see hidden elements in their simplest form. Futhermore, he clearly demonstrated that the phenomenon is intrinsically a perceptual one, while such factors as experience, knowledge and deductive ability are less important.

It should be emphasized that amodal perception is significant in our everyday lives because it enables us to make the necessary integrations—which for the most part we do correctly—when it is impossible to rely solely on our senses to grasp a particular reality. This takes us back to the issue of our perception "adjusting"—we might say completing—the world around us to our satisfaction on the basis of certain principles. Some of these principles, as described by Hilgard, are listed below.

"a) Mainly, we perceive things and we perceive environmental objects as thing-like, that is as stable and enduring. The stability of perceived objects depends on various constancies: color and brightness constancy, shape constancy, size constancy and location constancy. In the choice between perspective size and object size, perception tends usually to conform more nearly to object size unless the contextual cues are greatly reduced. When they are, perception comes close to perspective . . . b) Perception is selective so that we attend at once to only part of the influx of sensory stimulation. Factors of advantage, favoring attention to one pattern of stimuli over another, reside in part in the stimuli themselves, but they depend also on both the habitual and the momentary interests of the individual. Preparatory set is one condition for perception . . . c) The satisfying of individual needs and values may lead to perceptual distortion. Personality characteristics such as rigidity and intolerance of ambiguity may likewise determine how the individual perceives."

Item	not at all	not much	quite	very
the physical and emotional pain of your fellowmen.	☐	☐	☐	☐
52. Knowing why certain plants grow on coastlines, hills, in desert regions, forests, etc.	☐	☐	☐	☐
53. Being able to assess a rational road system with an efficient traffic-light network and traffic flow.	☐	☐	☐	☐
54. Taking a vacation with the main objective being visits to museums and art galleries.	☐	☐	☐	☐
55. Studying ancient Greek.	☐	☐	☐	☐
56. Formulating theories about soil fertility and methods to improve fertility without dangerously affecting the natural balance.	☐	☐	☐	☐
57. Learning why certain cities have larger populations and are more prosperous than others.	☐	☐	☐	☐
58. Understanding why boys behave differently from girls.	☐	☐	☐	☐
59. Spending hours digging for traces of an ancient civilization.	☐	☐	☐	☐
60. Seeing the inside of a slaughterhouse.	☐	☐	☐	☐
61. Studying the relationship between pay raises, unemployment and devaluation.	☐	☐	☐	☐
62. Trying to solve a court case.	☐	☐	☐	☐
63. Trying to understand the conditions plants need to flower.	☐	☐	☐	☐
64. Working in a small drugstore where medicines are still made at the back of the shop.	☐	☐	☐	☐
65. Understanding scientifically why an object falls from your hands, or a balloon tends to rise.	☐	☐	☐	☐
66. Examining a boat's engine room, even when you are on a short trip.	☐	☐	☐	☐

Item	not at all	not much	quite	very

67. Constructing an electrical system at home. ☐ ☐ ☐ ☐

68. Being able to ascertain the degree of danger of chemical preservatives in food. ☐ ☐ ☐ ☐

69. Following what happens in space from the ground-control center. ☐ ☐ ☐ ☐

70. Knowing about the variations in quality of daytime radio reception and understanding why this happens. ☐ ☐ ☐ ☐

71. Understanding the theory of probability. ☐ ☐ ☐ ☐

72. Studying the various applications of an abstract mathematical formula. ☐ ☐ ☐ ☐

73. Being able to choose between two similar medicines and selecting the more suitable one for a particular case. ☐ ☐ ☐ ☐

74. Understanding as much as possible about the planet earth, its movements, rotation, revolutions, the pattern of the seasons, and the elements on which the climate depends. ☐ ☐ ☐ ☐

75. Visiting the control tower of an airport and learning how contact is made with pilots and automatic landings are made. ☐ ☐ ☐ ☐

76. Learning about the formation of the earth's surface. ☐ ☐ ☐ ☐

77. Understanding the various systems to acquire and elaborate data. ☐ ☐ ☐ ☐

78. Promulgating your views in public as politicians do. ☐ ☐ ☐ ☐

79. Dedicating your maturity and professional life to sports. ☐ ☐ ☐ ☐

80. Conceiving new and interesting forms of artificial lighting. ☐ ☐ ☐ ☐

81. Studying philosophy because it affords the opportunity to reflect on what might

otherwise be merely passing thoughts. ☐ ☐ ☐ ☐

82. Seeking plausible explanations of events, be they events with worldwide implications or everyday occurrences. ☐ ☐ ☐ ☐

83. Working on a newspaper. ☐ ☐ ☐ ☐

84. Understanding the specific functions of insects, even troublesome ones. ☐ ☐ ☐ ☐

85. Knowing whether a building was designed by an undistinguished architect or one thought to be a genius. ☐ ☐ ☐ ☐

86. Merging your interests with the common cause in order to promote a just society in which people can enjoy a reasonable sense of well-being. ☐ ☐ ☐ ☐

87. Staying in a stable for a stretch of time to see if anything unexpected happens. ☐ ☐ ☐ ☐

88. Studying the rules by which different events can be interpreted and classified. ☐ ☐ ☐ ☐

89. Handling a boat, either with sails or an engine, and taking a measure of responsibility for its navigation. ☐ ☐ ☐ ☐

90. Conducting a research survey in your neighborhood. ☐ ☐ ☐ ☐

91. Finding ways to restore old houses. ☐ ☐ ☐ ☐

92. Living abroad for a time to perfect your command of the language. ☐ ☐ ☐ ☐

93. Thinking up new uses for old valves, condensers, transistors, printed curcuits and such, and implementing your ideas. ☐ ☐ ☐ ☐

94. Knowing each and every organ of the human body. ☐ ☐ ☐ ☐

95. Listening to a literary program on the radio. ☐ ☐ ☐ ☐

Item	not at all	not much	quite	very

96. Suffering the discomforts of cold nights in an observatory in order to study the movement of a star or the path of a comet. ☐ ☐ ☐ ☐

97. Knowing why certain areas are famous for good wines. ☐ ☐ ☐ ☐

98. Examining the mechanics of a camera and understanding the various technical features which distinguish one camera from another. ☐ ☐ ☐ ☐

99. Being able to explain the way some people behave when they are confronted by unknown natural phenomena. ☐ ☐ ☐ ☐

100. Working in the pharmaceutical industry or in a hospital laboratory. ☐ ☐ ☐ ☐

101. Knowing why at different stages of life, there are different ways of thinking. ☐ ☐ ☐ ☐

102. Knowing when you look at a field of wheat, the natural process by which an ear of grain grows from the seed. ☐ ☐ ☐ ☐

103. Designing or improving laboratory machinery for chemical reactions and processes. ☐ ☐ ☐ ☐

104. Studying the area of physics that deals with communicating basins, syphons, underground streams, and artesian wells among other things. ☐ ☐ ☐ ☐

105. Conducting research studies about computers, writing programs and finding new applications for computers. ☐ ☐ ☐ ☐

106. Being able to use a camera artistically. ☐ ☐ ☐ ☐

107. Being able to date an archeological find. ☐ ☐ ☐ ☐

108. Discovering which chemical elements make up a substance, or identifying a microorganism. ☐ ☐ ☐ ☐

109. Knowing why people behave in one way when they are alone and in another when they are part of a group. ☐ ☐ ☐ ☐

110. Studying rare old books or manuscripts. ☐ ☐ ☐ ☐

111. Training a sports team. ☐ ☐ ☐ ☐

112. Studying space exploits from a technical point of view. ☐ ☐ ☐ ☐

113. Finding scientific ways to improve the techniques of breeding. ☐ ☐ ☐ ☐

114. Visiting a chemical laboratory. ☐ ☐ ☐ ☐

115. Trying to find ways to improve unhealthy work environments. ☐ ☐ ☐ ☐

116. Being directly involved in the problems of a large railroad station. ☐ ☐ ☐ ☐

117. Learning more about the various forms of life that exist in the woods when you are walking through them. ☐ ☐ ☐ ☐

118. Taking apart an old radio, examining its parts and making it functional. ☐ ☐ ☐ ☐

119. Learning about the world's countless monetary systems. ☐ ☐ ☐ ☐

120. Looking for the expression of man's sentiment in a work of art. ☐ ☐ ☐ ☐

121. Learning as much as possible about the exploits of the great navigators. ☐ ☐ ☐ ☐

122. Asking technical questions when you look at a dam, and trying to discern on your own, on what physical laws its retaining quality and strength are based. ☐ ☐ ☐ ☐

123. Being able to identify the exact element when you smell gas. ☐ ☐ ☐ ☐

124. Being able to give a scientific answer when asked why there is no danger of the moon falling to earth. ☐ ☐ ☐ ☐

Item	not at all	not much	quite	very

125. Collecting mushrooms in order to classify them according to their species. ☐ ☐ ☐ ☐

126. Doing research on nuclear energy to discover possible new applications. ☐ ☐ ☐ ☐

127. Using electronic equipment in chemistry. ☐ ☐ ☐ ☐

128. Working in a legal office of a private association, a county or municipal council, a bank, corporation, etc. ☐ ☐ ☐ ☐

129. Helping locate underground raw materials on which the economy and the population's survival often depend. ☐ ☐ ☐ ☐

130. Working in a consulate as an interpreter. ☐ ☐ ☐ ☐

131. Being able to explain why there were a certain number of road accidents three years ago, during the August holidays, practically the same number last year and nearly the same this year. ☐ ☐ ☐ ☐

132. Calculating the insurance premiums on the precise values of certain goods. ☐ ☐ ☐ ☐

133. Keeping abreast with the latest discoveries in the world of chemistry. ☐ ☐ ☐ ☐

134. Working in a bank and dealing with other banks. ☐ ☐ ☐ ☐

135. Recognizing the different types of ears of grain. ☐ ☐ ☐ ☐

136. Being part of a team engaged in a statistical survey of the insurance field, the economy, the population, and industrial production. ☐ ☐ ☐ ☐

137. Looking at and admiring a building of great architectural value. ☐ ☐ ☐ ☐

138. Being a director in the civil service. ☐ ☐ ☐ ☐

139. Working with developing economies which are trying to establish themselves and wish to collaborate with other existing economies. ☐ ☐ ☐ ☐

140. Developing a relationship between aeronautical/mechanical engineering and design, in order to study how to create an aerodynamic car body. ☐ ☐ ☐ ☐

141. Sailing at night, guided only by the stars. ☐ ☐ ☐ ☐

142. Understanding why apparently similar people act differently in similar situations. ☐ ☐ ☐ ☐

143. Designing modern buildings so they will blend harmoniously with older buildings. ☐ ☐ ☐ ☐

144. Understanding the historical evolution of the legislative institutions and laws of a nation. ☐ ☐ ☐ ☐

145. Dealing with international economic problems. ☐ ☐ ☐ ☐

146. Being directly involved in the problem of meat supply. ☐ ☐ ☐ ☐

147. Acting as a judge of someone accused of a crime. ☐ ☐ ☐ ☐

148. Being able to form abstract judgements of beauty so you can define various objects as "beautiful" within their own context. ☐ ☐ ☐ ☐

149. Being able to construct abstract images on which abstract reasoning can be based. ☐ ☐ ☐ ☐

150. Studying the differences in the behaviour of people, in the family, at school, at work, and in society. ☐ ☐ ☐ ☐

151. Following the European and world monetary market. ☐ ☐ ☐ ☐

152. Contributing as a professional to the smooth running of an organization, and making certain that legal regulations are properly adhered to. ☐ ☐ ☐ ☐

Item	not at all	not much	quite	very

153. Finding the meaning of certain words by going back to the languages of origin. ☐ ☐ ☐ ☐

154. Finding the points of contact between geology, chemistry and engineering in order to exploit mineral deposits rationally. ☐ ☐ ☐ ☐

155. Being able to understand an artist's personality from his work. ☐ ☐ ☐ ☐

156. Establishing the period in which a city was founded. ☐ ☐ ☐ ☐

157. Admiring flowers, grass and plants. ☐ ☐ ☐ ☐

158. Studying floods and learning how to predict and prevent them. ☐ ☐ ☐ ☐

159. Using sophisticated chemical analysis equipment. ☐ ☐ ☐ ☐

160. Knowing the processes that take place in the refineries, and chemical or pharmaceutical establishments, learning about the processing of certain raw materials. ☐ ☐ ☐ ☐

161. Learning about the infinite range of small animals which live in the underbrush. ☐ ☐ ☐ ☐

162. Dedicating yourself to sport and giving free rein to your physical energy. ☐ ☐ ☐ ☐

163. Being able to explain the essence of the work of modern authors. ☐ ☐ ☐ ☐

164. Determining, on the basis of statistical calculation, whether a product or a publicity campaign will be successful. ☐ ☐ ☐ ☐

165. Understanding the principal origins of terrestrial phenomena. ☐ ☐ ☐ ☐

166. Working professionally in the area of corrective gymnastics. ☐ ☐ ☐ ☐

167. Being able to predict the probable effects of a medicine through a knowledge of its constituent elements. ☐ ☐ ☐ ☐

168. Constructing or maintaining refineries, pharmaceutical industries, purification systems and similar plants. ☐ ☐ ☐ ☐

169. Gaining a full understanding of the operation of a power station, supply station, or a television relay station. ☐ ☐ ☐ ☐

170. Working solely with numbers, drawings and calculations. ☐ ☐ ☐ ☐

171. Visiting botanical gardens with a measure of interest. ☐ ☐ ☐ ☐

172. Studying Greek or Latin in an effort to understand and gain a better command of the languages that derive from them. ☐ ☐ ☐ ☐

173. Visiting a printer to learn how the essential parts of the machinery operate. ☐ ☐ ☐ ☐

174. Analyzing human emotions and studying the motivations that determine modes of behaviour. ☐ ☐ ☐ ☐

175. Studying the history of music or the theater. ☐ ☐ ☐ ☐

176. Being able to solve a variety of problems in the many aspects of engineering. ☐ ☐ ☐ ☐

177. Trying to change what is wrong in the political and legislative systems. ☐ ☐ ☐ ☐

178. Being responsible for certain decisions on traffic problems. ☐ ☐ ☐ ☐

179. Being able to analyze the words you hear spoken in a particular dialect, and then being able to compare those words with words in different dialects or languages. ☐ ☐ ☐ ☐

Item

Item

180. Being involved in geological surveys with a view to preventing landslides, floods and other such natural disasters. ☐ ☐ ☐ ☐

181. Being able to treat babies, old people and the mentally ill with the same care you would bring to adults. ☐ ☐ ☐ ☐

182. Following the stock market in the daily papers. ☐ ☐ ☐ ☐

183. Using modern equipment to diagnose and cure illnesses. ☐ ☐ ☐ ☐

184. Living in contact with nature. ☐ ☐ ☐ ☐

185. Handling the foreign relations of a large company. ☐ ☐ ☐ ☐

186. Making a contribution to society from a position that is demanding but socially useful. ☐ ☐ ☐ ☐

187. Knowing exactly what to do when confronted with a problem in electrical equipment. ☐ ☐ ☐ ☐

188. Learning about different peoples and their environments; understanding the elements that characterize and differentiate the various civilizations. ☐ ☐ ☐ ☐

189. Being able to identify the exact provenance of a piece of marble. ☐ ☐ ☐ ☐

190. Visiting an astrophysics laboratory. ☐ ☐ ☐ ☐

191. Studying the subsoil with a view to using the resources. ☐ ☐ ☐ ☐

192. Working with art history; examining the emotions that have inspired art throughout time and its contribution to man's history. ☐ ☐ ☐ ☐

193. Knowing how a flower grows, why it has a particular colour and smell. ☐ ☐ ☐ ☐

194. Knowing what a man-made satellite can do. ☐ ☐ ☐ ☐

195. Relieving the suffering of a wounded animal. ☐ ☐ ☐ ☐

196. Working on statistical programs designed to produce appropriate decisions regarding the future. ☐ ☐ ☐ ☐

197. Working with the complex economies of highly developed countries. ☐ ☐ ☐ ☐

198. Being able to keep a critically ill person alive. ☐ ☐ ☐ ☐

199. Cultivating a plant you particularly like. ☐ ☐ ☐ ☐

200. Working out long-term plans for the economy. ☐ ☐ ☐ ☐

201. Collecting and cataloging fossils. ☐ ☐ ☐ ☐

202. Studying the words and phrases of a foreign language as they are used in everyday speech and in literature. ☐ ☐ ☐ ☐

203. Understanding the mechanical loading and unloading systems used in airports, as well as their passenger control systems. ☐ ☐ ☐ ☐

204. Comparing the budget and balances of a company or association. ☐ ☐ ☐ ☐

205. Dealing with school medical systems and general systems designed for preventive medicine. ☐ ☐ ☐ ☐

206. Working in the classical theater. ☐ ☐ ☐ ☐

207. Being able to appreciate the scenery and sets in a play in addition to its story. ☐ ☐ ☐ ☐

208. Frequenting libraries specializing in old manuscripts. ☐ ☐ ☐ ☐

Item	not at all	not much	quite	very

209. Learning about the principal parts of a boat and how to use the navigation equipment. ☐ ☐ ☐ ☐

210. Building a model plane which can actually fly. ☐ ☐ ☐ ☐

211. Working with electronics in order to solve problems of mechanization. ☐ ☐ ☐ ☐

212. Seeing a play of great literary value. ☐ ☐ ☐ ☐

213. Trying to restore a person's health by operating. ☐ ☐ ☐ ☐

214. Watching a baby playing alone when he is unaware he is being observed and that his behaviour is being studied. ☐ ☐ ☐ ☐

215. Delving into the mysteries of the universe and the laws governing it. ☐ ☐ ☐ ☐

216. Being involved in the planning and organization of a refinery, foundry or dye works. ☐ ☐ ☐ ☐

217. Working with systems for the prevention of floods, fire or pollution. ☐ ☐ ☐ ☐

218. Living in a forest year-round. ☐ ☐ ☐ ☐

219. Making a useful contribution to the formation of just laws. ☐ ☐ ☐ ☐

220. Dealing with the adjustment of the handicapped to normal schools. ☐ ☐ ☐ ☐

221. Learning more about minerals, rocks and crystals. ☐ ☐ ☐ ☐

222. Translating an idea into an image that can be appreciated aesthetically. ☐ ☐ ☐ ☐

223. Acquiring the mathematical knowledge needed to use electronic equipment correctly. ☐ ☐ ☐ ☐

224. Handling the budgets and accounts of a small firm or association. ☐ ☐ ☐ ☐

Score Grouping Table

1. G1	**57.** E2	**113.** A1	**169.** D4
2. D2	**58.** E4	**114.** G2	**170.** B3
3. E1	**59.** E1	**115.** F	**171.** A2
4. B3	**60.** A1	**116.** D2	**172.** E1
5. A2	**61.** B1	**117.** A2	**173.** D2
6. B1	**62.** C	**118.** D4	**174.** E4
7. B2	**63.** A2	**119.** B1	**175.** E1
8. D2	**64.** G2	**120.** E1	**176.** D2
9. D1	**65.** G1	**121.** E2	**177.** B2
10. D3	**66.** D2	**122.** D1	**178.** D1
11. G1	**67.** D4	**123.** G2	**179.** E1
12. A2	**68.** G2	**124.** G1	**180.** G5
13. B3	**69.** D2	**125.** A2	**181.** F
14. D2	**70.** D2	**126.** D5	**182.** B1
15. A1	**71.** B3	**127.** G2	**183.** F
16. G5	**72.** B3	**128.** C	**184.** A2
17. D2	**73.** G2	**129.** D3	**185.** B1
18. C	**74.** E2	**130.** E3	**186.** C
19. B1	**75.** D2	**131.** B3	**187.** D4
20. E1	**76.** E2	**132.** B3	**188.** E2
21. D2	**77.** G4	**133.** G2	**189.** G5
22. E1	**78.** B2	**134.** B1	**190.** G1
23. G3	**79.** H	**135.** A2	**191.** D3
24. D1	**80.** D4	**136.** B3	**192.** E1
25. A1	**81.** E1	**137.** D1	**193.** A2
26. G1	**82.** D2	**138.** C	**194.** D2
27. B2	**83.** E1	**139.** B1	**195.** A1
28. G5	**84.** G5	**140.** D2	**196.** B3
29. D2	**85.** D1	**141.** G3	**197.** B1
30. E1	**86.** B1	**142.** E4	**198.** F
31. D4	**87.** A1	**143.** D1	**199.** A2
32. D2	**88.** B3	**144.** C	**200.** B1
33. D5	**89.** D2	**145.** B1	**201.** G5
34. F	**90.** B2	**146.** A1	**202.** E3
35. D1	**91.** D1	**147.** C	**203.** D2
36. D1	**92.** E3	**148.** E1	**204.** B1
37. B2	**93.** D4	**149.** G4	**205.** F
38. D4	**94.** F	**150.** E4	**206.** E1
39. G2	**95.** E1	**151.** B1	**207.** D1
40. C	**96.** G1	**152.** C	**208.** E1
41. D1	**97.** A2	**153.** E3	**209.** G3
42. G1	**98.** D2	**154.** D3	**210.** D2
43. A1	**99.** E4	**155.** E1	**211.** D4
44. G5	**100.** G2	**156.** E1	**212.** E1
45. E3	**101.** E4	**157.** A2	**213.** F
46. B1	**102.** A2	**158.** E2	**214.** E4
47. E4	**103.** D3	**159.** G2	**215.** G1
48. D5	**104.** G1	**160.** D3	**216.** D3
49. G5	**105.** G4	**161.** G5	**217.** G5
50. G5	**106.** E1	**162.** H	**218.** A2
51. F	**107.** E1	**163.** E1	**219.** B2
52. A2	**108.** F	**164.** B3	**220.** E1
53. D1	**109.** E4	**165.** G5	**221.** D3
54. E1	**110.** E1	**166.** H	**222.** D1
55. E1	**111.** H	**167.** F	**223.** G4
56. A2	**112.** D2	**168.** D3	**224.** B1

Score Interpretation Tables

Group A: AGRICULTURE

A1

Veterinary medicine
Animal production sciences
Feed preparation science   24

A2

Agricultural science
Forestry
Tropical and subtropical
  agriculture   48

Group B: ECONOMICS

B1

Economics and social
  disciplines
Finance and business
Political economics
Banking and insurance   48
Economics and banking
Economics and social
  sciences
Economic-marine sciences

B2

Political science
Sociology   24

B3

Statistical and actuarial
  sciences
Statistical and economic
  sciences   33
Statistical and demographic
  sciences
Statistics

Group C: LAW

C

Law   27

Group D: ENGINEERING

D1

Architecture
Civil engineering (construction)
Civil engineering (soil
  conservation and rural
  planning)   42
Town planning
Civil engineering (water and
  transport)

D2

Aeronautical engineering
Aerospace engineering
Mechanical engineering
Marine and mechanical
  engineering   63

D3

Chemical engineering
Mining engineering
Industrial technology   27
  engineering

D4

Electronic engineering
Electrical engineering   27

D5

Nuclear engineering   9

Group E: ARTS

E1

Philosophy
Humanities
Literature
Conservation of the cultural
  heritage
Fine arts, music and drama
Philology and the history of
  Western Europe   70
Teaching
History
Elementary school supervision
The history and didactics of
  music

E2

Geography   18

E3

Interpreting and translating
Oriental languages and   15
  literature
Foreign languages and
  literature
Modern languages and
  literature

E4

Psychology   27

Group F: MEDICINE

F

Medicine and surgery   33

Group G: SCIENCE

G1

Astronomy
Physics   30

G2

Chemistry
Chemistry and pharmaceutical
  technology   30
Pharmacology

G3

Naval disciplines   9

G4

Mathematics
Computer sciences   12

G5

Biology
Geology
Natural science   36

Group H: SPORT

H

Physical education   12

Summary Table

Calculate your percentages by multiplying the total number of points (the number of Xs) by 100 and divide the product by the number given under each set of boxes.

Group	Percentage	Group	Percentage
A1	_____%	E1	_____%
A2	_____%	E2	_____%
B1	_____%	E3	_____%
B2	_____%	E4	_____%
B3	_____%	F	_____%
C	_____%	G1	_____%
D1	_____%	G2	_____%
D2	_____%	G3	_____%
D3	_____%	G4	_____%
D4	_____%	G5	_____%
D5	_____%	H	_____%

used by an eighteen-year-old who is just entering and wants to register for an academic course, by a graduate student, or by those who simply want to find out where their talents lie.

Let's end this chapter on a creative note, for creativity is important to one's success, be it in business, in a career or emotionally. Figures 48 and 49 are designed as outlets for your creativity. Compare your results with those of your friends and family. Finally, we return to our indefatigable koala who has now progressed from his pulleys to a device designed to free a monkey, a parrot and a rabbit. Will he do it?

Fig. 48   **Find the Comparison**

Instructions
Complete the following comparisons with as many suitable qualifying adjectives as possible. For example, the incomplete comparison, "as ... as a wheel," could be completed with "round," "fast," etc.

You have thirteen minutes to complete the comparisons.

1. **As ..... as a bird**

2. **As ..... as a gold coin.**

3. **As ..... as a rogue.**

4. **As ..... as a wire.**

5. **As ..... as a punishment.**

6. **As ..... as success.**

Fig. 50   **The Mechanical Koala**

The koala has invented a contraption to free his three friends. He needs to use it because the cage doors are very heavy, but he has made a mistake and only two of the doors will open. Which two?

(Answer in Figure 45)

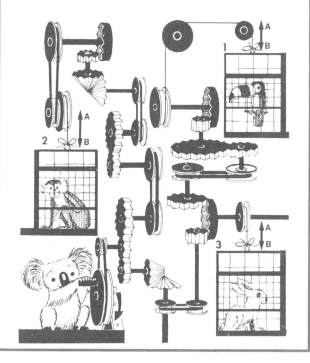

Fig. 49   **Life Stories**

Instructions
A given situation can often be
interpreted in a number of ways.
List all the explanations you can
think of for the following.

1. A young woman is sitting
in the corner of a restaurant. She is drinking coffee and every now and
then wipes away a tear.

2. Mr. R. buys two bottles of
whisky because he wants
to get drunk.

3. Mr. V., who has always
been silent and serious,
appears to be a changed
man now. He seems to
have shed a great burden
and he often smiles to
himself.

4. Mr. L. is on the second
day of his vacation. The
hotel receptionist tells
him, "Your company
called and said it is ur-
gent that you call them
back this afternoon."

You have twenty minutes for the
four situations.

Theories of personality

"Medley: heterogenous mixture" (Concise Oxford Dictionary 1978).
This term is often used to express the complex interaction of temperament, character, intelligence, creativity, social adjustment, conflicts, motivation, interests, feelings, aspirations, attitudes and opinions, all of which play a part in human life.

Beyond the primary abilities

To be sure, Lady Macbeth was an intelligent woman, but in Shakespeare's play, this does not grant absolution, nor is she any more likeable because of it. Indeed, it is her very capacity to reason and scheme that renders her so disturbing and sinister a figure. Through the ages writers have attempted to portray their characters in their entirety, and intelligence, as we all know, is but one characteristic of the human condition. It is true that the definition of "intelligence" as it is used in everyday language, is far broader than the one we adopted, which is an operational definition used as a yardstick to analyze intellectual ability scientifically. When a researcher takes test results as a measure of intellectual level, and therefore as a clear demonstration of intelligence, he does not endow the latter with its multifaceted meanings as this would render the results too intricate to check against valid empirical controls.

It is precisely through the use of operational definitions, i.e., ones that allow the possibility of establishing controls by restricting the subject matter and the methods employed, that a large number of scientific advances are made in the field of psychology.

We can, however, extend the scope of investigation into intelligence and still keep within the bounds of science. The psychologist J. P. Guilford, also an expert on factorial analysis, added to the work of Thurstone and developed a theory postulating the existence of a substantial number of factors; as yet not all have been shown to have an empirical base, but many experiments are currently under way to this end. According to Guilford, the value of 120, which he uses to express the number of intellectual dimensions, could be easily enlarged, but we will limit ourselves to the cube in Figure 51 which he created on the basis of distinguishing three aspects of every intellectual activity: operation, product and content.

If we consider five types of operation (evaluation, convergent production, divergent production, memory, and cognition), six categories of product (unit, class, relation, systems, transformations, and implications) and four types of content (figurative, symbolic, semantic, and behavioural) the cube contains 120—$5 \times 6 \times 4$—specific intellectual factors.

A fundamental contribution of Guilford's theory of the three dimensions common to all intellectual activity, is that it increases the areas of interest used by Thurstone as the basis for his research.

According to Hilgard, Guilford extended the concept of intelligence beyond that considered in normal intelligence tests. The traditional test determined the accuracy of a child's answer in relation to "truth" and "reality." This is known as "convergent production": the information leads to a single correct answer. One of Guilford's fundamental concepts, on the other hand, is "divergent production," which is characterized by greater creativity. This means various answers are possible instead of a single correct answer. Tests of divergent thinking include questions like: What uses can you think of for a brick? The child who gives the most varied answers—Heat it to warm a bed; As a weapon; To hold the shelves of a bookcase.—will gain the highest score on divergent thinking. This way of thinking has been neglected in intelligence tests and Guilford rightly believes that it is actually an important part of overall intellectual activity.

Figure 52 gives examples of items (proposed by Hilgard, et al) used to evaluate divergent thinking; if the instructions seem rather sketchy, they too are an exercise in creativity.

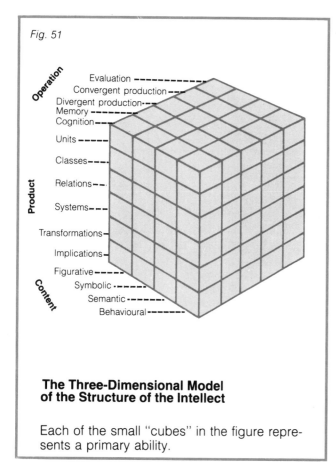

The Three-Dimensional Model of the Structure of the Intellect

Each of the small "cubes" in the figure represents a primary ability.

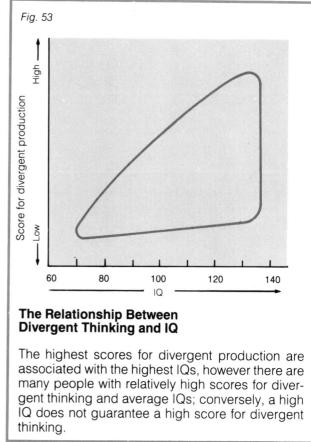

The Relationship Between Divergent Thinking and IQ

The highest scores for divergent production are associated with the highest IQs, however there are many people with relatively high scores for divergent thinking and average IQs; conversely, a high IQ does not guarantee a high score for divergent thinking.

An interesting point is that there is a clear relationship between the results on a standard intelligence test and those on a test of divergent thinking. This is plainly set out in Figure 53.

Intelligence and personality

A further distinction of intellectual activity into a *fluid* and a *crystallized* aspect was made by J. M. Cattell, the noted researcher on intelligence: The first category appears to be little influenced by what has been learned and thus is peculiar (we could say innate) to a particular person; the second category embraces the education received, the schools attended and the environment in which one lives.

Once again we choose to steer clear of the fruitless argument over heredity and environment: What interests us particularly about Cattell's theory is his attempt to show how the intellect "works," rather than to evaluate specific abilities, for surely it remains a persistent but often frustrated ambition of man to understand how

the mind functions, and how emotions, feelings and abilities combine and interact.

Theories of personality

Which is the more intense and commonly felt, the desire to understand our fellow man's behaviour or to predict and control him? We do not pretend to know the answer. Philosophers and moralists are probably more sensitive to the first whereas politicians, businessmen and those who associate knowledge with practical results are more inclined to the latter. Teachers, we believe, fall somewhere in between.

Psychology provides everyone with a "theory" and a set of operational techniques, though frequently the results are not very satisfactory when dealing with the personality. You can select from many different, yet closely interwoven, elements: a vast range of genetic and interacting factors including temperament, character, intelligence, creativity and social adaptability, as well as conflict and aggression; motivational factors

Fig. 52   **Examples of Items Used in Tests of Creativity**

Ingenuity
A. During a storm, wind destroyed the transmission tower of a TV station. The station was located in a small town in a flat plain with no other tall buildings. Its 300-foot tower enabled it to serve a large farming community and the management wanted to restore service while a new tower was being built. The problem was temporarily solved by using a . . .

B. As part of a manufacturing process, the inside lip of a deep cup-shaped casting is threaded by machine. It was found that the metal chips produced by the threading operation were difficult to remove from the bottom of the casting without scratching the sides. An engineer solved this problem by . . .

Unusual Uses
Name as many uses as you can think of for:
A. a toothpick   B. a brick   C. a paper clip.

Consequences
Imagine everything that could possibly happen if all national and local laws were suddenly abolished.

Fable Endings
Write three endings for the following fable, one moralistic, one humorous, one sad:

The Mischievous Dog

A rascally dog used to run quietly to the heels of every passerby and bite them without warning, so his master was obliged to tie a bell on the cur's collar to make certain he was noticed wherever he went. The dog thought this was very fine indeed, and he went about tinkling his bell in pride all over town. But an old hound said . . . .

Product Improvement
The subject is presented with a series of objects, such as children's toys or instruments, used in his or her particular occupation and asked to suggest ways to improve them.

Pattern Meanings
The subject is shown a series of patterns of geometric forms (like the samples shown below) and asked to imagine all the things they could represent.

Remote Associations
Find a fourth word that is asociated with each group of three words:
a) rat—blue—cottage   b) out—dog—cat   c) wheel—electric—high   d) surprise—line—birthday.

Word Association
Write as many meanings as you can for each of the following words:
a) duck   b) sack   c) pitch   d) fair.

rooted in a kind of personal bedrock, and others, more dynamic and influenced by education, experience and environment; attitudes and opinions, that is the propensity to take a stand for or against certain things, to form judgements and to create personal value systems, all of which are based on emotional evaluations, on knowledge and intention.

It is impossible to dissect the personality without using operational definitions. We have already discussed such definitions when dealing with the subject of intelligence, nevertheless it might be useful to cite an example of an operational definition of aggression: An experiment was conducted designed to observe the consequences of a gradual restriction of the space available to a group of rats, leading, in turn, to an increase in aggression. The latter was measured by recording the number of times each rat bit the others. Just as tests of intellectual level do not yield anything close to a full picture of an individual's potential, so this experiment measured aggression only in a limited sense.

When a researcher attempts to isolate a personality trait, the results can certainly be of value for the specific and immediate purpose, but as a contribution to our overall understanding, they usually prove wanting. In addition, no human action can be defined in terms of simply one trait, such as aggression, without considering interrelated factors of reason, education, rivalry, jealousy, etc.. But how can these factors be taken into account?

The tendency is to relate the individual traits to their "natural" environment which is, of course, the personality itself—not the psychologist's laboratory. This helps to explain the global terms in which the various theories tend to be couched, be they psychoanalytic, typological theorizations of traits, or the specificity of behaviour. The emphasis on the importance of the subconscious in everyday life is due, above all, to Sigmund Freud (1856–1939), the father of psychoanalysis, and to other scholars who were mainly interested in its clinical implications, including C. G. Jung (1875–1961) and Alfred Adler (1870–1937). According to classical Freudian theory, the human personality is divided into three functional parts: the *ego,* the *id,* and the *superego.* They determine our every action, thought, dream, desire or regret and our mental health depends on the extent to which a balance is maintained between them.

The id is the source of man's basic instinctual impulses, which include sexual drives, and it seeks immediate gratification of those impulses. The purpose of the ego—which is the largely conscious part of the personality and is derived from the id—is to contain these forces and channel them into the attainment of more mature and lasting goals such as a harmonious coexistence between one's affective and family life and the libidinal demands for pleasure and instant gratification.

The superego, in turn, derives from the interaction between the ego and the rules governing the family and society; it also has the function of regulating the other two elements, and, in its appraisal of good and evil, acts as a censor, a kind of conscience.

Another major psychoanalytic theory distinguishes the stages of psychosexual development through which each individual's personality is formed: the oral, anal, phallic, latency and genital stages. It would be arduous to give an account of the infinite number of assumptions and implications that have been drawn from the basic tenets of psychoanalysis through the years; the history of psychoanalysis as a school of thought, and of the movement to which it gave rise, is fraught with doctrinal disputes (a notorious example being that between Freud and Jung) which in turn have led to the new schools of *dynamic* and *depth* psychology in addition to a variety of other clinical trends. It is difficult to know exactly who is right and who is wrong, but different psychotherapists, depending on the school of thought to which they belong, associate particular personality disorders with particular aspects of maladapative development; the form of therapy is then prescribed accordingly. The aim is to help the patient become aware of how he feels and behaves, both in the present and in the past, thus laying the foundation for change. It should be emphasized that psychoanalytical theory tries to give a global explanation for the feelings, aspirations and behaviour of human beings. The specialist uses the theoretical framework of psychoanalysis to interpret his patient's situation, and hence to recognize the disorder and treat it.

This interaction between the general and the specific analysis makes the psychoanalyst's role a difficult one to control on an empirical experimental basis of diagnosis and treatment. As a result, many in the scientific community consider psychoanalysis and its various branches to be outside the realm of science and to be more akin to an art, a philosophy, or a faith.

However, the theories of personality traits, among which Cattell's is especially important, are based on an attempt to be nothing less than scientific: Factorial analysis is used to isolate a certain number of pairs of opposing dimensions, such as the *force of the ego* and *emotivity, dynamism* and *depression, dominance* and *submission, integrity* and *dishonesty, cordiality* and *timidity,* etc. which can then be used to explain and predict behaviour.

Eysenck's two-dimensional personality model is similar: He sets the various possible types of personality along the two axes of introversion-extroversion and emotional stability-instability, producing an interesting analogy to the four basic temperaments in which the ancient Greeks believed (see Figure 54).

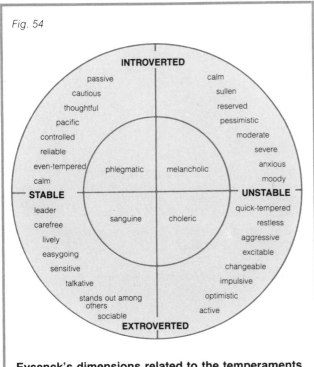

Fig. 54

Eysenck's dimensions related to the temperaments and personality traits

The inner ring reveals the four temperaments as defined by the ancient Greeks; the outer circle shows the arrangement of the different personality traits, worked out through factorial analysis, in relation to the two main axes postulated by Eysenck.

It is therefore conceivable to use factorial analysis, which is based on a consideration of the characteristics observed in individual behaviour, to confirm the ancient typologies based on a surfeit or lack of the four "humours"—blood (the sanguine type), lymph (the phlegmatic), black bile (the melancholic) and bile (the choleric).

With Eysenck's questionnaires, which are given below, we too can classify and evaluate our temperaments.

Extroversion-introversion

The first of the major typologies of temperament is extroversion–introversion. In turn this fundamental area can be broken down into at least seven component characteristics of "subfactors." These will be described, together with a method for scoring them and comparing yourself with other people, at the end of the questionnaire.

Now work through the 210 questions given below, putting an X in the "Yes" or "No" boxes. If, for any reason, you find it impossible to make a decision, put an X in the "?" box. It is best if you work quickly and don't dwell too much on the exact wording of the questions. If some of them seem repetitive, remember there are valid reasons for posing the same question in slightly different ways.

Yes ? No

1. Are you happiest when you become involved in a project calling for rapid action? ☐ ☐ ☐

2. Do you like going out a lot? ☐ ☐ ☐

3. Would you prefer a job involving change, travel and variety even though it is risky and insecure? ☐ ☐ ☐

4. Do you like planning things well ahead of time? ☐ ☐ ☐

5. Do you sit quietly when you are watching a race or a competitive sport? ☐ ☐ ☐

6. Do you like to have time to be alone with your thoughts? ☐ ☐ ☐

7. Are you inclined to be overconscientious? ☐ ☐ ☐

8. Do you become restless when working at something in which there is little action? ☐ ☐ ☐

9. Do you often need understanding friends to cheer you up? ☐ ☐ ☐

10. Do you enjoy taking risks? ☐ ☐ ☐

11. Do you usually make up your mind quickly? ☐ ☐ ☐

12. If you are watching a slapstick film or a farce, do you laugh louder than most of the people around you? ☐ ☐ ☐

13. Do you frequently take the time just to meditate about things in general? ☐ ☐ ☐

14. Are you normally on time for appointments? ☐☐☐

15. When climbing stairs, do you usually take them two at a time? ☐☐☐

16. Generally, do you prefer reading to meeting people? ☐☐☐

17. Do you lock up your house carefully at night? ☐☐☐

18. Do you often change your interests? ☐☐☐

19. Is your anger quick and short? ☐☐☐

20. Do you often reflect on the purpose of human existence? ☐☐☐

21. Do you live by the maxim that a job worth doing is worth doing well? ☐☐☐

22. When you are driving in a car, do you get very frustrated by slow-moving traffic? ☐☐☐

23. Are you fairly talkative when you are with a group of people? ☐☐☐

24. Do you think young children should have to learn to cross roads by themselves? ☐☐☐

25. Before making up your mind, do you carefully consider all the advantages and disadvantages? ☐☐☐

26. Does a sentimental film easily move you to tears? ☐☐☐

27. Do you often try to find the underlying motives for the actions of other people? ☐☐☐

28. Can you always be relied on? ☐☐☐

29. Are you inclined to be slow and deliberate in your actions? ☐☐☐

30. Can you usually let yourself go, and have a good time at a party? ☐☐☐

31. When the odds are against you, do you usually still think it worth taking a chance? ☐☐☐

32. Do you often buy things on impulse? ☐☐☐

33. Are you able to maintain outer calm in the face

of an emergency? ☐☐☐

34. Would you rather read a newspaper's sports page than its editorial page? ☐☐☐

35. Are you inclined to live each day as it comes? ☐☐☐

36. Do you usually finish your meals faster than anyone else even though there is no reason to hurry? ☐☐☐

37. Do you dislike being with a crowd that plays practical jokes on one another? ☐☐☐

38. When you are catching a train, do you often arrive at the last minute? ☐☐☐

39. Do you know what you will be doing for your next vacation? ☐☐☐

40. Do you get very upset when watching documentaries about living conditions in less fortunate countries? ☐☐☐

41. Do you seldom stop to analyze your own thoughts and feelings? ☐☐☐

42. Do you often leave things to the last minute? ☐☐☐

43. Do other people regard you as very lively? ☐☐☐

44. Do you enjoy talking to people so much that you never miss a chance of talking to a stranger? ☐☐☐

45. Would life that held no danger be too dull for you? ☐☐☐

46. Can you make decisions quickly? ☐☐☐

47. Would you say your temper is well under control? ☐☐☐

48. Are you keen about learning things even though they may have no relevance to your everyday life? ☐☐☐

49. Do you have a tendency to "let things slide" occasionally? ☐☐☐

50. Are you always "on the go" when you're not sleeping? ☐☐☐

51. If you were making a business inquiry would you rather do so by letter than by telephone? ☐☐☐

52. Do you save regularly? ☐☐☐

53. Do you often get into a jam because you do things without thinking? ☐☐☐

54. Are you so carried away by music that you often feel compelled to conduct, or to dance in time with it? ☐☐☐

55. Do you like to solve "brain teasers"? ☐☐☐

56. Do you have difficulty applying yourself to work that requires sustained concentration? ☐☐☐

57. Do you like organizing and initiating leisure-time activities? ☐☐☐

58. Do you enjoy spending long periods of time by yourself? ☐☐☐

59. Do you enjoy driving fast? ☐☐☐

60. Do you generally do and say things without stopping to think? ☐☐☐

61. Do you prefer early classical music to jazz? ☐☐☐

62. Do you frequently become so involved with a question or problem that you must keep thinking about it until you arrive at a satisfactory solution? ☐☐☐

63. Does it often take you a long time to get started on something? ☐☐☐

64. Are you generally very enthusiastic about starting a new project or endeavour? ☐☐☐

65. Are you relaxed and self-confident in the company of other people? ☐☐☐

66. Would you make quite sure you had another job before giving up your old one? ☐☐☐

67. Do you usually think carefully before doing anything? ☐☐☐

68. Do you like to play pranks on other people? ☐☐☐

69. After you have seen a play or movie, do you like going over it in your mind for a long time? ☐☐☐

70. Do you often forget little things you are supposed to do? ☐☐☐

71. When you are walking with other people, do they often have trouble keeping up with you? ☐☐☐

72. Are you more distant and reserved than most people? ☐☐☐

73. Do people who drive carefully annoy you? ☐☐☐

74. Would you rather plan things than do things? ☐☐☐

75. Do you subscribe to the philosophy of, "Eat, drink and be merry for tomorrow we die"? ☐☐☐

76. Are you frequently so lost in thought that you do not notice what is going on around you? ☐☐☐

77. Are you ordinarily a carefree person? ☐☐☐

78. Do other people find it hard to keep up with the pace you set either at work or at play? ☐☐☐

79. Do you like mixing with lots of other people? ☐☐☐

80. Are you rather cautious in new situations? ☐☐☐

81. Are you an impulsive person? ☐☐☐

82. Do you tell your friends what you think is wrong with them? ☐☐☐

83. Do you ever walk across the street against a red light? ☐☐☐

84. Would you enjoy writing a critical essay on a book? ☐☐☐

85. Are you inclined to rush from one activity to another without stopping to rest? ☐☐☐

86. Do you easily make new friends with people of your own sex? ☐☐☐

87. Would you do almost anything on a dare? ☐☐☐

88. Do you prefer activities that just happen to those planned in advance? ☐☐☐

89. If you were visiting Rio de Janeiro during carnival time, would you rather observe the festivities than participate in them? □□□

90. Do you react to new ideas by analyzing them to see how they mesh with your own point of view? □□□

91. Would you say that generally you have a serious and responsible attitude toward the world? □□□

92. Do you often find yourself hurrying to get to places even when there is plenty of time? □□□

93. Do you like to tell jokes and stories to groups of friends? □□□

94. When buying things, do you usually examine the guarantee? □□□

95. When you meet new people, do you quickly decide whether you like them or not? □□□

96. Are you usually among the last to stop clapping at the end of a concert or stage performance? □□□

97. Have you ever tried to write poetry? □□□

98. Are you considered easygoing? □□□

99. Do you frequently lack the energy and motivation to do things? □□□

100. Do you enjoy talking and playing with young children? □□□

101. Do you think people expend too much effort safeguarding their future with savings and insurance? □□□

102. Do you often do things on the spur of the moment? □□□

103. Do you find it easy to discuss intimate matters with members of your family? □□□

104. Would you enjoy working on a project that involved a great deal of library research? □□□

105. If you say you will do something, do you always keep your promise no matter how inconvenient it might turn out to be? □□□

106. Do you like to stay in bed late on weekends? □□□

107. Are you apprehensive about going into a room full of strange people? □□□

108. Do you have regular physical checkups? □□□

109. If it were practical and possible, would you like to live each day as it comes? □□□

110. Have you ever performed in amateur theatrics or with musical groups? □□□

111. Do you read a newspaper regularly? □□□

112. Do you sometimes have a tendency to be "slapdash" in your work? □□□

113. Do you prefer vacations that are quiet and restful without a good deal of rushing about? □□□

114. Have you ever seriously felt you might be happier living by yourself on a desert island? □□□

115. Do you always wear a safety belt when travelling in a car? □□□

116. Do you like doing things in which you have to act quickly? □□□

117. Would you refrain from expressing your attitudes and opinions if you thought that others present might be offended by them? □□□

118. Do you enjoy solving problems even when they have no practical application? □□□

119. Do you usually answer a personal letter immediately after receiving it? □□□

120. Do you generally move about at a leisurely pace? □□□

121. Do you sometimes feel uncomfortable when people get too close to you physically? □□□

122. Do you sometimes bet money on races, elections and the like? □□□

123. Do you often get involved in things that later you want to get out of? □□□

124. Do you choose your words carefully when discussing business matters? □□□

125. Are you so thoughtful and reflective that your friends sometimes call you a dreamer? ☐ ☐ ☐

126. Are you generally unconcerned about the future? ☐ ☐ ☐

127. When you wake up in the morning are you usually ready to "get cracking"? ☐ ☐ ☐

128. Is it important to you to be liked by a wide range of people? ☐ ☐ ☐

129. Would you agree that an element of risk adds spice to life? ☐ ☐ ☐

130. Are you an easygoing person, not generally bothered about having everything "just so"? ☐ ☐ ☐

131. When you are angry with someone do you wait until you have "cooled off" before talking to them about the incident? ☐ ☐ ☐

132. Are you overcome by a sense of wonder and excitement when visiting historical monuments? ☐ ☐ ☐

133. Can you honestly say that you honour your commitments more than most people? ☐ ☐ ☐

134. Are you usually full of pep and vigour? ☐ ☐ ☐

135. Do you spontaneously introduce yourself to strangers at social gatherings? ☐ ☐ ☐

136. Do you agree that one should "neither a borrower nor a lender be"? ☐ ☐ ☐

137. When you go on a trip do you like to plan routes and timetables carefully? ☐ ☐ ☐

138. Can you keep an exciting secret for a long time? ☐ ☐ ☐

139. Do you frequently discuss the causes and possible solutions of social and political problems with your friends? ☐ ☐ ☐

140. Do you set an alarm clock if you have to be up at a particular time in the morning? ☐ ☐ ☐

141. Do you often feel tired and listless? ☐ ☐ ☐

142. Would you rather spend an evening talking to one interesting member of your own sex than singing and dancing with a large crowd of friends? ☐ ☐ ☐

143. Would being in debt worry you? ☐ ☐ ☐

144. Do you usually speak before thinking things out? ☐ ☐ ☐

145. Do you get so excited that you gesticulate when you talk? ☐ ☐ ☐

146. Do you often spend an evening just reading a book? ☐ ☐ ☐

147. Do you always follow the rule "business before pleasure"? ☐ ☐ ☐

148. Do you like to have a lot of things to do all the time? ☐ ☐ ☐

149. Do you like to be right in the middle of things socially? ☐ ☐ ☐

150. Do you often find you cross a road leaving your more cautious companions on the other side? ☐ ☐ ☐

151. Do you think an evening out is more successful if it is arranged at the last minute? ☐ ☐ ☐

152. If somebody expresses an opinion with which you disagree, do you tell them so immediately? ☐ ☐ ☐

153. Would you rather see a comedy than a TV documentary? ☐ ☐ ☐

154. Do you often not bother to vote in an election? ☐ ☐ ☐

155. Do other people seem to get more done in a day than you do? ☐ ☐ ☐

156. Do you enjoy lone activities such as playing solitaire and solving crossword puzzles? ☐ ☐ ☐

157. Do you think the risk of lung cancer from smoking has been exaggerated? ☐ ☐ ☐

158. Do you get so "carried away" by new and exciting ideas that you never think of the potential problems? ☐ ☐ ☐

159. Would you find it impossible to make a speech "off the cuff"? ☐ ☐ ☐

160. Do you think it is pointless to analyze your own value system and morality? ☐☐☐

161. Did you occasionally play truant in your school days? ☐☐☐

162. On most days, are there times when you enjoy just sitting and doing nothing? ☐☐☐

163. Are you inclined to avoid people whenever possible? ☐☐☐

164. Would you always read the small print before signing a contract? ☐☐☐

165. Do you prefer to "sleep on it" before making decisions? ☐☐☐

166. Are you given to making outrageous threats even though you have no intention of carrying them out? ☐☐☐

167. Do you enjoy essays on serious, philosophical subjects? ☐☐☐

168. Do you sometimes drink alcohol till you reach a state of intoxication? ☐☐☐

169. Would you rather watch sports than play them? ☐☐☐

170. Would you be very unhappy if you were prevented from making numerous social contacts? ☐☐☐

171. When travelling in an airplane, bus or train, do you choose your seat with safety in mind? ☐☐☐

172. Do you prefer work that needs close attention most of the time? ☐☐☐

173. Do you wish you could "let yourself go" and have a good time more often? ☐☐☐

174. Do you think it is a waste of time to formulate plans for an ideal society or Utopia? ☐☐☐

175. Would you go out of your way to find a trash can rather than throw a wrapper on the street? ☐☐☐

176. Do you frequently take a nap in the middle of the day? ☐☐☐

177. Do you usually prefer to take your recreation with companions rather than alone? ☐☐☐

178. Are you careful to swim within the area marked by safety flags at the beach? ☐☐☐

179. Do you need to use a lot of self-control to keep out of trouble? ☐☐☐

180. Are you hesitant about asking strangers for street directions? ☐☐☐

181. Are you bored by discussions of what life might be like in the future? ☐☐☐

182. Do you have regular dental checkups? ☐☐☐

183. Do you get agitated if you have to wait for someone? ☐☐☐

184. Do you like to have a number of social engagements? ☐☐☐

185. Do you avoid "thrill" rides such as roller coasters and ferris wheels when you go to an amusement park? ☐☐☐

186. When you want to buy something expensive, can you save patiently for a period of time? ☐☐☐

187. Are you likely to swear loudly if you trip over something or hit your finger with a hammer? ☐☐☐

188. Do you like work that involves action rather than profound thought and study? ☐☐☐

189. Have you occasionally "played sick" to avoid an unpleasant responsibility? ☐☐☐

190. If you think you might have to wait a few minutes for an elevator, are you inclined to take the stairs? ☐☐☐

191. Do you enjoy entertaining? ☐☐☐

192. If you travel abroad, are you always careful to declare everything at customs? ☐☐☐

193. Would you agree that planning things ahead takes the fun out of life? ☐☐☐

194. Are you prone to exaggeration and elaboration when relating a story to your friends? ☐☐☐

195. Are you bored by museums that feature archaeology and classical history? ☐☐☐

196. Do you think it is pointless to provide for your old age? ☐ ☐ ☐

197. Normally, do you tend to do things at a rapid rate? ☐ ☐ ☐

198. Are you inclined to limit your acquaintances to a select few? ☐ ☐ ☐

199. Do you arrive at appointments with plenty of time to spare? ☐ ☐ ☐

200. Do you hate standing in a long line for anything? ☐ ☐ ☐

201. Do you like colourful modern paintings more than discreet classical works? ☐ ☐ ☐

202. Do you think it is futile to wonder about what there is in outer space? ☐ ☐ ☐

203. If you found something valuable in the street would you pass it on to the police? ☐ ☐ ☐

204. Do you often feel full of excess energy? ☐ ☐ ☐

205. Do you often feel ill at ease with other people? ☐ ☐ ☐

206. Do you think insurance plans are a good idea? ☐ ☐ ☐

207. Do you get bored more easily than most people doing the same old things? ☐ ☐ ☐

208. Are you forever buying silly little gifts for people even when no occasion calls for it? ☐ ☐ ☐

209. Do you spend much time reflecting on the past and the shape your life is taking? ☐ ☐ ☐

210. Would you describe yourself as "happy-go-lucky"? ☐ ☐ ☐

The first factor from the above questionnaire that can be scored is called "activity." People scoring high on this scale are generally active and energetic. They enjoy all forms of physical activity including hard work and exercise. They tend to awaken early and easily in the morning, move rapidly from one activity to another, and pursue a wide variety of interests. People with low scores on this scale are inclined to tire easily and to be physically inactive and lethargic. They move at a leisurely pace and prefer quiet, restful holidays. A high degree of activity is characteristic of the extrovert and low activity of the introvert.

The key for scoring yourself on this scale is given below. The numbers refer to the question numbers and the sign indicates whether a "Yes" or "No" answer scores a point. For example, consider Question 1: "Are you happiest when you become involved in a project calling for rapid action?" Because there is a plus sign after the number 1 in the key, you give yourself one point if you answered "Yes." If you said "No" you score nothing; if you responded with a "?" you score one-half. Questions 2–7 are not scored on this scale as they do not appear in the key. The next question scored on the activity scale is number 8. Again it is a "Yes" answer that scores 1 because the sign is positive; "No" scores zero and "?" scores one-half. The first question in the key to be scored in reverse is number 29: "Are you inclined to be slow and deliberate in your actions?" This time, because the sign is a minus, it is the "No" that scores 1 and the "Yes" that scores zero. As before, the "?" scores one-half.

To summarize then: Only those question numbers appearing in the key are scored. If there is a plus sign, "Yes" scores 1; if there is a minus sign, "No" scores 1. In either case a "?" is scored one-half. Each of the seven keys to follow includes thirty items, so the possible range of scores is 0–30. To see if your scores are low, average or high in relation to other peoples, compare them with the profile sheet at the end of the tables. This will also indicate whether you tend to be extroverted or introverted.

1. Activity				
1 +	43 +	85 +	127 +	169 −
8 +	50 +	92 +	134 +	176 −
15 +	57 +	99 −	141 −	183 +
22 +	64 +	106 −	148 +	190 +
29 −	71 +	113 −	155 −	197 +
36 +	78 +	120 −	162 −	204 +

The second primary factor which can be scored is "sociability." This has a fairly straightforward interpretation. High scorers seek the company of other people; they like social functions such as parties and dances; they meet people easily and are generally happy and comfortable in social situations. By contrast, low scorers prefer to have only a few special friends. They enjoy solitary activities such as reading, have difficulty finding things to talk about to other people and are inclined to withdraw from social contact.

High sociability is an aspect of extroversion, low sociability of introversion. The key to this scale is given below and is used in exactly the same fashion as the previous key.

2. Sociability				
2 +	44 +	86 +	128 +	170 +
9 +	51 −	93 +	135 +	177 +
16 −	58 −	100 +	142 −	184 +
23 +	65 +	107 −	149 +	191 +
30 +	72 −	114 +	156 −	198 −
37 −	79 +	121 −	163 −	205 −

The third scale is "risk-taking" and this is again fairly self-explanatory. High scorers like to live dangerously and seem little concerned with the possibility of adverse consequences. Typical examples are gamblers who believe "an element of risk adds spice fo life." Low scores indicate a preference for the familiar, for safety and security, even if this means sacrificing a measure of excitement. The "risk-taking" factor is quite closely related to "impulsiveness," the next factor in the extroversion group. It is also akin to "sensation-seeking" which, it may surprise you to learn, falls into the "tough-mindedness" group of factors. This illustrates one of the complexities of personality classification—a primary factor can fall diagonally between two major factors, just as the same item can contribute to two or more primary factors. The fact is that risk-taking and sensation-seeking can be used as measures of both extroversion and tough-mindedness; they fall almost midway between the two independent major factors. However, because risk-taking is somewhat closer to the extroversion axis and sensation-seeking to the tough-mindedness axis, they have been classified accordingly.

3. Risk-taking				
3 +	45 +	87 +	129 +	171 −
10 +	52 −	94 −	136 −	178 −
17 −	59 +	101 −	143 −	185 −
24 +	66 −	108 −	150 +	192 −
31 +	73 +	115 −	157 +	199 −
38 +	80 −	122 +	164 −	206 −

The fourth scale gives a measure of impulsiveness. High scorers tend to act on the spur of the moment, make hurried, often premature decisions and are usually carefree, changeable and unpredictable. Low scorers deliberate carefully before making a decision. They are systematic, orderly, cautious, and plan their lives; they think before they speak and "look before they leap."

4. Impulsiveness				
4 −	46 +	88 +	130 +	172 −
11 +	53 +	95 +	137 −	179 +
18 +	60 +	102 +	144 +	186 −
25 −	67 −	109 +	151 +	193 +
32 +	74 −	116 +	158 +	200 +
39 −	81 −	123 +	165 −	207 +

The fifth factor contributing to extroversion is "expressiveness." This refers to a general tendency to display one's emotions openly, be they feelings of sorrow, anger, fear, love or hate. High scorers are inclined to be sentimental, sympathetic, volatile and demonstrative; low scorers are reserved, even-tempered, cool, detached and generally controlled. Expressiveness, when carried to extremes, relates to behaviour that is classically called "hysterical." It is not surprising then that, even though it is primarily a component of extroversion, it also leans slightly toward emotional instability.

5. Expressiveness				
5 −	47 −	89 −	131 −	173 −
12 +	54 +	96 +	138 −	180 −
19 +	61 −	103 +	145 +	187 +
26 +	68 +	110 +	152 +	194 +
33 −	75 +	117 −	159 −	201 +
40 +	82 +	124 −	166 +	208 +

The sixth component of extroversion is "reflectiveness." This scale is slightly complicated as it is the high scores that indicate introversion and the low scores that indicate extroversion. In fact, some theorists have called this factor "thinking introversion," a useful definition because it not only signifies its emphasis on the extroversion-introversion scale, but it also distinguishes the trait from social introversion and emotional introversion (the counterparts of which are sociability and expressiveness). High scorers on the reflectiveness scale are drawn to ideas, abstractions, philosophical discussion, speculation and "knowledge for the sake of knowledge." In short, they are generally thoughtful (in the literal sense of the word) and introspective. Low scorers, on the other hand, have a practical bent. They are interested in doing things rather than thinking about them and are often impatient with "ivory tower" theorizing.

6. Reflectiveness				
6 +	48 +	90 +	132 +	174 −
13 +	55 +	97 +	139 +	181 −
20 +	62 +	104 +	146 +	188 −
27 +	69 +	111 +	153 −	195 −
34 −	76 +	118 +	160 −	202 −
41 −	83 +	125 +	167 +	209 −

The last scale in this first group is called "responsibility" and this too is closer to the introverted end of the spectrum than to the extroverted. Those who score high on this factor are apt to be conscientious, reliable, trustworthy and serious-minded, and possibly a bit compulsive (see obsessionality in the next group of traits). By contrast, low scorers tend to be casual, careless of protocol, late meeting commitments, unpredictable and perhaps socially irresponsible. All this is within the normal range, however, and no "deviance" is implied, even for rock-bottom scores.

7. Responsibility				
7 +	49 −	91 +	133 +	175 +
14 +	56 −	98 −	140 +	182 +
21 +	63 −	105 +	147 +	189 −
28 +	70 −	112 −	154 −	196 −
35 −	77 −	119 +	161 −	203 +
42 −	84 −	126 −	168 −	210 −

By now you should have seven scores, each within the range of 0–30. To see how you compare with the majority, mark your scores on the profile sheet given below. For example, if you scored 18 on Activity, circle the number 18 in the appropriate column, and so on for each of the other traits. If you are to the left of the center line, you are above average on that trait; if you fall to the right, you are below average (except of course for the two reverse-scored traits). Think of the average, however, as covering a broad span.

Finally, if you connect your seven scores by straight lines between all adjacent pairs, and then look at the overall profile, you will see at a glance whether you tend to be extroverted or introverted. If all or most of your scores fall to the left of the center line, you are to a greater or lesser extent extroverted; if they consistently fall to the right of the center line, you can regard yourself as an introvert.

	Average		
	extroversion	introversion	
Activity	30 29 28 27 26 25 24 23 22 21 20 19 18 17	16 15 14 13 12 11 10 9 8 7 6 5 4 3 2 1	Inactivity
Sociability	30 29 28 27 26 25 24 23 22 21 20 19 18 17	16 15 14 13 12 11 10 9 8 7 6 5 4 3 2 1	Unsociability
Risk-taking	30 29 28 27 26 25 24 23 22 21 20 19 18 17 16	15 14 13 12 11 10 9 8 7 6 5 4 3 2 1 0	Carefulness
Impulsiveness	30 29 28 27 26 25 24 23 22 21 20 19 18	17 16 15 14 13 12 11 10 9 8 7 6 5 4 3 2	Control
Expressiveness	27 26 25 24 23 22 21 20 19 18 17 16 15 14 13 12	11 10 9 8 7 6 5 4 3 2	Inhibition
Practicality	2 3 4 5 6 7 8 9 10 11 12 13 14 15 16 17	18 19 20 21 22 23 24 25 26 27 28 29 30	Reflectiveness
Irresponsibility	0 1 2 3 4 5 6 7 8 9 10 11 12 13 14	15 16 17 18 19 20 21 22 23 24 25 26 27 28 29 30	Responsibility

Emotional instability—adjustment

This second group of major personality factors is concerned with the area of emotional instability versus adjustment. Its 210 questions should be answered following the same instructions given for the preceding scales; try to use the "Yes" or "No" if you can and resort to the "?" only when you find it really impossible to decide. Again, do not ponder over precise shades of meaning; your first reaction is generally the best one.

Yes ? No

1. Do you think you are able to do things as well as most other people? ☐ ☐ ☐

2. Do you seem to have more than your share of bad luck? ☐ ☐ ☐

3. Do you blush more often than most people? ☐ ☐ ☐

4. Do you sometimes have ideas repeatedly running through your head which you would like to stop but cannot? ☐ ☐ ☐

5. Is there a habit such as smoking that you would like to break but cannot? ☐ ☐ ☐

6. Do you usually feel well and strong? ☐ ☐ ☐

7. Are you often troubled by feelings of guilt? ☐ ☐ ☐

8. Do you feel you have little to be proud of? ☐ ☐ ☐

9. Do you often feel depressed when you wake up in the morning? ☐ ☐ ☐

10. Would you say you seldom lose sleep over your worries? ☐ ☐ ☐

11. Are you often acutely aware of a clock ticking? ☐ ☐ ☐

12. If you see a game that you would like to be good at, are you usually able to acquire the necessary skill to play it well? ☐ ☐ ☐

13. Do you often suffer from a poor appetite? ☐ ☐ ☐

14. Do you often catch yourself apologizing when you are not really at fault? ☐ ☐ ☐

15. Do you often think of yourself as a failure? ☐ ☐ ☐

16. In general, would you say you are satisfied with your life? ☐ ☐ ☐

17. Are you usually calm and not easily upset? ☐ ☐ ☐

18. If you are reading something that contains errors of spelling and punctuation, do you find it difficult to concentrate on what is being said? ☐ ☐ ☐

19. Do you take steps to control your figure by exercise or diet? ☐ ☐ ☐

20. Is your skin very sensitive and tender? ☐ ☐ ☐

21. Do you sometimes think you have disappointed your parents by the life you have led? ☐ ☐ ☐

22. Do you suffer from inferiority feelings? ☐ ☐ ☐

23. Do you find a good deal of happiness in life? ☐ ☐ ☐

24. Do you sometimes feel you have so many difficulties you cannot possibly overcome them? ☐ ☐ ☐

25. Are you sometimes compelled to wash your hands even though you know they are perfectly clean? ☐ ☐ ☐

26. Do you believe your personality was firmly shaped by what happened to you as a child, so there is little you can do to change it? ☐ ☐ ☐

27. Do you frequently feel faint? ☐ ☐ ☐

28. Do you believe you have committed unpardonable sins? ☐ ☐ ☐

29. In general are you pretty confident of yourself? ☐ ☐ ☐

30. Do you sometimes feel you don't care what happens to you? ☐ ☐ ☐

31. Is life often a strain for you? ☐ ☐ ☐

32. Are you sometimes bothered by an unimportant thought that runs through your mind for days? ☐ ☐ ☐

33. Do you make your own decisions regardless of what other people say? ☐ ☐ ☐

34. Do you have more headaches than most people? ☐ ☐ ☐

35. Do you often feel a strong need to confess something you have done? ☐☐☐

36. Do you often wish you were someone else? ☐☐☐

37. Do you generally feel in good spirits? ☐☐☐

38. As a child were you afraid of the dark? ☐☐☐

39. Do you indluge in superstitious little rituals like avoiding the cracks in the pavement? ☐☐☐

40. Do you find it difficult to control your weight? ☐☐☐

41. Do you sometimes feel a twitching of the face, head or shoulders? ☐☐☐

42. Do you often feel people disapprove of you? ☐☐☐

43. Would you be troubled by feelings of inadequacy if you had to make a speech? ☐☐☐

44. Do you ever feel "just miserable" for no reason? ☐☐☐

45. Do you often feel restless as though you want something but do not really know what? ☐☐☐

46. Are you obsessional about locking drawers, windows, suitcases and such things? ☐☐☐

47. Do you place your trust in supernatural powers such as God or fate to see you through safely? ☐☐☐

48. Do you worry a good deal about contracting a disease? ☐☐☐

49. Do you believe that the pleasure you have in the here and now will have to be paid for eventually? ☐☐☐

50. Are there a lot of things about yourself you would change if you could? ☐☐☐

51. Do you see your future as quite bright? ☐☐☐

52. Are you apt to tremble and perspire when you are faced with a difficult task? ☐☐☐

53. Do you routinely make certain that all the lights, appliances and taps are off before you go to bed? ☐☐☐

54. If something goes wrong do you usually attribute it to bad luck rather than bad management? ☐☐☐

55. Do you make a point of visiting your doctor even if you think you only have a cold? ☐☐☐

56. Does it concern you a great deal that you are living better than the majority of people in the world? ☐☐☐

57. Do you think that generally you are quite popular? ☐☐☐

58. Have you ever wished you were dead? ☐☐☐

59. Are you often afraid of things and people even when you know they will not hurt you? ☐☐☐

60. Are you careful to keep a supply of canned or dried food in your house in case of an emergency food shortage? ☐☐☐

61. Have you ever felt as though you were possessed by evil spirits? ☐☐☐

62. Do you suffer from nervous exhaustion? ☐☐☐

63. Is there something you have done you will regret all your life? ☐☐☐

64. Do you have a great deal of confidence in your decisions? ☐☐☐

65. Do you often feel down in the dumps? ☐☐☐

66. Are you less prone to anxiety than most of your friends? ☐☐☐

67. Does dirt frighten and disgust you to an exceptional degree? ☐☐☐

68. Do you often feel you are a victim of outside forces you cannot control? ☐☐☐

69. Are you considered a sickly person? ☐☐☐

70. Do you often get blamed or punished when you don't deserve it? ☐☐☐

71. Would you say you have a high opinion of yourself? ☐☐☐

72. Do things often seem hopeless to you? ☐ ☐ ☐

73. Do you often worry unreasonably over things that do not really matter? ☐ ☐ ☐

74. If you are staying somewhere other than your own house, do you make a point of figuring out how to escape in the event of a fire? ☐ ☐ ☐

75. Do you set out with a definite course of action to get what you want rather than trust to luck? ☐ ☐ ☐

76. Do you keep the remains of a variety of old prescriptions in your medicine chest? ☐ ☐ ☐

77. Are you immediately offended if somebody scolds you? ☐ ☐ ☐

78. Do you often feel ashamed of things you have done? ☐ ☐ ☐

79. Do you smile and laugh as much as most people? ☐ ☐ ☐

80. Are you anxious about something or somebody most of the time? ☐ ☐ ☐

81. Are you easily irritated by things that are out of place? ☐ ☐ ☐

82. Do you ever make decisions by tossing a coin, or a similar practice that leaves things entirely to chance? ☐ ☐ ☐

83. Do you worry a lot about your health? ☐ ☐ ☐

84. If you have an accident do you assume you deserved it because of something you did? ☐ ☐ ☐

85. Do you feel embarrassed when looking at photographs of yourself and think how awkward you look? ☐ ☐ ☐

86. Have you often felt listless and tired for no good reason? ☐ ☐ ☐

87. If you have made an awkward social error can you forget it quite easily? ☐ ☐ ☐

88. Do you keep careful accounts of the money you spend? ☐ ☐ ☐

89. Do you often act contrary to custom or the wishes of your parents? ☐ ☐ ☐

It is an accepted fact that clothes of a dark colour make the person wearing them look slimmer than clothes of a light colour. This is reflected in a general principle well-known to perceptologists. A black shape looks smaller than an identical white one. Of course it is rare for women to base their choice of dresses on a knowledge of perception psychology, although such knowledge could certainly be useful. As the subject is broken down further, it becomes even more complex; horizontal or vertical stripes, the type of material and how it is cut, and the figure of the person wearing the dress all combine to form a composite reality which can vary in ways almost impossible to predict scientifically.

Furthermore, it goes without saying that the creations of fashion designers are not the result of laboratory experiments, but rather, the product of the sensitivity, intuition and acumen of those skilled in fashioning successful styles. It is no coincidence that a celebrated tailor or a designer is considered an artist. In fact, it is their job to consider the many variables which determine the success or failure of a given effect, and channel them in such a manner that the public can do no less than applaud the result. This is also precisely what is asked of the architect, say, or those who create "designer" products: To start with certain materials (in specific price brackets) and to produce innovative and estimable results—and "artists," as we well know, do not spring from research laboratories.

Let's return to fashion, and consider the most complex of the variables, the effect of horizontal or vertical stripes on a dress. We would probably all agree, for example, that in the photograph the model looks thinner in black than in white. The vertical stripes give a similar effect, but we must ask ourselves if this is due to the stripes, or more to the girl's position (which is different) and hence to the different arrangement of the material. In truth, we cannot claim that as a general rule, horizontal stripes make a figure appear heavier. At most, such matters are fleeting impressions and do not lend themselves to controlled experiments. The many inconstants, from how wide and how close together the stripes are, to the person's figure, the type of material, how it is cut and its colour, can be combined in a number of ways to produce a wide range of effects. For instance, horizontal lines can make the figure look broader, but if the skirt or dress is cut wide, they can actually make the body appear slimmer.

Hence, it is all but impossible to give a precise rule other than the "dark-light" one (actually known to perception psychology since the early 19th century), so we must content ourselves with evaluating the effects in each situation as it arises. As we have said, the perceptologist's normal empirical-experimental methods do not encourage predictions in this area, an area which really belongs more to the artist who, with knowledge, skill and imagination can create a successful formula in each particular case.

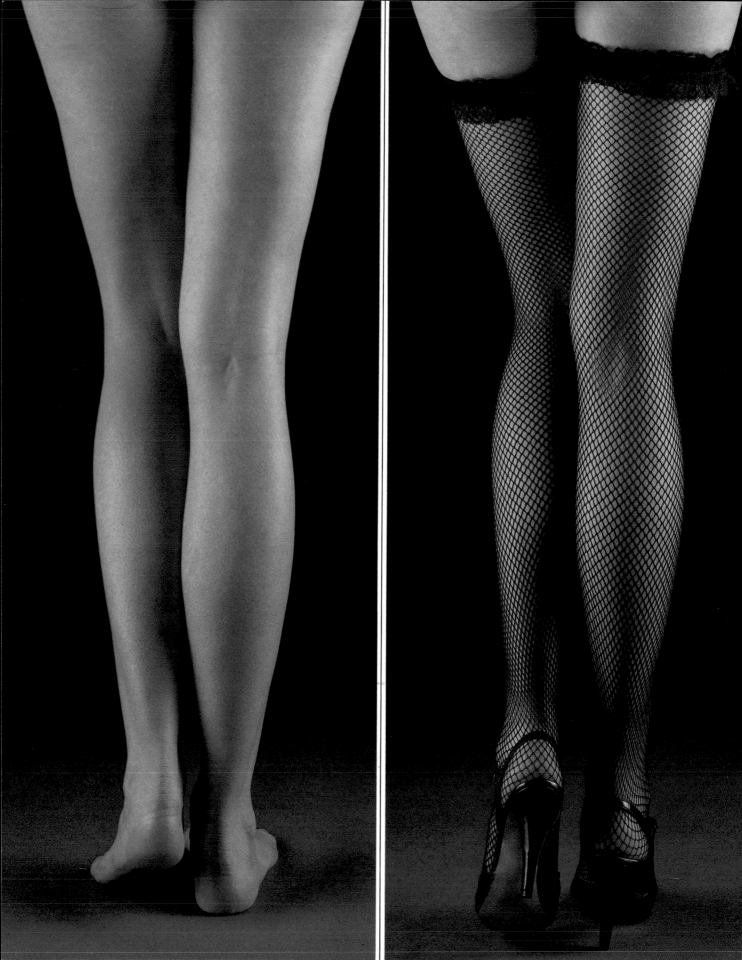

No one can be completely insensitive to the fascination of superstimuli. Bertold Brecht (1898–1966), the German dramatist, poet and outspoken Marxist, is said to have insisted that his hair be cut short on his forehead in order to emphasize its width, an apt choice for an intellectual whose mind aroused the curiosity, and occasionally the ire, of others.

The attractions of Marylin Monroe are of another stamp. Generations of women have tried to imitate her blend of sensuousness and innocence. On the other hand, Brigitte Bardot's sexuality and Humphrey Bogart's penchant for manifestly virile roles are most direct and imperious statements. In citing these particular examples, we are not simply being prurient, but reflecting modern life which is liberally spiced with superstimuli. The long legs of drum majorettes kick off American football games, blue jeans are modelled by nymphets, and there is hardly a summer drink which is not offered to us by slender, attractive and slightly clad girls. Indeed according to ethologists, those who study the behaviour of animals and humans in their own environments, many of the superstimuli exalt the physical characteristics that emphasize sexuality. There are even "supernormal" stimuli, not a linguistically felicitous expression, but one which clearly conveys the attendant exaggeration of shape, proportions and colour. Such stimuli are not just sexually oriented but are manifest on many levels. Dolls, for instance, are frequently made with a supernormal roundness of the head, legs and stomach, designed to visibly dramatize childhood. And, most certainly, exaggeration is the stuff of advertisements: Only X laundry soap can return the whiteness to your dingy clothes, even though we know that all laundry soaps are more or less the same.

Superstimuli are not peculiar to the modern age, or, for that matter, to Western society. According to ethologists, superstimuli have existed throughout man's history, though we lack an abundance of information on the evolution of many patterns of behaviour and customs, one of them being women's shoes.

Why, for instance, do women wear high heels? Ethologists suggest that it is because of a superstimulus. The legs of young girls, like their figures as a whole, tend to appear slender, thus there is no need to elongate them further. However, as the proportions of the body change, and as the figure gets fuller and heavier, the legs begin to look shorter. At this point, high heels help to recreate that much-admired image of youth. A woman who takes care to choose stockings and shoes that make her legs look slimmer and longer (see the photograph on the facing page) is not simply acting out of vanity; even if she is not fully aware of doing so, she is obeying a desire to regain that harmony so epitomized by youth.

90. Do severe aches and pains make it impossible for you to concentrate on your work? ☐ ☐ ☐

91. Are you full of regret about your early sexual experiences? ☐ ☐ ☐

92. Are there some members of your family who make you feel you are not good enough? ☐ ☐ ☐

93. Are you often bothered by noise? ☐ ☐ ☐

94. Can you relax quite easily when sitting or lying down? ☐ ☐ ☐

95. Do you worry a good deal about catching germs from people in public? ☐ ☐ ☐

96. If you were feeling lonely would you make an effort to be friendly to people? ☐ ☐ ☐

97. Are you often bothered by severe itching? ☐ ☐ ☐

98. Do you have some habits that are really inexcusable? ☐ ☐ ☐

99. Do you get very upset if someone criticizes you? ☐ ☐ ☐

100. Do you feel you often get a raw deal out of life? ☐ ☐ ☐

101. Are you easily startled by someone appearing unexpectedly? ☐ ☐ ☐

102. Are you always careful to pay back even the most trivial debt? ☐ ☐ ☐

103. Do you often feel you have little influence over the things that happen to you? ☐ ☐ ☐

104. Are you normally in good health? ☐ ☐ ☐

105. Are you often bothered by pangs of conscience? ☐ ☐ ☐

106. Do people regard you as useful to have around? ☐ ☐ ☐

107. Do you feel people really don't care what happens to you? ☐ ☐ ☐

108. Do you find it difficult to sit still without fidgeting? ☐ ☐ ☐

109. Do you often do a job yourself rather than trust someone else to do it properly? ☐ ☐ ☐

110. Are you easily persuaded by the arguments of others? ☐ ☐ ☐

111. Does stomach trouble run in your family? ☐ ☐ ☐

112. Do you regard your youth as misspent? ☐ ☐ ☐

113. Are you often inclined to question your worth as a person? ☐ ☐ ☐

114. Do you often suffer from loneliness? ☐ ☐ ☐

115. Do you worry a lot about money matters? ☐ ☐ ☐

116. Would you walk under a ladder on the street rather than go out of your way to go around it? ☐ ☐ ☐

117. Do you often find life difficult to cope with? ☐ ☐ ☐

118. Are other people unsympathetic when you are feeling sick? ☐ ☐ ☐

119. Do you think you are undeserving of other people's trust and affection? ☐ ☐ ☐

120. When people say nice things about you do you find it difficult to believe they are really sincere? ☐ ☐ ☐

121. Do you think you are contributing to the world and leading a useful life? ☐ ☐ ☐

122. Can you fall asleep quite easily at night? ☐ ☐ ☐

123. Can you easily disregard minor mistakes and inaccuracies? ☐ ☐ ☐

124. Are most of the things you do geared to pleasing other people? ☐ ☐ ☐

125. Do you constantly suffer from constipation? ☐ ☐ ☐

126. Do you spend a lot of time going over things that happened in the past and wishing you had behaved more responsibly? ☐ ☐ ☐

127. Do you sometimes withhold your opinions for fear people will laugh at you, or be critical? ☐ ☐ ☐

128. Is there at least one person in the world who really loves you? ☐ ☐ ☐

129. Are you easily embarrassed in a social situation? ☐ ☐ ☐

130. Do you keep all kinds of discards in case they might one day come in handy? ☐ ☐ ☐

131. Do you believe your future is really in your own hands? ☐ ☐ ☐

132. Did you ever have a nervous breakdown? ☐ ☐ ☐

133. Are you harbouring a guilty secret that you fear might come out some day? ☐ ☐ ☐

134. Are you shy and self-conscious in social situations? ☐ ☐ ☐

135. Would you agree that it is hardly fair to bring a child into the world the way things are today? ☐ ☐ ☐

136. Are you easily "rattled" if things don't go according to plan? ☐ ☐ ☐

137. Do you feel very uncomfortable if your house gets messy? ☐ ☐ ☐

138. Have you as much will power as the next person? ☐ ☐ ☐

139. Are you often bothered by heart palpitations? ☐ ☐ ☐

140. Do you believe bad behaviour will always be punished in the long run? ☐ ☐ ☐

141. Do you have a tendency to feel inferior to people you meet? ☐ ☐ ☐

142. Generally speaking have you been successful in achieving your aims and goals in life? ☐ ☐ ☐

143. Do you often wake up sweating after a bad dream? ☐ ☐ ☐

144. Are you repelled if someone's pet dog licks you on the face? ☐ ☐ ☐

145. Do you find planning ahead a waste of time because something always happens to make you change your plans? ☐ ☐ ☐

146. Do you worry a lot about other members of your family getting sick? ☐ ☐ ☐

147. If you have done something morally reprehensible can you forget it quickly and direct your thoughts to the future? ☐☐☐

148. Do you feel that, on the whole, you can accomplish the things you want to? ☐☐☐

149. Are you overcome by sadness? ☐☐☐

150. Does your voice get shaky if you are talking to someone you particularly want to impress? ☐☐☐

151. Would you rather go without something than feel obliged to another person? ☐☐☐

152. Would you prefer a job in which somebody else made the decisions and told you what to do? ☐☐☐

153. Are you troubled by cold hands and feet even in warm weather? ☐☐☐

154. Do you often pray for forgiveness? ☐☐☐

155. Are you satisfied with your appearance? ☐☐☐

156. Does it seem to you that it is always other people who get the breaks? ☐☐☐

157. Would you stay calm and collected in the face of an emergency? ☐☐☐

158. Do you make a point of writing down every appointment in a notebook, even those things you have to do later the same day? ☐☐☐

159. Do you often have the feeling that it's no use trying to get anywhere in life? ☐☐☐

160. Do you often have difficulty in breathing? ☐☐☐

161. Are you embarrassed by dirty stories? ☐☐☐

162. Are you often reticent with other people because you think they will not like you? ☐☐☐

163. Is it a long time since you last felt on top of the world? ☐☐☐

164. Do you sometimes get into a state of tension and turmoil when thinking about your difficulties? ☐☐☐

165. Do you usually adjust your hair and clothing before you open the door to a visitor? ☐☐☐

166. Do you often feel you don't have enough control over the direction your life is taking? ☐☐☐

167. Do you think it is a waste of time to go to the doctor with most mild complaints, like coughs and colds? ☐☐☐

168. Do you often feel you have done something wrong and wicked even when you know the feeling is not justified? ☐☐☐

169. Do you find it hard to do things in a way that wins the attention and approval of others? ☐☐☐

170. Do you feel cheated when you look back on what has happened to you? ☐☐☐

171. Do you torment yourself for a long time after a humiliating experience? ☐☐☐

172. Are you often tempted to correct people's grammar (even though politeness might stop you from doing so)? ☐☐☐

173. Do you find things are changing so rapidly today that it is hard to know what rules to follow? ☐☐☐

174. Do you always go straight to bed if you have caught a cold? ☐☐☐

175. Do you think you must have disappointed your teachers at school by not working hard enough? ☐☐☐

176. Do you often catch yourself pretending to be a better person than you really are? ☐☐☐

177. Are you about as happy as the next person? ☐☐☐

178. Would you describe yourself as self-conscious? ☐☐☐

179. Would you describe yourself as a perfectionist? ☐☐☐

180. Do you usually have clear-cut goals and a sense of purpose in life? ☐☐☐

181. Do you look at the colour of your tongue most mornings? ☐☐☐

182. Do you often think back on how badly you treated people in the past? ☐ ☐ ☐

183. Do you sometimes feel you can never do anything right? ☐ ☐ ☐

184. Do you often get the feeling you are just not a part of things? ☐ ☐ ☐

185. Do you worry unnecessarily over things that might happen? ☐ ☐ ☐

186. Do you follow a set routine at bedtime that if broken, would make it hard for you to get to sleep? ☐ ☐ ☐

187. Do you often have the feeling other people are using you? ☐ ☐ ☐

188. Do you weigh yourself every day? ☐ ☐ ☐

189. Do you expect God to punish you for your sins in the afterlife? ☐ ☐ ☐

190. Do you often have doubts about your sexual prowess? ☐ ☐ ☐

191. Is your sleep usually fitful and disturbed? ☐ ☐ ☐

192. Are you inclined to get yourself all worked up over nothing? ☐ ☐ ☐

193. Is it very important to you that everything be neat and tidy? ☐ ☐ ☐

194. Are you sometimes persuaded by advertisements to buy something you don't really want? ☐ ☐ ☐

195. Are you often troubled by noises in your ears? ☐ ☐ ☐

196. Do you usually blame yourself if something goes wrong in your personal relationships? ☐ ☐ ☐

197. Have you at least a normal amount of self-respect? ☐ ☐ ☐

198. Do you often feel lonely even when you are with other people? ☐ ☐ ☐

199. Have you ever felt you needed to take tranquillizers? ☐ ☐ ☐

200. Are you very upset if your daily habits are disturbed by unforeseen events? ☐ ☐ ☐

201. Do you read horoscopes with the hope of obtaining some guidance in your life? ☐ ☐ ☐

202. Do you often feel a choking lump in your throat? ☐ ☐ ☐

203. Are you sometimes disgusted by your own sexual desires and fantasies? ☐ ☐ ☐

204. Do you think your personality is attractive to the opposite sex? ☐ ☐ ☐

205. Do you feel a sense of inner calm and contentment most of the time? ☐ ☐ ☐

206. Are you nervous? ☐ ☐ ☐

207. Do you spend a good deal of time filing and arranging your papers so you will know where everything is should you want it? ☐ ☐ ☐

208. Do other people usually decide what play or movie you are going to see? ☐ ☐ ☐

209. Do you have hot or cold spells? ☐ ☐ ☐

210. Is it easy for you to forget the things you have done wrong? ☐ ☐ ☐

The first scale derived from this questionnaire is "self-esteem." People who score high on self-esteem are inclined to an ample measure of confidence in themselves and their abilities. They consider themselves worthy, useful human beings and believe they are well liked. Without implying a cockiness or conceit on their parts, it could be said they like themselves a lot. Low scorers, on the other hand, undervalue themselves, believing they are unattractive and failures.

The key for this scale is given below. It is used in the same fashion as the preceding key; when the sign is plus, score 1 for a "Yes"; when the sign is minus score 1 for a "No." The "?" scores one-half regardless of the sign. Remember to score only for the question numbers listed in the key.

1. Self-Esteem

1 +	43 −	85 −	127 −	169 −
8 −	50 −	92 −	134 −	176 −
15 −	57 +	99 −	141 −	183 −
22 −	64 +	106 +	148 +	190 −
29 +	71 +	113 −	155 +	197 +
36 −	78 −	120 −	162 −	204 +

We have called the second scale "happiness" and its meaning is very straightforward. In the main, high scorers are cheerful, optimistic and enjoy good health. They are satisfied with their existence, find life rewarding and are at peace with the world. Low scorers are characteristically pessimistic, gloomy and depressed, disappointed with their existence and at odds with the world.

The key for this scale appears below and should be used in the same way we previously described. Our scale was constructed to cover the normal range of "happiness-unhappiness." The reader with a low score should not automatically consider himself clinically depressed, as there is no cutoff point that signals this condition.

2. Happiness

2 −	44 −	86 −	128 +	170 −
9 −	51 +	93 −	135 −	177 +
16 +	58 −	100 −	142 +	184 −
23 +	65 −	107 −	149 −	191 −
30 −	72 −	114 −	156 −	198 −
37 +	79 +	121 +	163 −	205 +

The third scale is labelled "anxiety." High scorers are easily upset when things go wrong and are inclined to worry unnecessarily about what may or may not happen. Such people are responsible for much of the consumption of minor tranquillizers like Librium and Valium. Low scorers are placid, serene and resistant to irrational fears and anxieties. On the average, women experience a greater degree of fear and anxiety than men, however the difference is not such that it necessitates separate keys for the two sexes.

3. Anxiety

3 +	45 +	87 −	129 +	171 +
10 −	52 +	94 −	136 +	178 +
17 −	59 +	101 +	143 +	185 +
24 +	66 −	108 +	150 +	192 +
31 +	73 +	115 +	157 −	199 +
38 +	80 +	122 −	164 +	206 +

The fourth type of "maladjustment" represented in our questionnaire is "obsessiveness." High scorers are careful, conscientious, highly disciplined, staid, meticulous and easily irritated by things that are unclean, untidy or out of place. Low scorers are casual and easygoing with less need for order, routine, or ritual.

4. Obsessiveness

4 +	46 +	88 +	130 +	172 +
11 +	53 +	95 +	137 +	179 +
18 +	60 +	102 +	144 +	186 +
25 +	67 +	109 +	151 +	193 +
32 +	74 +	116 −	158 +	200 +
39 +	81 +	123 −	165 +	207 +

The fifth scale is "autonomy." The autonomous person (high scorer) enjoys a good measure of independence, makes his own decisions, sees himself as master of his fate, and takes realistic action to solve his problems. The low scorer considers himself a helpless pawn of fate, is easily influenced by other people and events, and exhibits a high degree of what is described as "authoritarian submission"—the unquestioning obedience to institutional power. Men tend to score slightly higher on this scale, but again not so strikingly that separate norms need be provided.

5. Autonomy

5 −	47 −	89 +	131 +	173 −
12 +	54 −	96 +	138 +	180 +
19 +	61 −	103 −	145 −	187 −
26 −	68 −	110 −	152 −	194 −
33 +	75 +	117 −	159 −	201 −
40 −	82 −	124 −	166 −	208 −

The sixth scale, "hypochondriasis" measures a tendency to acquire psychosomatic symptoms and to imagine oneself ill. High scorers complain of a variety of diffuse physical symptoms, are excessively concerned about their state of health, and frequently demand the sympathetic attention of their doctor, family and friends. Low scorers are seldom ill and are not unduly concerned about their health.

7. Guilt				
7 +	49 +	91 +	133 +	175 +
14 +	56 +	98 +	140 +	182 +
21 +	63 +	105 +	147 −	189 +
28 +	70 −	112 +	154 +	196 +
35 +	77 +	119 +	161 +	203 +
42 +	84 +	126 +	168 +	210 −

6. Hypochondriasis				
6 −	48 +	90 +	132 +	174 +
13 +	55 +	97 +	139 +	181 +
20 +	62 +	104 −	146 +	188 +
27 +	69 +	111 +	153 +	195 +
34 +	76 +	118 +	160 +	202 +
41 +	83 +	125 +	167 −	209 +

Finally we have included a scale for guilt. High scorers are self-accusing, self-abasing and troubled by their conscience regardless of whether or not their behaviour is, in fact, morally reprehensible. Low scorers are little inclined to punish themselves or regret their past behaviour.

Having obtained seven scores from the questionnaire, these can be entered on the profile sheet below, in the same manner as the previous test; one's overall emotional stability or instability can then be assessed at a glance. If the scores fall clearly and consistently to the left of the center line, a certain degree of instability is indicated. If, however, the scores are around the center line or to the right of it, the reader can regard himself or herself as reasonably stable or "well-balanced."

Most people would agree that stability is preferable to emotionality which is often accompanied by suffering and unhappiness. On the other hand, some would argue that excessive stability is also undesirable because to live is to experience, and the person who feels nothing is deadened. Remember too that it is the very intensity of emotions that leads some people to artistic pursuits. As in many cases, it might well be that the middle (normal) ground is the more satisfactory one, but this is such a complex debate we are loath to take sides, one way or the other.

Average

	emotional instability	stability/adjustment	
Inferiority feelings	6 7 8 9 10 11 12 13 14 15 16 17 18 19 29 21	22 23 24 25 26 27 28 29 30	Self-esteem
Depressiveness	7 8 9 10 11 12 13 14 15 16 17 18 19 20 21 22	23 24 25 26 27 28 29 30	Happiness
Anxiety	30 29 28 27 26 25 24 23 22 21 20 19 18 17 16	15 14 13 12 11 10 9 8 7 6 5 4 3 2 1 0	Calm
Obsessiveness	25 24 23 22 21 20 19 18 17 16 15 14 13 12 11 10	9 8 7 6 5 4 3 2 1	Casualness
Dependence	5 6 7 8 9 10 11 12 13 14 15 16 17 18 19 20	21 22 23 24 25 26 27 28 29	Autonomy
Hypochondriasis	21 20 19 18 17 16 15 14 13 12 11 10 9 8 7 6	5 4 3 2 1	Sense of health
Guilt	23 22 21 20 19 18 17 16 15 14 13 12 11 10 9 8	7 6 5 4 3 2 1 0	Guiltless

Some results will probably come as no surprise, others perhaps will. It could be interesting to compare our own or other people's results with any judgements we might have formed before doing the questionnaire. Then again, it could also prove disturbing. Which is right, your personal judgement or the score? And can we now predict our future actions?

But there is no need to fret about this. Both the personality-trait approach and the typological approach are forms of classification; the former is predominantly descriptive and the latter more closely linked to biological and genetic factors. Although they generate assessments worthy of consideration, neither is sufficient in itself to explain individual behaviour patterns in a given set of circumstances. There is always the risk that they may create stereotypes which would prove to be more limiting than explanatory, for the results of the interaction between an individual and society, and between the diverse characteristics within the same person, are not easy to predict and often are quite the opposite of what one might expect. This is the case with the two brothers (Figure 55) in the Sinclair Lewis novel, *Work of Art,* which was quoted by the well-known psychologist and theorist, F. H. Allport (1897–1967) to demonstrate that, "the same fire that melts butter also hardens eggs."

Although a teenager's personality may exhibit marked traits of sociability, self-confidence and calmness at a given moment, who can say how these qualities will be affected by a long illness, or a move to a new environment, or the loss of a parent. Hence, any typological approach must consider the different experiences each of us undergoes. And the reactions to those experiences cannot always be predicted. The inspiring teacher or, conversely, the provocative colleague can evoke quite different reactions from each of us.

This does not mean everything is a matter of chance and we are therefore justified in neglecting the quality of our education or our work. Quite the contrary. These are obligations we cannot ignore if we are to increase the satisfactions in our private and professional lives. It simply means the results of such commitments are in no way foregone conclusions.

We must also remember that a person's characteristics alter as he grows older. Certain traits become ingrained while others give way to new ones; one's personality is not carved in stone.

Methods and techniques

Interviews, questionnaires, projective tests and direct observation of behaviour are all used to study the personality, but for a more detailed description of techniques, we refer again to Anastasi. These diverse methods enable researchers to collect data on the subjects under study which they can then interpret in light of the particular theories they are using.

We have already had a taste of questionnaires. For an example of projective tests, see Figure 56, from Hilgard et al. Although there is now a degree of skepticism regarding the assumption on which these tests are based—that subjects "project" their personalities onto their interpretations of the visual stimuli, and hence open themselves to analysis by the psychologist—they are still quite commonly used in clinical settings, particularly the Rorschach test which employs a reliable and articulate method of evaluation, making positive comparisons possible.

Methods that include interviews with a subject and observation of his behaviour are closely linked to the

---

Fig. 55	**The Role of Experience**

"My father," said Oral, "was a sloppy, lazy, boozing old bum, and my mother didn't know much besides cooking, and she was too busy to give me much attention. And the kids I knew were a bunch fo foulmouthed loafers who hung around the bums up near the water tank, and I never had a chance to get any formal schooling and just got thrown on my own. So naturally I've become a kind of vagabond who can't be bothered thinking about his "debts" to a lot of little shopkeeping lice, and I suppose I'm inclined to be lazy and not too scrupulous about the dames and the liquor. But my early rearing did have one swell result. Brought up so unconventionally, I'll always be anti-Puritan. I'll never deny the joys of the flesh."

"My father," said Myron, "was pretty easygoing and always liked drinking and swapping stories with the boys, and my mother didn't have time to take care of us, and I heard a lot of filth from the bums up near the water tank. Maybe just as a sort of reaction I'm scared of liquor and women, and I've become almost too much of a crab about paying my debts and fussing over my work. But my rearing did have one swell result. Just by way of contrast, it made me a good, sound, old-fashioned Puritan."

The Inkblot Test

Fig. 56

These inkblots are similar to the ones used in the Rorschach and Holtzman tests. The subject has to describe everything he sees in the blots, looking at them from any angle.

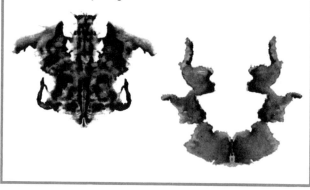

skill and cultural background of the researcher, particularly in the interpretative stage. Indeed the researcher's flexibility and sensitivity can determine whether the results are useful, or distorted and superfluous.

The specific nature of behaviour

A child may lie to his teacher, but to avoid being ostracized he is careful to show loyalty to his peers. In much the same fashion, while it is considered almost natural not to tell the whole truth on an income tax return, such behaviour is not countenanced in the confessional. By the same token, at any given moment in history, magistrates tend to look upon some offenses with more severity than others, even though, under the law they merit identical penalties.

This is the kind of argument social behaviourists often use to criticize the psychoanalytical, typological and personality-trait approaches. Their basic assumption is that human behaviour varies according to environmental stimuli, thus little is gained by an analysis of the personality. A subject under examination is in an artificial situation, they maintain, therefore the psychologist gleans only the slightest notion of his true conduct. Conversations, questionnaires, tests, statistical evaluations, and all other techniques generally employed in empirical and experimental psychology, are

misleading because they generate what are, on the whole, illusory insights.

This is a stimulating point of view, but one guilty of the same schematic approach it condemns—and often quite rightly—in other systems. In fact we too, have consistently recommended caution in evaluating the test results for they are merely indications, and serve to explain and predict behaviour patterns only to a limited degree. Without question, it is a mistake to put too much faith in them, and an even greater mistake to use them for mechanistic ends. However, if a psychologist is aware of the tests' limitations, and does not permit himself fantasies of omnipotence, there is no reason not to use the traditional procedures and still be mindful of the social behaviourists' well-taken position.

The social behaviorists endeavor to interpret human behaviour in broader, more articulate terms than those traditionally employed by scientific psychology, which tends to be more reductive. An example of their approach is the *ethogenic* theory of behaviour recently developed by R. Harré, the well-known scientific philosopher of Oxford University and P. F. Secord, the equally noted American social psychologist. By combining articulate observation and analytical procedures as well as contributions from such diverse disciplines as psychology, philosophy, history, sociology, anthropology and ethnography, ethogenic theory lays the groundwork for a wider and more complete study of the human character.

For instance, an analysis of the manner in which people are introduced to one another in modern Western society, reveals the importance attached to social status: The names of those being introduced are frequently coupled with their professional, academic or honorary titles. Muslim societies, on the other hand, do not emphasize status in their rituals of introduction.

This kind of orientation serves to place human actions (in the above case, the way in which one is introduced and introduces oneself), in an appropriate context and thus avoids the fragmentary picture that is obtained from simply observing the meeting of two people. If the latter approach is followed, it is only possible to learn the specific words and forms of expression that are used. What we do not learn is their significance in a broader social context. In short, wider considerations, of an anthropological, historical and sociological nature, are needed for true evaluation; only by combining perspectives and methods can we understand motivations and actions with sufficient clarity.

Games appendix

Filling in the corners

Eventually, when the steaming first courses and countless second courses, accompaniments, ice creams, cakes, etc. are all finished, The Hobbit (very small and peaceable people who were fond of green vests, and were born of J. R. R. Tolkien's imagination) sip coffee and munch biscuits just to make certain they leave their stomachs with no empty spaces. This final state of their banquet is called "filling in the corners," which is precisely what this appendix is meant to do.

How Many Squares Can You See?

Creativity often involves looking at a situation or a problem with fresh eyes and seeing something others have failed to see.
How many squares can you see?

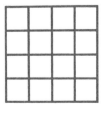

The Thumbprint

Here is your chance to be creative with even simple stimuli. Ink your thumb on an ink pad and make your thumbprint on a piece of paper. Using this as a starting point, you can now draw a variety of designs.

Example

Now do the same with the rest of your fingers (individually or together) and draw other pictures (more examples are given with the solutions).

Obvious!

Although the creative person likes the challenge of the complex, chaotic, obscure and disorderly, he doesn't overlook the obvious and simple. The tendency, however, is frequently to search for the difficult when a simple solution would be sufficient. We are so conditioned to intricate processes that we have become almost blind to the "obvious."

The following fifteen mini-problems have been designed to test your capacity to find simple solutions to situations that at first glance seem complicated.

1. You go to bed at 8 p.m. and set the alarm to get up at 9 a.m. How many hours of sleep will you get?
2. One month has twenty-eight days. Of the remaining eleven months, how many have thirty days?
3. A woman gave a beggar 10 cents. The woman is the beggar's sister, but the beggar is not the woman's brother. What is their relationship?
4. Why can't a man living in New York be buried west of the Mississippi?
5. Do they have a fourth of July in England?
6. How can you throw a tennis ball with all your strength and have it stop and come right back to you without it hitting a wall or net, or any other obstruction?
7. If you stand on a hard marble floor, how can you drop a raw egg five feet without breaking its shell?
8. Two fathers and two sons shot three deer. Each took home one deer. How was that possible?
9. How many times can you subtract the number 2 from the number 24?
10. Seven cars were lined up in a dealer's showroom bumper-to-bumper. How many bumpers were actually touching each other?
11. Would it be cheaper for you to take one girl friend to the movies twice or two girl friends at the same time?
12. Take five apples from seven apples and what have you got?
13. Visualize four horizontal lines, one above the other. Now visualize four vertical lines, each one cutting through the horizontal lines. How many squares did you form? (Do not use paper or pencil.)
14. Six men drove over 150 miles in a car. The trip took two hours, yet no one in the car noticed that they had a flat tire the whole time. How was this possible?
15. You are sitting in a room with twelve friends. Can any of them sit in a particular place in the room where it would be impossible for you to sit?

The Mysterious Number

Find the number that follows in each series.

a) **2, 3, 4, 6, 8, 12, 14, 18, 20, ?**

b) **3, 6, 13, 26, 33, 66, ?**

c) **9, 10, 12, 14, 15, 16, 18, 20, 21, 22, 24, 25, 26, 27, 28, ?**

d) **22, 20, 10, 8, 4, 2, ?**

e) **4, 8, 32, 512, ?**

f) **364, 361, 19, 16, 4, 1, ?**

g) **15, 15, 13, 13, 13, 14, ?**

Scribbles

Look at the twenty-one squares, each marked with a letter. How many types of scribble are there?

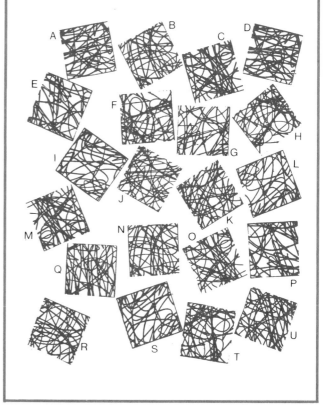

Boundaries, Shapes and Sizes

Here's another chance to test your powers of visualization. The following problems are designed to exercise a number of important capacities such as the ability to perceive implications, to be flexible and to restructure and transform figures.

1. Trace the lines in this diagram without lifting your pen from the paper and without retracing any lines.

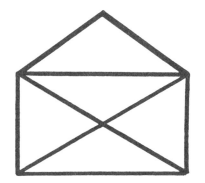

2. Arrange the seven dots so they make five straight rows with three dots in each row.

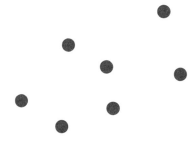

3. Put these seven dots into seven squares. You can draw only three squares, and no more than four of the squares can be the same size.

4. A man had a lucky horseshoe which he wanted to divide among his six sons. He did it by cutting only two straight lines. How did he do it?

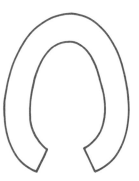

5. Copy this design onto a piece of paper, then cut it into three parts with two straight cuts so the individual parts will form a square when they are reassembled.

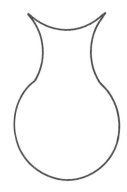

6. Copy the letter E, cut it into seven parts with four straight cuts; form a square out of the parts.

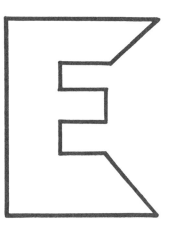

A Piece of Cake

This problem tests your perseverance. Eleven members of a family, all of different ages and with different appetites, turn up suddenly on Sunday afternoon. You have only one large cake to divide among them. How can you cut the cake into eleven parts, not necessarily of equal size, by making just four straight-line cuts?

Squares and Numbers

Divide this numbered sheet into four parts, each with the same number of squares. The numbers in each part must total forty-five.

3	9	5	1	4	3
8	6	2	7	5	8
9	7	1	8	3	1
4	5	3	9	7	6
2	6	8	6	1	2
7	4	5	2	9	4

A particularly interesting area of psychology is ethology, even though it has produced sundry arguments and misunderstandings among theorists. As we have said, ethology is the study of human and animal behaviour. Preferably subjects are studied in their natural environments with methods that do not in any way influence their behaviour. Telephoto lenses and telescopes are used, for example, to observe certain animals so their behaviour will not alter with the presence of humans. An analogous situation exists with people; we need only become aware of a strange presence to change our gestures, actions and often, the order in which we do things.

In 1973, zoologist Konrad Lorenz was awarded the Nobel Prize for his work in establishing the science of ethology, particularly his studies on different species of animals including wild ducks and small coral reef fish. Indeed, his studies clearly demonstrated the important role of aggression in nature.

As for human behaviour, a great deal of research has been done and continues to be done, on the numerous forms of expression and communication—including the smile—some of which are universal while others are distinctive to specific environments and cultures (including those discussed earlier on pp. 17 and 18 with particular reference to expressive, schematic and symbolic gestures).

Here again it must be stressed that there are fervid disputes (which will be discussed in more detail later) surrounding the "biological" interpretation of human behaviour. According to its advocates, those actions generally defined either as altruistic or egotistical are by nature, geared to the survival of an individual's genes and hence the survival of the species. Thus the role of morality, religion and politics is to abet and make possible the one true objective in life, the reproduction and the passing on of one's characteristics to the next generation. Yet, setting aside the heated tones and extreme opinions which attend such far-reaching theories on behaviour and which have risen to a fevered pitch in the case of the sociobiological approach (understandable given the subjects' vast emotional implications), the fundamental importance of ethology in this area cannot be denied.

For example, any consideration of the enormously expressive flexibility of the face must include a recognition of the complexity of the facial muscles. It is then natural to wonder why these particular characteristics exist in humans; any search for the answer must involve further observation in different situations as well as increased theoretical speculation. The behaviourist cannot, therefore, help but use this combination of approaches.

Furthermore, psychology draws on the findings of other sciences, such as physiology and the computer sciences, and hence operates in a dynamic and essentially interdisciplinary dimension. Indeed, there are many who suggest that science not be separated into distinct areas, but that each problem be engaged in an interdisciplinary fashion. Although we have concentrated on ethology's thought-provoking hypotheses, there are objections to them which deserve noting: 1)In the main, human behaviour is determined by the cultural environment and the learning process. 2)Man's propensity to adapt to his environment was operative when conditions of life were "primitive"

continued on page 173

and is of no significance in a highly organized and technological society. 3)Each animal species is unique, hence what is learned about one cannot be applied to others.

In answer to these objections, we must state our belief that: 1)Human behaviour cannot be explained solely on the basis of environment and learning. To do so would be to deny the existence of a relationship between man's biological development and the activities (including cultural activities) he pursues. 2)As a variety of animal species have adapted through time to a succession of new environments, it is difficult to support the notion that man had to start "from scratch" with regard to contemporary society. 3)We would point to the valid argument that if it were impossible to transfer what is known about one species to others, biology itself would not exist.

To sum up, it would appear that while the three objections cited can certainly be countered, the need for accurate controls must be stressed, as well as the need for extreme caution in transferring acquired data on animal behaviour to the area of human behaviour.

"...the suggestion that psychologists should study what is more typically 'human' in man cannot be accepted," wrote Mario Zanforlin, a scholar of comparative psychology and ethology, "for it is in fact impossible to know what is 'more typically' human if you do not also study other animal species. It would be interesting to analyze the reasons behind the refusal and reluctance to accept a human ethology in the sense of a comparative study of behaviour, considering man as one of the great number of interesting animal species (even if only by way of hypothesis), but I think this could be rather indiscreet."

In conclusion, the ethological prespective could be very useful in psychology which is a discipline labouring under a weight of "atomized" observations, particularly evident in its theoretical approach. The capacity to offer global explanations is, in fact, one of the more important characteristics of ethology and could permit the formulation of wide-ranging explanatory hypotheses about mankind (although as always we stress the need for extreme caution). An analysis of the structure and biology of behaviour could make it possible to identify the general laws governing them. To continue in the words of Mario Zanforlin, "the only real hope of reconstructing the biological evolution of human behaviour lies in a comparative study of the many other animal species with a view to grasping the underlying general laws of biological evolution which control behaviour... Just as every individual is unique and cannot be repeated, so is every species. But if it is possible to turn human psychology into a science with general laws by which an individual's behaviour can be identified and interpreted within a certain range of probability despite his uniqueness and inimitability, so the laws of a general theory of behaviour evolution could be used to identify and interpret the characteristic behaviour patterns of each species. Obviously, the degree of probability with which the trends in the behaviour patterns of each species could be predicted, as in the case of individuals, will depend not only on the general law regarding that particular mode of behaviour, but also on what is peculiar to each species."

Number Games

Although the eight games below are presented in numerical terms, they require no special mathematical training. They provide an excellent means for inventive manipulation and combination, and they involve several functions necessary for effective problem solving, such as the perception of relations and implications.

1. Place numbers from 1 to 16 in the small squares so each vertical and horizontal column and one diagonal column equals 34. Use all the numbers from 1 to 16 but use each only one time. To get you off to a good start five numbers have already been placed.

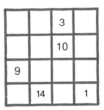

2. When my mother was 41 years old, I was 9. Now she is twice as old as I am. How old am I?

3. Here are two columns of numbers. The numbers in both columns are the same, but in the right column, they are inverted and in reverse order. Can you tell at a glance which column has the larger total?

123456789	1
12345678	21
1234567	321
123456	4321
12345	54321
1234	654321
123	7654321
12	87654321
1	987654321

4. How can you obtain 100 using four 9s?

5. How can you obtain 100 using six 9s?

6. Can you obtain 1,000 using eight 8s?

7. Add the following numbers to obtain 1111.

4, 5, 1, 6, 7, 9, 8,

(There are several solutions.)

8. Express 100 with five 1s.
   Express 100 three ways with five 5s.

Hot Shots

You have seven shots to get a total of 225 points. You can do it by hitting two targets on each row, saving the seventh shot for the gong.

Dots and Lines

These puzzles might not be particularly easy for you. They illustrate how subconsciously we often refuse to see any solutions to our problems and thus remain enclosed by them (in the case of the puzzles, entrapped in the imaginary square and rectangular-shaped boundaries formed by the dots). Many of our problems can be resolved if we approach them with a broader perspective, and if we have the courage to "kick at the fences."

1. Draw six straight lines without lifting your pen from the paper and without retracing, that will cross through all sixteen dots.

2. Draw five straight lines without raising your pen or retracing, that will connect all twelve dots.

The Principle

All these shapes are different, but there is a principle underlying their arrangement. Which of the lettered shapes in the second line goes where the question mark (?) is on the first line?

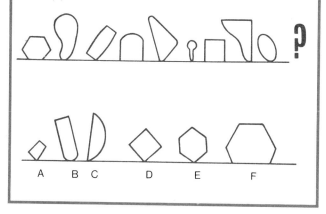

Menu, Please

Five old friends had a reunion at their favourite restaurant. Each man ordered something to drink, an entree and a dessert. John and Mr. Jackson had martinis and James and Mr. Jones ordered scotch. Mr. Jenkins had coke since he was driving. John and Mr. Jennings ordered steak, Joe and Mr. Jenkins had roast beef. For dessert, Joe and Mr. Jordan ate chocolate cake, while Jerry and Mr. Jenkins had pie. The other man had ice cream. No two men sitting next to each other were served the same things. Who had pheasant and what did Jack eat? The answer to this can be worked out in five minutes.

Small Changes

Place two coins heads up on circles three and eight and two coins tails up on five and ten. By moving the coins one at a time in straight lines, and only along the dotted lines, make the heads and tails switch places. No two coins can occupy the same circle at the same time. You can move the coins one, two or three spaces, but you cannot pass a space already occupied. This can be done in ten moves.

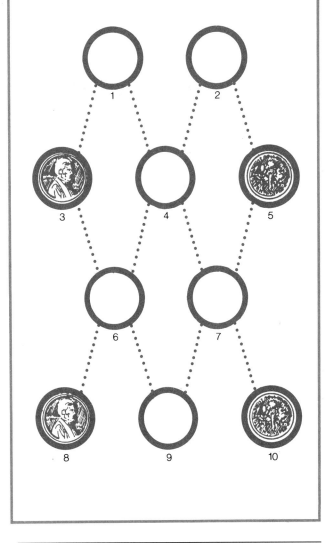

Answers

How Many Squares Can You See?

There are 30 squares. The immediate answer is 16, or 17 if you count the big square which contains all the smaller ones. There are, however, squares within squares which you need patience to find. A satisfactory solution to a problem is rarely found in a hurry.

The Thumbprint

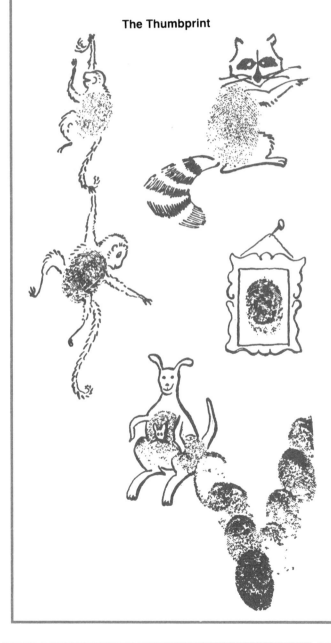

Obvious!

1. One hour. The alarm would go off at 9 o'clock, but in the evening.
2. All eleven.
3. They're sisters.
4. He's still alive.
5. Yes
6. If you throw it straight up into the air.
7. Hold the egg up and drop it from a height of six feet. It will drop five feet without breaking. After that you'll have to clean up the mess.
8. They are son, father and grandfather.
9. Only once. After that, you're subtracting from 22, 20, 18, and so on.
10. Twelve
11. Two girl friends at the same time: three tickets. If you take one twice: four tickets.
12. Five apples, naturally.
13. Nine
14. The spare tire was flat.
15. Yes, on your lap.

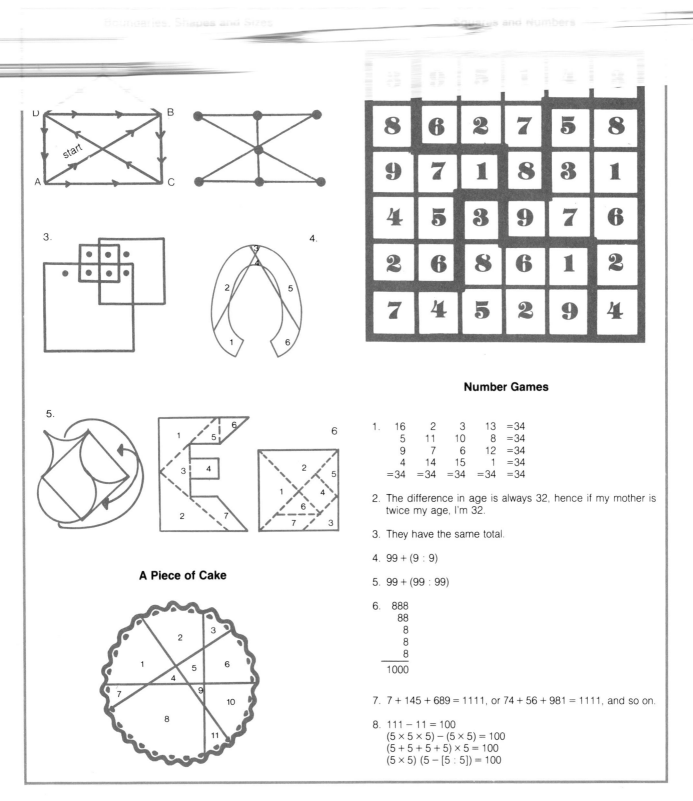

A Piece of Cake

Number Games

1.

16	2	3	13	=34
5	11	10	8	=34
9	7	6	12	=34
4	14	15	1	=34
=34	=34	=34	=34	=34

2. The difference in age is always 32, hence if my mother is twice my age, I'm 32.

3. They have the same total.

4. $99 + (9 : 9)$

5. $99 + (99 : 99)$

6.
```
 888
  88
   8
   8
   8
————
1000
```

7. $7 + 145 + 689 = 1111$, or $74 + 56 + 981 = 1111$, and so on.

8. $111 - 11 = 100$
$(5 \times 5 \times 5) - (5 \times 5) = 100$
$(5 + 5 + 5 + 5) \times 5 = 100$
$(5 \times 5)(5 - [5 : 5]) = 100$

Hot Shots

First row: + 52 × 6 = 312
Second row: 312 − 32 = 280 : 2 = 140
Third row: 140 − 73 = 67 × 3 = 201
Gong: 201 + 24 = 225

The Principle

F: The series is made up of one "stable" figure and two "unstable" ones.

Dots and Lines

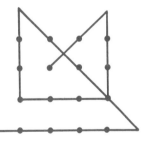

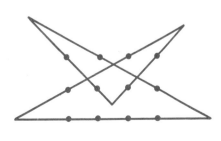

Menu, Please

1. Joe Jackson had a martini, roast beef and cake.
2. Jerry Jones had scotch, pheasant and pie.
3. John Jordan had a martini, steak and cake.
4. Jack Jenkins had a coke, roast beef and pie.
5. James Jennings had scotch, steak and ice cream.

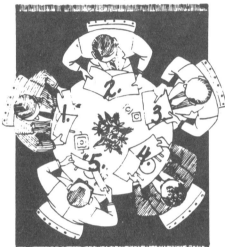

Small Changes

Move the coins as follows: 8 to 2, 3 to 6, 5 to 9, 10 to 1, 2 to 5, 6 to 4, 9 to 6, 1 to 3, 4 to 10 and, finally, 6 to 8.

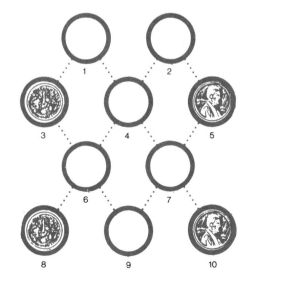

Sources of the Games and Tests

The games, tests and experiments included in this book have been taken from the following books:

W. Kirst, U. Diekmeyer, *Creativitätstraining,* Deutsche Verlags-Anstalt, Stuttgart, 1971.

P. Berloquin, *Testez votre intelligence,* Librairie Générale Francaise, Paris, 1974.

E. Ott, *Optimales Denken,* © 1971, Deutsche Verlags-Anstalt GMBH, Stuttgart.

E. R. Hilgard, R. C. Atkinson, R. L. Atkinson, *Introduction to Psychology,* Harcourt Brace Jovanovich, New York, 1971.

H. J. Eysenck, *Know Your Own I.Q.,* Penguin Books, Harmondsworth, 1966.

H. J. Eysenck, *Check Your Own I.Q.,* Penguin Books, Harmondsworth, 1966.

P. Lauster, *Begabungstests,* Deutsche Verlags-Anstalt, Stuttgart, 1971.

A. Bragdon, L. Fellows, *Diabolical Diversions,* Muller, London, 1981, pp. 89, 20–21, 28–29, 36–37, 60–61, 80–81, 96–97.

H. J. Eysenck, G. Wilson, *Know Your Own Personality,* Penguin Books, Harmondsworth, 1976, pp. 42–66, 67–90.

E. Raudsepp, *Brain Stretchers,* Muller, London, 1982 (© 1980 by Eugene Raudsepp. Excerpted from *More Creative Growth Games,* published by Perigree Books and used by permission), pp. 14–5, 31, 40–1, 50–1, 54, 56, 61–3, 137.

V. Serebriakoff, *A Mensa Puzzle Book,* Muller, London, 1982, pp. 6, 33–5, 36.

M. Massironi, *Verder con il disegno,* Franco Muzzio & C. Editore, Padua, 1982, p. 21.

G. Sartoratti, *Una scelta per l'università,* Alborg, Padua, 1980, questionnaire-form.

Sources

Chapter 1

Fromm, E. *To Have Or To Be?* New York: Harper & Row, 1976, pp. 167–168.

Goffman, E. *Encounters.* New York: Bobbs-Merrill, 1961.

Arnold, W., Eysenck, H.J., and Meili, R., eds. *Lexikon der Psychologie.* Freiburg im Breisgau: Herder, 1971–1972.

Rubini, V. *La creatività.* Florence: Giunti Barbera, 1980, p. 17.

Lorenz, K. *Das sogenannte Böse.* Vienna: G. Borotha-Schoeler, 1963.

Eibl-Eibesfeldt, I. *Grundriss der vergleichenden Veraltensforschung: Ethologie.* Munich: Piper, 1967.

With particular reference to human behaviour and its possible interpretations, see Morris, D. *Manwatching: A Field Guide to Human Behaviour.* Oxford: Elsevier, 1977.

Schultz, D.P. *A History of Modern Psychology.* New York: Academic Press, 1969.

Anastasi, A. *Psychological Testing.* New York: Macmillan, 1961, p. 11.

Gardner, M. *"La storia fantastica e le possibilità creative del rompicapo tangram."* Le scienze 76, 1974, pp. 100–106.

Gardner, M. *"Ancora sui tangram: Problemi combinatori e possibilità di gioco offerte dai tangram compatti."* Le scienze 77, 1975, pp. 96–100.

Chapter 2

Hilgard, E.R. *Introduction to Psychology.* New York: Harcourt Brace Jovanovich, 1962.

Arnold, Eysenck and Meili, *op. city.*

Eysenck, H.J. and Kamin, L, *Intelligence: The Battle for the Mind.* Willemstad: Multimedia, n.d.

With reference to transparency, see: for grey surfaces, Metelli, F. "The Perception of Transparency." *Scientific American*, April 1974, pp. 91–97; for coloured surfaces, Da Pos, O. "Contributo teorico-sperimentale alla percezione della trasparenza equilibrata con colori." Venice Institute of Sciences and Arts, Acts CXXXIV, 1975–1976, pp. 701–724.

Zanforlin, M. "Perception of the Apparent by Using Adjacent Surfaces." University of Padua, Institute of Psychology, *Report* 37, 1981, pp. 1–33.

Eysenck and Kamin, *op. cit.*

Hilgard, E.R., Atkinson, R.C., and Atkinson, R.L., *Introduction to Psychology.* New York: Harcourt Brace Jovanovich, 1971.

Angela, Piero, Preface to Eysenck and Kamin, *op. cit.*

Anastasi, *op. cit.*

De Carlo, N.A. *La scelta del campione.* Padua: Liviana, 1983, p. 167.

Sartoratti, G. *Una scelta per l'università.* Padua: Alborg, 1980.

Michotte, A., Thines, G. and Crabbé, G. *Les compléments amodaux des structures perceptives.* Louvain: Publications Universitaires de Louvain, 1964.

Kanizsa, G. *Grammatica del vedere: Saggi su percezione e Gestalt.* Bologna: Il Mulino, 1981.

Chapter 3

Antiseri, D. and De Carlo, N.A. *Epistemologia e metodica della ricerca in psicologia.* Padua: Liviana, 1981.

Arnold, Eysenck and Meili, *op. cit.*

Hilgard, Atkinson and Atkinson, *op. cit.*

Morris, *op. cit.*

Anastasi, *op. cit.*

Hilgard, *op. cit.*

Harré, R. and Secord, P.F. *The Explanation of Social Behaviour.* Oxford: Blackwell, 1972.

Harré, R., ed. *Life Sentences.* London: Wiley, 1976.

Lorenz, *op. cit.*

Stent, G.S., ed. *Morality as a Biological Phenomenon.* Dahlem Konferenzen. Berlin: 1978.

Zanforlin, M. *Psicologia animale e psicologia umana.* [A Report Presented to the XVIII Congress of Italian Psychologists.] Acireale: 1979, p. 5.

Index of Games